The First Oscar Hammerstein
and New York's Golden Age
of Theater and Music

The First Oscar Hammerstein and New York's Golden Age of Theater and Music

ADOLPH S. TOMARS

McFarland & Company, Inc., Publishers
Jefferson, North Carolina

All images are from the author's collection unless otherwise noted.

LIBRARY OF CONGRESS CATALOGUING-IN-PUBLICATION DATA

Names: Tomars, Adolph S., 1908–1985, author.
Title: The first Oscar Hammerstein and New York's golden age of theater and music / Adolph S. Tomars.
Description: Jefferson : McFarland & Company, Inc., Publishers, 2020. | Includes index.
Identifiers: LCCN 2020009867 | ISBN 9780786496150 (paperback : acid free paper) ∞
ISBN 9781476639130 (ebook)
Subjects: LCSH: Hammerstein, Oscar, 1846-1919. | Impresarios—New York (State)—New York—Biography. | Musical theater—New York (State)—New York—History—19th century. | Musical theater—New York (State)—New York—History—20th century.
Classification: LCC ML429.H25 S66 2020 | DDC 792.6092 [B]—dc23
LC record available at https://lccn.loc.gov/2020009867

BRITISH LIBRARY CATALOGUING DATA ARE AVAILABLE

ISBN (print) 978-0-7864-9615-0
ISBN (ebook) 978-1-4766-3913-0

© 2020 Adrea Tomars Nairne. All rights reserved

No part of this book may be reproduced or transmitted in any form or by any means, electronic or mechanical, including photocopying or recording, or by any information storage and retrieval system, without permission in writing from the publisher.

On the cover: Front cover: Oscar Hammerstein I, 1908 (Library of Congress); 1911 photograph of Longacre Square, New York City (Library of Congress)

Printed in the United States of America

McFarland & Company, Inc., Publishers
Box 611, Jefferson, North Carolina 28640
www.mcfarlandpub.com

To my father, Semion Tomars,
friend and associate of Oscar Hammerstein,
who made that legendary figure real to me and even
arranged my one and only interview with him in London,
lasting three minutes, during which the great man shook my hand
and patted my head—my age being four and a half.

Adolph S. Tomars, 1985

To the public of New York, to all who love the arts,
and to all those who love effort and enterprise of any sort…
—Oscar Hammerstein I, 1906

Table of Contents

Acknowledgments by Adrea Tomars Nairne   viii
Preface by Adolph S. Tomars   1
Editor's Note by Adrea Tomars Nairne   3

1. Mr. Show Business   7
2. The Grand Alliance   25
3. The Prisoner in the Gilsey House   35
4. Glorifying the Human Form   49
5. Gala Performance—Unscheduled   65
6. Lawmen, Showmen and Shysters   78
7. Hammerstein's Folly   94
8. Olympian Splendor   107
9. The Great Guilbert   120
10. The War of the Music Halls   142
11. "Stop Hammerstein!"   147
12. Counterattack—Thrust and Parry   157
13. Mechanization of the Living Picture   171
14. Broadway Hits and Misses   175
15. The Great Fregoli   181

Epilogue   202
Chapter Notes   203
Index   205

Acknowledgments
by Adrea Tomars Nairne

My heartfelt thanks go out to Lisa Camp at McFarland & Co. for recognizing the merits of this material in 2014, and also to Dylan Lightfoot, a wonderful editor who stayed with the project for six years until we could make it happen. His dedication, diligence and respect for my father's work is appreciated beyond words.

To my friend Paula Keller, who took on the tedious task of retyping all the old, sometimes damaged pages in preparation for publication, you were the missing link to moving forward. I thank you so much for your generosity.

And to friends old and new, some who knew my father and some who came along later, your encouragement always kept me going. You know who you are.

Most of all, I am amazed that my mother never included the manuscript when she donated the research. She kept it safe for me to find so many years ago. She must have had a vision of its future.

Preface
by Adolph S. Tomars

(*date unknown*)

This is a book about New York's Golden Age of theater and music—the period of the eighteen eighties, the Gay Nineties and the glittering years up to the First World War. The entire gamut of show business and its glamorous personalities are highlighted, from vaudeville to grand opera. It is seen, however, through the colorful life of a single individual whose activities epitomize the entire theatrical era.

This is simultaneously a biography of a period and a biography of a man. The period was a magnificent era in show business. The man—the fabulous Oscar Hammerstein—was Mr. Show Business as no single individual has ever been before or since.

The opening chapter, titled "Mr. Show Business," provides a conspectus of the scope and variety of the material gathered in forty years of research.

Editor's Note
by Adrea Tomars Nairne

This book represents a lifetime of work, researched and written by my father Adolph S. Tomars over many decades—but, regrettably, never completed. His love of opera and the theater had deep roots, beginning with his parents and their association with Oscar Hammerstein the First. With personal knowledge and family history, he never stopped learning and, as with most scholars, the work was never done. My father died suddenly on March 1, 1985, of a heart attack at age 77.

All the research material, notes, newspaper clippings and photos were donated to the New York Public Library but the handwritten manuscript was typed out by my mother on an old Emerson portable typewriter and kept at home. I discovered it after she passed in 1993.

The amazing story and history of musical theater, its creativity, masterful stage engineering, humor, unlikely associations and the turbulence of the period are told around a most unusual character. Forces came together to create entertainment as never before, all led by Hammerstein and his brilliant imagination. Everything he did was an event and all of New York City celebrated his triumphs and witnessed his antics.

It is also clear from the research and other materials that have never before been published that things were not always as they seemed. It was believed Hammerstein had been forced out of some partnerships, but he masterfully constructed scenarios so it only appeared that way. In fact, he orchestrated events in such a way that he wound up with money and freedom to do as he pleased.

Oscar Hammerstein I was also known as the Father of Times Square for this is the site of the Olympia, his crowning achievement, in an unknown part of the city, very inconvenient and removed from the heartbeat of New York City at the time.

And so my father's years of writing began in the 1950s and never actually ended. I have come to believe he may have enjoyed all the research more and probably wasn't in a hurry to finish. This story was also his family history and now, in a distant way, mine too.

My grandfather, Semion Tomars, born in Russia around 1876, was a concert singer in Russia, Vienna and London before coming to the Metropolitan Opera Company as a stage director around 1900. In 1908 he became the stage manager for the opera productions of Oscar Hammerstein at the Manhattan Opera House and also Hammerstein's London Opera House 1912–1913. Under his direction at different times were singers like Caruso and Tetrazzini. His numerous other credits included the Chicago-Philadelphia Opera Company, the Century Opera Company, the Society of American Singers and his own companies in London 1913 and New York 1920.

My grandmother, Rose Tomars, was also a singer and voice teacher and performed in many of the productions during this same period.

It is not easy to write about my father objectively. In my eyes he could do no wrong. He was elegant, soft spoken and a true gentleman in perfectly pressed suits or a silk robe, smoked L&Ms and had a martini with my mother every evening before dinner. He had beautiful, smiling blue eyes and hardly ever raised his voice. When I was older, he was the one who stayed up late waiting for me to come home and we would talk into the night.

Saturday afternoons belonged to us. My mother taught piano at Julliard on Saturday so we did something special together like Radio City Music Hall or a museum or even a walk in the park. Those mornings always began with WNYC radio playing Milton Cross and the Metropolitan Opera, which I disliked intensely. After that, we could have our time together. I still have the old Zenith radio.

Known by most as a sociologist,

Adolph as a child with his parents, Rose and Semion Tomars, ca. 1910.

Dr. Adolph S. Tomars had numerous credentials and authored many publications, beginning with *The Introduction to the Sociology of Art*, a pioneering study in 1941. Other published works include *Human Relations in a Changing Society* in 1949. Over the years he lectured at Hofstra College and New York University among others.

As a faculty member of the City College of the City University of New York for 41 years, he retired in 1971 as professor emeritus. His specialties were sociological theory, the sociology of art, urban sociology and the family.

He was a graduate of Columbia University receiving his A.B. in philosophy in 1929, M.A. in history in 1930, and Ph.D in sociology in 1941. He was a member of Phi Beta Kappa.

In 1959 he received a Guggenheim Fellowship to pursue the history of opera in the United States

The author, Adolph S. Tomars, 1965.

and abroad, particularly relating to the Manhattan Opera Company, which brought together all the family history. We lived overseas for a little over a year and he visited opera houses, libraries and every place they could find related to the project. For me it was kind of scary and exciting at the same time.

In later years, he was a University Seminar Associate of Columbia University, a member of the Public Affairs Committee, an officer of the Retirees Chapter of the Professional Staff Congress of the City University and a member of the American Sociological Association.

I miss my parents every day but when I read this book, I can feel the joy he must have felt while writing it. It is filled with wonderful stories and colorful characters of a time when the theater suddenly exploded with vision and talent.

1

Mr. Show Business

On August 1, 1919, one of the most famous men in America died—and one of the most spectacularly successful. For Oscar Hammerstein, born in Stettin, Prussia in 1846 (possibly 1848), came to America in 1863 or 1864, a runaway immigrant lad in with a dollar and a half in his pocket and became a millionaire. During twenty-five years he made and lost a number of modest fortunes until at the end he was worth several millions. Ten years later he was penniless. Within another eight years he had acquired another million.

For a quarter of a century, his colorful doings were constantly discussed in the daily papers and often he was front page news. There was a period during the era of Theodore Roosevelt, when, as Gilbert Seldes[1] noted, Hammerstein appeared in the news more often than any man in America except "T.R." himself—and this only because Roosevelt had the unfair advantage of being president.

Already a legend in his own lifetime, Hammerstein's face, habit of dress and personal characteristics were familiar to everyone. To the public on both sides of the Atlantic, the small, pointed beard, long cigar and flat-brimmed silk hat were a virtual trademark

Among other things, he founded a great theatrical dynasty now in the fourth generation—the Hammerstein dynasty of Broadway. For sixty years there have always been Hammersteins active on Broadway. Our generation knows best the grandson, Oscar Hammerstein II, the brilliant and successful lyricist, librettist and producer, collaborator with Jerome Kern in *Showboat*, with Richard Rodgers in *Oklahoma*, *South Pacific*, *The King and I*.

Longer memories recall Oscar II's father, Willie Hammerstein, a beloved figure in the world of vaudeville, his uncle Arthur Hammerstein, producer of such musical successes as the indestructible *Rose Marie*, and Arthur's daughter Elaine Hammerstein, lovely film star of the silent movies. Towering over them all looms the legendary figure of grandfather Oscar Hammerstein, the first and greatest of the line, a colossus of the theater and much else besides.

The front pages of the newspapers of August 2, 1919, carried the news of Hammerstein's death in large headlines and full columns. The inside pages continued with further columns, illustrations, editorials on his life. The Sunday editions broke out in feature articles. The weekly magazines followed with more articles, more editorials, and in their wake came the monthlies. The total newsprint in the American press was staggering but the papers of New York led the rest. For New York claimed Hammerstein as its own. He was more than a celebrity, more than one of the city's fabulous personalities. For years he had been a virtual civil institution, one of the liveliest and most colorful of which the metropolis could boast.

If the length of a man's newspaper obituaries is the measure of his fame, their content should provide the summary of his achievement. The facts should all be there, spread out in black and white, easy to read. The record is there, column upon column of it, but it is not easy to grasp. Not only because of the sheer bulk. The story itself is bewildering.

Hammerstein made his first fortune as a businessman, manufacturing cigars. He began as a worker at the bench, later selling cigars, then buying and selling tobacco. A business career in which he climbed the ladder of success rung by rung from apprentice at $2 a week to a prosperous merchant.

A decade after arriving in New York he was a successful editor and publisher. This career he began by founding a trade paper with a capital of $8. Fifteen years later, when he sold it, it was the leading journal for the tobacco trade, responsible for much of the organization of the industry. It became so well established that today the *United States Tobacco Journal* is still the leading weekly of the industry.[2] Hammerstein became known as the trade's foremost expert and powerful force in its development.

Hammerstein had an outstandingly successful career as an inventor. Fifty-six inventions were patented in his name, many more unregistered or sold outright for others to patent. He invented all sorts of devices, but mostly machinery for the manufacture of cigars, machinery which proved crucial in revolutionizing cigar making from purely a handicraft to a largely mechanized industry and which brought him several large fortunes. He was one of the tribe of Edison—a mechanical genius.

Oscar Hammerstein I, photograph from *Who's Who on the Stage*, published 1906 (public domain).

He was one of New York's most prominent and far-sighted figures in real estate and building operations. It was Hammerstein who developed West Harlem when it was thought too far uptown ever to be fit for anything but grazing land for goats. He put it on the path of its colorful career as a bustling residential and commercial area of Manhattan. As a builder he erected almost every kind of structure, single homes, apartment houses—whole blocks of them—banks, stores, offices. But mostly he concentrated on building theaters, and before he was through he had built fourteen of them, chiefly in New York, although his building operations even reached across the Atlantic to England.

He not only built theaters, he designed them, and some of his patents were inventions embodying novel features in the construction of theaters. Another of his achievements was his development of a seedy and disreputable area called Longacre Square. Here he built the greatest theatrical structure in the country. He followed it with another theater at the corner of Forty-Second Street and Seventh Avenue, where soon, settling as his neighbor across the street, the *New York Times* gave the square its new name and Times Square became and has remained the hub of theatrical life for New York and the nation. George M. Cohan called him "the man who made Times Square," and proposed that his statue be erected there, a suggestion that met with general approval. Nevertheless, the man who made Times Square has no monument there or anywhere.

Yet he was much more than the most famous builder of theaters in America. As the obituary editorial of the *New York Sun* puts it: "Hammerstein could not be content with controlling the bodies of his theatres. He wanted to shape the destinies of their souls." He directed the theaters he had built, as manager, producer, and impresario. Above all, he was a showman.

At various times all the great acting personalities of the age trod the boards of his Harlem Opera House, Columbus, Olympia and Victoria theaters—Edwin Booth and Helena Modjeska, Richard Mansfield and Robert B. Mantell, E. H. Sothern and Julia Marlowe, Joseph Jefferson (the immortal Rip Van Winkle), Otis Skinner, Henry Miller and David Warfield. On his stages Eleanora Duse worked her tragic spells and Ada Rehan, Mrs. Leslie Carter, Olga Nethersole, Henrietta Crossman and Grace George, each in her own way, radiated glamor and charm. Almost the whole of the Barrymore and Drew clan graced his stages—suave John Drew; Mrs. John Drew, the grand old lady of the American stage; her son-in-law and daughter, Maurice Barrymore and Georgie Drew Barrymore (parents of Ethel, Lionel and John). It was in a Hammerstein theater that Lionel Barrymore first appeared in a good part in New York, as did Chrystal Herne on the same night.

All sorts of "firsts" dot the record. The distinguished English actress, Mrs. Patrick Campbell and the brilliant English actor, George Arliss made their first American appearance at one of his theaters. On his stages were presented new and important plays of D'Annunzio, Bjornsterne and others, including the first American presentation of Maeterlinck's *Pelleas and Melisande*. He produced and gave the first performance in America of Ibsen's Pillars of Society (it was the second Ibsen play to be presented in the U.S.) and he produced the first dramatization of Tolstoy's Resurrection. A shining record of theatrical enterprise in the legitimate drama, it was matched only by his presentations of musical comedy and comic opera.

Again a parade of glamorous show people across his stages, now tripping more lightly and more tunefully before his footlights—Chauncey Olcott, the sweet Irish singer, those masters of musical mirth, Francis Wilson and De Wolf Hopper, Frank Daniels, The Rogers Brothers, Edna Wallace Hopper, the ever youthful, dainty Della Fox, the versatile Fay Templeton, the one and only Lillian Russell, the golden beauty with the silver voice.

Again "firsts" come thick and fast—American premiers of French operettas by Planquette and Audran, of musical comedies by John Philip Sousa and Harry Von Tilzer, and the first presentation of Victor Herbert's finest operetta, *Naughty Marietta*. It was in Hammerstein's theater that Eva Tanguay first appeared in New York in a sizeable stage part and then again for the first time in a featured part. He gave Anna Held her first role in a musical show, and the winsome Edna May, who came "The Belle of New York" and the toast of London, was one of his discoveries plucked from his chorus for her first stage role in his own production.

And here a new factor emerges on the record. Hammerstein was not satisfied to engage musical shows nor even to produce his own shows. He created them as well, writing the libretto and the lyrics and composing the music. He wrote individual songs, ballets, reviews and complete musical comedies and operettas and staged them himself with numerous novel scenic and stage effects of his own invention. Some of them were highly successful, as his musical, *Marguerite*, a genuine hit at the Olympia, or his summer pantomime-revue, *Punch, Judy and Co.*, which "stood them up" at the Victoria all summer.

Dancers and dancing were usually featured in his shows and he delighted to compose ballet music for the dancers he presented. Loie Fuller's sensational "serpentine" dances were first seen in his theater. He imported the first troupe of Tiller Girls from England and he made Gertrude Hoffman a star.

The credits for some of his musicals might have read as follows:

Oscar Hammerstein presents "_____"; book and lyrics written by Oscar Hammerstein, music composed by Oscar Hammerstein, produced by Oscar Hammerstein, staged and directed by Oscar Hammerstein in a theatre designed and built by Oscar Hammerstein, owned, operated and managed by Oscar Hammerstein.

Parenthesis after specific numbers might have noted "with special costumes, stage and scenic effects designed by Oscar Hammerstein" and asterisks after the names of some of the cast might have provided the information "this performer discovered and developed by Oscar Hammerstein." The mere words "An Oscar Hammerstein Production" would have been a gross understatement.

Once, on a bet, he composed a complete comic opera, plot, words and music, in forty-eight hours while locked in a room and produced it for a successful run, a feat duly celebrated in newspaper headlines and play-by-play accounts of its accomplishment.

In the less "legitimate" but livelier arts of the theater where joy is unconfined—in the music hall, vaudeville and variety stage—the record again speaks with eloquence. Hammer-

Hammerstein's Victoria Theater and Roof Garden, at the corner of Seventh Avenue and 42nd Street in Manhattan, 1908 (public domain).

stein's Olympia Music Hall was the greatest music hall ever known in America and probably in the world. His Victoria Theatre of Varieties was acknowledged the greatest vaudeville house in America by the profession itself. It was in its day and era what the Palace Theatre was in the next and it was Hammerstein who by deliberate act passed the succession to the Palace.

What a variegated array of great performers and personalities passed before his music hall and vaudeville footlights—singers, dancers, comedians, athletes, acrobats, daredevils, jugglers, magicians—specialists of every kind and each an artist in his line. To merely call the role is to sum up a whole word of the theater and allied arts—the comedian Sam Bernard; Virginia Aragon, lovely queen of the high wire; Sousa's Band; the cartoonist Outcault, creator of the comic strip and of Buster Brown; Bert Williams, perhaps the greatest of all black performers; Fred Stone of the rubber legs; Irene Franklin, singer and comedienne; Adgie the lion tamer, who did a sensational strip tease in a cageful of lions; the singers Louise Dresser and Nora Bayes; Blanche Ring and Maggie Cline (of "Throw Him Down, McCloskey" fame); Henry E. Dixey, the versatile actor; Pat Rooney, dancer; Ella Bradna, equestrienne; Victor Moore, comedian; Cissie Loftus; Josephine Cohan—the names crowd one another in a veritable torrent of talent—Cinquevalli, king of jugglers; Gus Edwards; Julius Tannen; Marie Dressler; Vesta Victoria (singing "Waiting at the Church"); Alice Lloyd; Julia Sandersonm; Julian Eltinge. The list could go on and on.

The successful vaudeville careers that were launched upon Hammerstein's stages, the new songs and dances that first became hits there, the great performers first introduced to America there, and the unknowns who became stars once they could bill themselves "Direct from Hammerstein's in New York"—this is a fascinating story in itself.

Here Weber and Fields, beloved monarchs of comedy and burlesque, were first established as Broadway stars. At the Olympia first appeared that supreme artist, Yvette Guilbert, greatest chanteuse of all time, whom Hammerstein brought from Europe at the staggering salary of $3,000 a week in 1895—a record not equaled for years after.

Hammerstein could even turn lack of talent into stardom. He brought an obscure troupe from Iowa, billed them as "The Cherry Sisters—the World's Worst Actresses," made them a household word and assured them a fabulous career. (His judgment was later backed by a judicial decision when the sisters became the only act ever to be certified as atrocious by the Iowa state supreme court.)[3]

A Hammerstein audience first heard the song so beloved of barbershop quartets—*Sweet Adeline*—and a Hammerstein stage first presented the sensational Creatore's Band. Motion pictures (the early Eidoloscope, Biograph, etc.) were shown for the first time in 1896 in a Hammerstein theater one week after the historic first showing of the Edison Vitagraph, and a Hammerstein stage first presented the talking pictures in 1907. Here was launched the fabulous vaudeville career of Eva Tanguay as a top-flight entertainer. Elsie Janis' first appearance as a full-fledged adult performer was at the Victoria, where Trixie Priganza, among many others, also made her first appearance in vaudeville. Here also were launched the careers of two young unknowns, W.C. Fields and Will Rogers, one a comic juggler, the other a trick lariat thrower. And here young Eddie Cantor made his debut in a Broadway theater.

Enough achievement in these fields to bring fame to at least a half dozen ordinary mortals. But not Hammerstein. His crowning achievement was grand opera, that most exalted and glamorous of the theater arts in which the high art of music is wedded to the arts of the stage. Grand opera is to the world of the theater what horse racing is to the world of sport—the show of kings and aristocrats and millionaires, where glamor is found on both sides of the footlights, on the boards and in the bows. The manager of such a theatrical enterprise is a king of showmen and bears the proud title—impresario.

It was as a grand opera impresario that Hammerstein won his greatest fame and gained a glory so bright that it cast into the shade all his other remarkable achievements. Nor is it surprising in a man who loved the theater and loved music that the combination of the two on the grandest scale should become his greatest passion. The record of his achievement in this field is one of unmatched daring.

Hammerstein gave grand opera in a number of his theaters, but when he was ready to devote himself fully to the operatic muse he built a great new house solely for grand opera and boldly challenged the great and powerful Metropolitan Opera itself. He said that single-handed he could produce grand opera better than that august institution with all its millionaires. And he proved it. His Manhattan Opera did outshine the Metropolitan. Alone, with his own resources and genius he shook the great entrenched institution to its foundations. He so humbled it that it was forced to reorganize completely and finally to sue for peace. He gave New York such brilliant productions as it had never seen before nor since and New York was grateful. The old newspaper clippings tell the story. The *Tribune* puts it well: "He pulled grand opera in New York from the marshes of routine and carried it into an atmosphere vibrant and alive."

"Until he flung himself into the production of grand opera," says a *Post* editorial, "the thing had been thought of as a sort of esoteric art, reserved for the select few." Hammerstein said that grand opera was too good a thing to be reserved for aristocrats and millionaires, or for highbrows. Opera was a good show, meant for all who could enjoy good theater and

Soprano and actress Lina Cavalieri (1874–1944), autographed photograph from 1918.

could be stirred by good music. And he proved it. For four years he made New York about opera. And he extended his operations beyond New York, building and running opera houses in Philadelphia and London.

The world famous singers he presented, the great artists he brought to America and the new talents he discovered and launched to stardom made him the world's most famous impresario. He did it without partners and backers. He never had a board of directors. He produced grand opera as he produced his musical comedies. He designed, built and owned the opera house, engaged the singers, conductors and staff, even to picking the chorus, chose the operas to be given, selected the casts and personally supervised every rehearsal and performance.

The list of the artists he presented during his career is a roll-call of some of the greatest voices, some of the most artistic singers and singing actors, and some of the most colorful personalities that ever appeared upon the grand opera stage. They included at various times, Adelina Patti, Lilli Lehmann, Nellie Melba, Lillian Nordica, Ernestine Schumann-Heink, Emma Calve, Lina Cavalieri. The singers he introduced to America included Allesandro Bonci, Mary Garden, Giovanni Zentaello, Clotilde Bressler-Gianoli, Mariette Mazarin, Adamo Didur, Hector Dufranne, Charles Dalmores, Luisa Tetrazzini, John McCormack. He brought to America the great conductor, Cleofante Campanini and he was indirectly responsible for the coming to America of Toscanini. He discovered talented Americans and raised them to stardom, as Felice Lyne and Alice Gentle, and Orville Harrold, the tenor whom he found in his own vaudeville house. He had persuaded Marguerite Sylva to begin a vaudeville career in his music hall and, some years later he launched her American operatic career in his opera house.

One of the top tenors of his time, Giovanni Zentaello (1876–1949) sang at the Manhattan Opera House 1907–1910.

Hammerstein presented to the public not only new and exciting opera singers but new and exciting operas. He gave the first public performance in New York of Mascagni's *Cavalleria Rusticana* and the first American performance of Offenbach's *Tales of Hoffmann* by a grand opera company. The operas which he presented for the first time in America included Massenet's *Thais* and *Jongleur de Notre Dame*, Charpentier's *Louise*, and that unique and supreme masterpiece of Debussy, *Pelleas and Melisande* (the operatic version of the Maeterlinck play which had had its American premiere in another of his theaters some years before.) He set New York by the ears with his sensational production of Strauss' *Salome*, which the Metropolitan had given but which was hastily withdrawn after one performance by the scandalized Metropolitan directors after a protest from J. P. Morgan. And he followed this with the American premiere of the even more radical music and action of Strauss' *Elektra*.

He produced the familiar operas in new and exciting ways, kicking aside traditions and precedents he thought useless and obsolete and opening the eyes of critics and public alike to new possibilities and methods of producing grand opera. His production of the thrice-familiar *Carmen* was so thrilling that it was given to packed houses nineteen times in a single season—a record for any opera in a repertory season of grand opera. The impact of Hammerstein's operatic reforms and policies upon grand opera in America was felt for years. He revitalized a branch of musical dramatic art that had become stodgy and moribund. He was, as the Times said editorially, "the regenerator of our musical life."

Nor were Hammerstein's musical interests confined wholly to the operatic stage. His concert stage presentations were many

Mezzo-soprano Alice Gentle (1885–1958) got her start in the opera chorus of Hammerstein's Manhattan Opera Company in 1908, and went on to star in three films (photograph ca. 1910).

and notable. Besides Campanini, he presented such orchestral conductors as Theodore Thomas, Walter Damrosch and Anton Seidl. He discovered and introduced to New York Fritz Scheel, who became the founder and conductor of the Philadelphia Orchestra. Pianists such as Lhevinne and Horzowski, violinists as Elman, appeared on his stages, and his concert programs included such works as Verdi's *Requiem*, numerous symphonies and orchestral compositions. And here we find the editor of Musical America calling him one of the great figures of American musical history, saying: "It is not merely operagoers who owe Oscar Hammerstein an undischargeable debt. It is music itself."

Despite the preponderant emphasis on the operatic theater in the press accounts, Hammerstein made notable contributions to each and every branch of the stage. It would not be correct to say that he gave every single type of theatrical representation known— there is no record, for instance, of his ever having presented a flea circus—but it is difficult to find a single major form of theater in which he was not active. He was undoubtedly the greatest showman America has known, the outstanding example of theatrical enterprise in

1. Mr. Show Business

Oscar Hammerstein I (left) with conductor Cleofonte Campanini in New York, 1908 (Library of Congress).

an era of great showmen. The heading of a *New York Globe* editorial reads—"The Arabian Nights Impresario"—and the text asserts: "He was Sinbad the Sailor and Aladdin rolled in one." A many-sided genius in show business, Hammerstein in his era was, in effect, Mr. Show Business.

Although the theater was his preference and his passion, he was as much a genius outside the theater as in it. Nor were his contributions in other fields less remarkable, as a builder, as a developer of real estate, as inventor of machinery, as journalist, as spokesman for an industry, as merchant and innovator of mercantile practices. When he began his real estate development in Harlem he was assured it was a foolish blunder to invest so far uptown. Who would go all the way out there to live? When he built the first theater in Times Square it was called "Hammerstein's folly." What audience would come to such an out of the way location? When it failed and he built another theater just across the square, they called him a madman until within a few years he could point to a great newspaper across the street and a subway entrance at his door.

Among the seeming contradictions and incongruities, the only common feature in all these successful careers appears to be the fact that Hammerstein was a genius in all of them. On this point all the accounts agree. "...a brain in which dreamer and realist combine. He was certainly a genius," a *Globe* editorial tells us. Carl Van Vechten[4] pays this tribute: "A genius. I have met few men who have seemed to me so great." And the *Sun* makes the assertion: "He was a natural genius in many directions and he had never any hesitation in making the statement… Oddly enough… what he said he demonstrated."

For Hammerstein did not pursue his several careers successively but largely simultaneously. While he was publishing and editing a trade paper, he was already writing songs and comedies and putting on shows; and while he was operating theaters he was building and renting apartment houses and inventing machinery. His Victoria was the only theater in the world that ever had a machine shop inside it where the manager of the theater developed mechanical inventions for manufacturing cigars and processing tobacco. The Manhattan Opera House was the only opera house in the world that, for a time, included a cigar rolling machine at which its silk-hatted impresario rolled his own cigars on a machine of his own invention.

The apparent contradictions mount. A real estate builder and speculator who built theaters not to sell them but to run them. He never sold a theater unless forced to and was ashamed to admit he once sold a theater site at a large profit. A tobacco expert who was considered the most renowned judge of singing and singers. Talent came from every corner of the country seeking his judgment. A manager of the leading vaudeville house in America, who was the country's most famous grand opera impresario, and ran his opera house most of the time from the office in his vaudeville theater. Here was a man who revolutionized two industries in America, but who could think of two more dissimilar industries—the manufacture of cigars and the production of grand opera.

The picture of his life that emerges from the newspaper summaries is confused. There are too many incongruous careers, the combinations too bizarre and contradictory. The news accounts devote much attention to the Hammerstein personality. Perhaps here are the clues to a clear pattern in the man's diverse achievements.

The *New York Tribune* describes Hammerstein as: "Inventor, editor, real estate speculator, composer, vaudeville manager, shrewd businessman, reckless plunger, humorist,... whimsical, temperamental, fearless, berating his audiences, condemning his critics, assailing his foes, cajoling his singers... ever in the limelight and often on the first page."

Hammerstein was considered a colossal self-advertiser, a deliberate and calculating publicity seeker. The *Sun* compares him to Barnum in this respect. The *Tribune* tells us "... he knew his public ... with all its strength and weakness and played upon it as a master musician plays upon his violin.... He played to the gallery but ... always with a color and an originality." And here is the *Times* editorial calling him "the amazing publicity expert who used his own eccentricities to their limit for public effect." Was he then purely the businessman whose business happened to be the theater, whose sole object is to attract paying customers? There were those who thought so all during his life.

Yet here we find Van Vechten assuring us: "He had ideals ... was an artist. He had no desire to make money except to spend it, and he spent it, not to make more money, but to further his gigantic projects." The *Musical Courier* speaks of his sincere wish to give the public the best. Others call him a dreamer, an idealist. The *Sun* editorializes on his artistic enterprise, the *Herald* on his artistic courage and on how the public always profited from his dreams, and it points out "The city enjoyed a period of music such as it may never have again. It owed it all to the witty little man who was always ready to take the risk and take the consequences." Others elaborate upon his contempt for money—an *Evening Mail* editorial, "He spared no money when it was a question of producing the best possible artistic results." James Gibbons Huneker[5] saying in the *Times*, "more prodigal with his own money than other managers with the capital of strangers." But the question remains. Which was he—reckless plunger or shrewd businessman?

Seldes assures us that he never deliberately made news, he naturally was news and the *Sun* admits, "no press agent living could compete with Oscar Hammerstein and the Hammerstein personality." It is true that he never sought out the reporters. They sought him. But was this only Hammerstein's use of the Hammerstein personality for its public effect?

The high-sounding "public relations consulatant" was then unknown, but the "press agent" was already in his heyday. Hammerstein employed a brilliant staff but he was always his own best press agent. The word "ballyhoo" was yet unborn; it was called "puffing" then, and Hammerstein was a master at puffing his shows and performers. He never hesitated to proclaim his theaters the finest, his artists the greatest. He advertised the tenor Bonci like a circus and puffed him into a celebrity rivalling the Metropolitan's Caruso until the Metropolitan was forced in self-defense to engage him at a fabulous fee. But, then again, his theaters and his artists were great and the critics agreed that Bonci did rival Caruso.

Again the evidence is contradictory. We find the *Herald* editor referring to the celebrated incident in which Hammerstein hissed an incompetent singer in his own theater, engaged in fisticuffs with one of her outraged admirers and precipitated a whole series of dramatic and hilarious incidents, including his own arrest for disturbing the peace. (The complete story of the incident and how it led to a culmination of lasting benefit to the city is a full and glorious chapter in itself.)

If an imported singer he had advertised failed to meet his standards on his first appearance he might send him packing on the next boat, his entire contract paid in full. On one occasion he brought over, sight unseen, an English tenor of great reputation who proved a dud. As Hammerstein described it later—"He sang for me one night and the next day I paid him $3,000 to stop." On numerous occasions he told the people lined up before his box office to save their money, the show wasn't good enough, he'd have a better one the next week. And once a first night audience came out to find Hammerstein mounting a chair in the lobby to make the following speech: "Ladies and gentlemen. This show is a fraud. I have it here for a week. I hope no one comes to see it."

Hammerstein was famous for his wit. The latest Hammersteinism was quickly quoted up and down Broadway and taken up by the reporters. Some of his sayings became part of the legendary heritage of the theater, and some, as is often the case, were later ascribed to others. Hammerstein's wit might almost be listed as another separate career, for men have made a public career out of being witty. Yet even Hammerstein's humor showed contradictory aspects. It could be blunt as a club or even too coarse for publication and at other times rapier-fine, eloquent. His wit could be caustic and cynical or of joyous hilarity. The sharp tongue came in handy in dealing with temperamental artists. Music critic Edward Moore once said that Hammerstein was the only one of his time or since whose tongue was warranted to be quicker than Mary Garden's.[6]

One of his very capable and very high-priced lawyers was a collector of books and fine editions. On one occasion he proudly showed Hammerstein some of his finest bindings. Hammerstein ran his fingers over the rich vellum, cocked an eyebrow and said, "The hides of your clients, no doubt."

When he was building his two million dollar opera house a vaudeville associate expressed his amazement. Why should a man with a fabulously successful vaudeville house want to give grand opera? The way to make more money was to build more vaudeville houses and multiply the profits. Hammerstein knew it was useless to try to explain and kept an exasperated silence. The fellow persisted. "But why go into grand opera? Is there any money in it?" "Of course," roared Hammerstein, "my money is in it."

And it was he, the cigar maker-theater manager who originally made the much-quoted epigram: "A show is like a cigar. If it is good everybody wants a box. If it isn't good no amount of puffing will make it draw."

Not only the Hammerstein humor but the Hammerstein *good* humor and charm were proverbial. There is evidence of his geniality in every account of his life. ".. a brilliant companion whose ordinary conversation sparkled," says the *Times*. "You had no way but to be his friend if he so willed it… He was picaresque and elfin—he numbered among his kin Till Eulenspiegel… and Peter Pan," says Pitts Sanborn[7] in the *Globe*. And here is James Huneker: "extraordinarily human. Charming… amazing wit," and Huneker chiming in with "shrewd, ever witty, good-tempered." And the *Herald* telling how "He made large fortunes and lost them with the same gentle smile," describing "his humor, his fortitude under adversity and quiet in success." The sweet smile, the merry twinkle in the eye, the drollery, the wit—a clear picture arises of a man who could charm a rhinoceros out of its hide, or a prima donna into a contract.

But, according to the *Tribune* "Hammerstein was an intense egoist, domineering, ruthless, unscrupulous when forced into a corner." And this in the *World*: "for more than a quarter of a century the storm center of musical and theatrical interest, accentuated by frequent appearances in the courts both as complainant and defendant." The *Post* says "his name… meant enterprise and daring and battle" with the *Sun* concurring, "He was a fighter always… never happy unless he was involved in litigation or verbal dispute with some one… Few men have been sued oftener or have brought more suits." And here is Van Vechten again: "His arrogance, his pride, his egoism assisted him to success; he allowed no obstacle to stand in his way." The editor of the *Evening Mail* tops them all: "His hat became a legend of two continents and it was in the ring most of the time."

His lawsuits—frequently a score of them simultaneously—were always exciting. Hammerstein on the witness stand was a delight, the assurance of a full courthouse. Once when being sworn in at a time when people were suing him in droves he replied to the routine question, "Occupation?" with "Professional defendant" The list of his legal counsel at various times is a story in itself. It includes Robert Ingersoll, the great orator, Elihu Root, and the brilliant and unscrupulous Abe Hummel of the rascally Howe and Hummel, lawyer for Lillian Russell and other stars of the stage and simultaneously "mouthpiece" for the criminals of the underworld.

But lawsuits were Hammerstein's most decorous quarrels. His tactful handling of temperamental singers was well known but he could also insult them publicly. He put a five inch waistline reduction clause into one of his singer's contracts and made it public. When he published an article on artistic temperament, he gave examples of the tantrums, manias and phobias of his own stars, naming their names. Some very famous faces were red. He had pointed out how the great stars used their temperamental outbursts to intimidate managers and tyrannize their co-workers and had concluded with a droll Shakespearian paraphrase: "The fault dear Public, is not in us but in our stars that we are underlings."

He did not hesitate to offend millionaires and society-leaders alike. The bigger they were the better he enjoyed it. He insulted Lady Cunard and the King of Portugal and he refused to make a deferential bow to the King of England—details that fall into their proper place as part of the incredible story of his invasion of England

Ironically, Hammerstein's own violent temper was a by-word, enough at times to send his entire staff into hiding in the "storm cellar." His physical courage was equal to his rage. He had numerous physical encounters, generally with men twice his size. It was no unusual sight to see someone ejected from his theaters, often with Hammerstein acting as his own bouncer. The ejectee might be an actor, an employee, a patron. It might on occasion be a critic or even one of his own sons. Willie was the son he was closest to and whose abilities he respected most but he had at one time banished him from his home. He horsewhipped his brother-in-law on the street and once put to rout a battalion of sheriff's bailiffs with a fire-axe.

His brushes with the law were legion. He was indicted several times, arrested numerous times. He was a thorn in the side of the police, always ready to challenge a law he didn't like by making himself a test case. He broke a grafting police captain and made a police commissioner look ridiculous. His feud with William Travers Jerome, the brilliant District Attorney of New York was memorable, and in Hammerstein the invincible Jerome met his match.

Nor was his private life smooth and tranquil. When tragedy struck him it was on a larger scale than with others. His first wife died in childbirth, leaving him with four young children. His second wife divorced him; his third survived him. When the boys were grown to manhood he saw three of his four sons die within the same year. His own death occurred under peculiarly poignant circumstances. But he lived with great gusto and a ready capacity for fun. He was always ready to flirt with a pretty face and plump figure. Besieged constantly by real and would-be actresses, singers, chorus girls, society women, his love affairs were casual and numerous. The mystery was where he found the time.

There is no end to the contradictions that could be listed in the life and personality of Oscar Hammerstein.

Here was a foreign-born immigrant who for many years spoke with a strong accent and never quite lost all trace of it. Yet a *Post* editorial called him "typically American," and the editor of the *Mail* describing him as "a type of the virile American with a passion for achievement."

Again and again his democracy is stressed, as in this *Sun* editorial: "He was above all democratic… the impresario of the people, known, loved and appreciated by them as no man of the theatre had ever been." A democrat who purveyed the most aristocratic and expensive of art forms and was always seen with a high silk hat and costly Havana cigar tilted under it—his virtual trademark.

Yet more contradictions. A man who was noted for never answering letters—he never had a secretary and said his secretary was his waste basket—and a man famed for his epistles. The letters he did write were almost always open letters, given to the press. They were usually intended to pillory someone, and that hapless someone would find himself a laughing stock for weeks.

A man who was amazingly well informed and could display unusual erudition—yet no one ever saw him buying a book or reading one.

A millionaire who lived in two dingy rooms under the balcony of a vaudeville theater; rooms that for those who had seen them were incredible. No cleaning woman was permitted to enter, the bed was usually unmade, the piano and floor littered with music, cigar boxes, empty bottles, everything covered with dust. And in the midst was Hammerstein, always scrupulously neat and clean, his clothes and linen fresh and immaculate.

During his life and after, it was the opinion of many that he was a man of impeccable taste and discrimination, an artist; and there was the opposite view held by others that he was really a vulgarian, a promoter of things he really did not understand at all. There was the theory that Hammerstein was an unpredictable screwball, governed by emotion, erratically flying on sudden impulse from one activity to another; and there was the theory that he was shrewdly, coldly calculating, that everything, even his most furious rages, were performances put on with an eye to the effect.

What was the secret of these incongruities? Can the jigsaw puzzle of Hammerstein's life be put together into a coherent picture? To do this it is necessary to leave off looking at death notices and to begin to look at the living man.

Even the casual reader of the stream of material set flowing on August 2, 1919, must realize how inadequate, indeed, how lopsided these accounts really are. Most of the things we have mentioned are only indicated or hinted at in the newsprint. The only part of the man's life really discussed is his career in the theater, and of that only his work in grand opera is given any real attention. Because his widest fame was won here the accounts were written by music reporters and music critics, men who knew little of the dramatic and musical comedy fields, who knew nothing and cared less about vaudeville, a field beneath their notice, and knew less than nothing of the great world of business and invention, of property and trade. The newspaper accounts contain numerous errors of fact, may of them since perpetuated in the standard biographical references. The accounts disagree with each other. Legend is frequently taken for fact. It was said that Hammerstein was a legend in his own lifetime. He was many and contradictory legends and when we follow the actual course of his life we find the source of many of them.

That notion some held that Hammerstein, for all his brilliant work in art, was really a vulgarian himself with no understanding of such high things; the source of that legend was none other than Hammerstein himself. It was a pose he loved to affect. He was just a cigar maker; he was only a vaudeville manager who exhibited trained dogs and monkeys, he would say. Many took him seriously. Huneker was taken in. Van Vechten knew better.

Then there were the two opposing views about his own musical compositions. There were many among the general public who had the notion he was also a towering genius as a composer, the equal of Wagner and Verdi, or at least, Puccini. (This was patently absurd; he never attempted anything but light music.) The other view, often repeated by sophisticates, was that Hammerstein's music was atrocious, his own shows the worst ever. That legend also was Hammerstein's own creation.

For all his egoism and self-assurance he had the saving grace of humor. He could laugh at himself. He made endless jests at his own expense, especially of his efforts as a composer. Once he discoursed solemnly on the power of music. He told of a friend so crippled by rheumatism as to be unable to walk. To cheer the poor fellow up, he had sat down at the piano and played for him his own compositions. In a few minutes the invalid was not only able to walk; he ran—such is the power of music! Even Van Vechten, who had never heard his music, was taken in. The verdict at the time, however, was that Hammerstein's music compared very favorably with other output of the same type.

The legends about Hammerstein were not only numerous and conflicting; they were highly colored, romantic, dramatic, fantastic. Yet when the facts of his life are discovered and the truth separated from the legends one rule holds consistently—the truth is almost invariably more interesting, more exciting, more dramatic and even more fantastic.

And when we follow the course of his life, the seemingly erratic leaps from one venture to another cease to appear bizarre. There is an inner logic that binds them together. The seemingly sudden, impulsive decisions cease to appear as volcanic eruptions when we trace their slow germination and follow the bold but careful planning that preceded them. That is not to say that all the contradictions disappear. In some respects Oscar Hammerstein remains an enigma. His friends did not understand him; his several wives and his children did not understand him. And he never bothered to try to understand himself; he was too busy being himself and following the dictates of his nature. But when we watch the unfolding of that nature in his day-to-day life we no longer feel that the contrasting traits of his character are contradictory. They seem complementary rather than conflicting sides of his many-sided nature.

Hammerstein was a complex character and yet, in some ways, a simple one. Certain guiding threads stand out connecting the tangle of his protean activities so clearly that even the superficial obituary accounts reveal some of them. There were, of course, his great and obvious twin passions—for the theater and for music—and his devotion to their combination in grand opera. Even greater as a motivating impulse was his passion for creative enterprise of any sort in the theater or elsewhere.

Three governing rules set the conditions for the tasks he wanted to accomplish. First, they had to be things no one had ever done before. He decided to invent a cigar-making machine precisely because everyone agreed this was the one industry that could never be mechanized. The tobacco leaf was too delicate for machine handling; only the sensitive fingers of the skilled artisan could roll a cigar properly. He accepted the challenge and found the principle upon which a machine could do the trick.

Secondly, the things he wanted to do must be on a larger and grander scale than ever done before. If a thing was worth doing it was worth going all the way to its maximum possibilities. Thirdly—and this was most important—what he did he must do alone. From beginning to end it must be all his, bearing the stamp of his personality in every part. He had to delegate authority in his huge undertakings but he insisted on supervising every detail. He never hesitated to praise his assistants but final credit for success was his and his alone. And when an enterprise failed he cheerfully took all the responsibility; not once did he blame a subordinate.

This was a point upon which he insisted again and again—sometimes humorously, sometimes seriously and at times angrily. His "Board of Directors" was his favorite joke. When the outlook for his greatest venture was darkest and he was even tempted to think of abandoning it, he said, "To drive away… dejection I held a meeting with myself in my office, elected myself president, vice-president and also a number of other officers, and respectfully tendered myself a unanimous vote of admiration and confidence."

The press made constant use of the jest. Whenever a reporter or cartoonist ran out of ideas, he could always write up a meeting of the "Hammerstein Board of Directors" or draw a cartoon which sometimes showed Hammerstein addressing a table and empty chairs and sometimes a dozen men about the table, each with silk hat, pointed beard and cigar.

When he was leaving for his London venture he declared, "The secret of my success in the past has been that I do not take anyone's advice. I rely on my own eyes, ears, and experience… I have confidence in my own judgment." Many called him an arrogant, conceited egotist to refuse the advice of experts. Yet it is difficult to see what other conclusion he could have come to from his own experience. All the things he had accomplished were things the experts had said could not be done and he had done them because he had refused to listen.

This principle of having to do it alone and do all of it from start to finish was best expressed in his theatrical enterprises. He would not produce a show except in a theater he himself had planned and built and he could not consider a show his own unless he had personally selected the cast from the first ranking star to the last member of the chorus. He never watched his own opera performances from a director's box as other impresarios did. He sat on the stage on a kitchen chair placed in the wings and his singers were always on their mettle because they were under his direct scrutiny. He once said he was in no hurry to go to heaven where there was sure to be a chorus he had not selected.

No one appreciated it more than his opera audiences. They never called his house the Manhattan Opera—it was always Hammerstein's Opera. They knew he had personally supervised the putting into place of each brick in the building they were sitting in, as they knew that from his kitchen chair he was personally supervising every note in the opera they were listening to.

A premiere at the Manhattan was an occasion without precedent or parallel in theatrical history. There were the enthusiastic curtain calls for the stars, the flowers for the prima donna, the resounding cries of "Bravo!" as the singers were called out again and again. Then the conductor would be brought out to a storm of applause fully equal to that given the stars. Then the stage director and more applause. Soon a new cry would be called out from all parts of the house and finally there would be brought before the curtain a stocky little man with a silk hat and cigar who had neither sung nor played nor conducted nor set the stage. And now the entire audience would rise up in a tremendous ovation dwarfing everything that had gone before. There never was another opera house like Hammerstein's. Great and glamorous were its stars—Nellie Melba, Maurice Renaud, Luiza Tetrazzini, Mary Garden—but its greatest star was Hammerstein himself.

One other thread runs through Hammerstein's life and work, one that none of his commentators seemed to notice, perhaps because it was so obvious. It was a sentiment, an emotion fully as strong as his passion for music and the theater. This was his life-long love affair with New York. He loved America as it can be loved only by an immigrant to whom it gave the opportunity to rise from a cigar-worker's bench at two dollars a week to a builder of two-million dollar theatrical structures handling receipts of sixty thousand dollars a week.

To one who loved creative enterprise as he did, the land of free enterprise was his natural element. They were made for each other and it was love at first sight.

But his America, his element and his love was New York. And when he developed Harlem, when he made Times Square and Forty-Second Street the theatrical hub, when he built the Manhattan Opera House, he saw them as installments on his great debt to New York, as gifts to its people, given with love and affection. And they knew it, for when one of his greatest enterprises failed and left him penniless, the entire theatrical profession, the newspapers, the musicians, and people from all walks of life showed him they knew it by joining hands and forcing him to accept, even against his will, a great testimonial benefit on such a colossal scale as the city had not yet seen. The story of that testimonial and how it came to be known as "the great cake-walk" is another chapter—a fascinating chapter in the life of a man and a chapter in the history of New York.

To follow the life of Oscar Hammerstein is to follow not merely the develop-

French baritone Maurice Renaud (1861–1933), internationally famed for his peerless singing and superb acting, played the Manhattan Opera House 1906–1910, roughly the date of this photograph.

1. Mr. Show Business

World-famous soprano Luisa Tetrazzini (1871–1940) joined the Manhattan Opera Company in 1908; autographed photo from 1910.

ment of a single man's life, incredible as that life was, but to follow the unfolding of the pulsing life of a great city in one of its periods of exuberant development. This is true, above all, of the theater and all its allied arts. The period 1883 to 1917—from the opening of Brooklyn Bridge and the Metropolitan Opera House to the plunge into the First World War—was New York's Golden Age of theater and music. In these years was concentrated the most glorious flowering of the best the nineteenth century had produced and in these years there burst open the revolt against the old conventions, the radical new trends, and the brave new talents that distinguished the new arts of the twentieth century.

All during the fabulous eighties, the Gay Nineties, and the dynamic pre-war era, the theater itself—show business—was in constant upheaval, artistic and economic. Those years saw the rise and fall of great managerial personalities and their colorful struggles with each other, great fortunes won and lost in the theater, wars of rival theaters waged on every level whether the level of grand opera (the period opens with the war between the Metropolitan Opera and the Academy of Music and closes with reverberations of the Metropolitan-Manhattan opera war still echoing) or the level of music-hall variety entertainment (as the great war of the music-halls between Koster and Bial and the Olympia).

The period witnessed the great trusts and combinations rising, the theater trust against the independent managers, the vaudeville trust against the independent houses, the opera trust, the war of the theater trust and the vaudeville trust for control of vaudeville, the struggle of trust and counter-trust and through it all plays, operas, great actors, dancers, musicians, beautiful actresses, glamorous opera singers, moved like pawns across a huge chessboard in the moves and countermoves of titanic struggles.

And Oscar Hammerstein, active in the theater during almost the entire period, is constantly in the picture—a storm center in a sea of tempests. Almost all the great and glamorous of the show world pass in review across his stages. There is hardly a struggle in the show world but he is in the thick of it, often leading it, now allied with this or that group of embattled forces, now singlehanded opposing them all.

Because he was a colossus of the theater, bestriding every one of its various fields—because he was Mr. Show Business—he stands out as the one individual most representative of an entire period of brilliant and turbulent activity. The life and legend of Oscar Hammerstein becomes an epitome of Broadway in its greatest and most glamorous era.

2

The Grand Alliance

With the conclusion of his season in July 1893, Hammerstein had to face some facts. From his fastness in the northern reaches of the city, he had launched his invasion of Broadway. He had built his magnificent $500,000 Manhattan Opera House on Thirty-Fourth Street.[1] One of the largest theaters in the city, it was the newest and most modern in construction, with his own patented novel arrangement of mezzanine boxes. It was considered the city's most beautiful theater. And it was a complete failure.

In the entire season there was only one financial fact from which he could take comfort. For the first time, his Harlem Opera House—built 125th Street in 1889—had not shown a loss. Finally, after three years, it had turned the corner. From now on it would be profitable as he had always believed it eventually would be. But for his new Manhattan Opera House he could not discern a ray of financial hope. It was time to take stock of his theatrical position.

Up to now he had seemed to possess the magic touch. He could review a succession of triumphs that had baffled his friends. When he built the Harlem Opera House, they had tried to dissuade him from such folly. Harlem could not support a theater. But he had expected to lose money at first and went ahead with it. When his first season's losses were enormous they begged him to give it up. How they had stared when he told them his conclusion that, since Harlem could not support one theater, perhaps it would support two, and that he was building the Columbus Theatre a few blocks down the street. Clearly they thought him deranged. But he had known exactly what he was doing; and when the Columbus opened and was profitable from the start they ceased to fear for his sanity and began to wonder about their own. He had solved the problem of the Harlem's losses—the Columbus' profits covered them. He had turned a defeat into a victory. And now both houses were to be profitable, as he had predicted all along.

Firmly established as the Napoleon of all theatrical enterprise north of Fifty-Ninth Street, he had turned to the attack on Broadway. Again the magic touch. The site for his proposed Murray Hill Theatre was so shrewdly selected that before the foundation was laid he had sold it. He had been offered a profit so large that the businessman within him could not resist despite the protests of the showman. But he had not been proud of that and resolved never to let it happen again. Then the new site on Thirty-Fourth Street and the construction and opening of the magnificent Manhattan of which he was so proud. And at that point, the magic touch had apparently deserted him.

He had tried everything and nothing had succeeded. Mrs. Bernard Beere, the distinguished British actress, and a company including Maurice Barrymore had been a fat failure. Alexander Salvini had been an artistic success but not a financial one; the theater was too large for drama. For long weeks the house had been dark, a total loss. His own production that had just closed—the French operetta, *The Talisman*, with the stunning ballet, *Versailles*—had been the talk of the town, but it had come too late in the season. So costly a production needed full houses and after a week two mortal blows struck it down—first the heat wave that descended on the city, then the disastrous crash that shook the stock market. People were only beginning to realize it was not just a financial panic but the onset of a national depression. Before the year was out almost five hundred banks and fifteen thousand business firms would fail.

Most imposing and most expensive of all was his own grand opera company, which should have had everything in its favor. There had been no productions at his Metropolitan Opera House since it was gutted by fire in 1892; and now he had presented a wholly new opera, all of it in English and at popular prices.

The Harlem Opera House, pictured in 1888 (public domain).

He had distinguished conductor Adolph Neuendorff in the pit, on the stage the conductor's glamorous wife, the lovely Georgine von Januschofsky—a fine singer and a woman who had once set his own heart aflame, though that was all past now. Nevertheless, the public did not come, and though the critics grudgingly granted him some artistic success, they were not friendly and some were hostile. They had refused to take seriously an impresario who gave opera without the backing of great wealth and social prestige. Well, some day he would make them take him seriously as a producer of grand opera. Perhaps if English impresario James Henry Mapleson—perhaps the most instrumental figure in the development of opera production in London and New York—had not reneged on his promise to let him have that new singer named Nellie Melba, who was electrifying European audiences he might have arrested the attention of critics and public. Perhaps it would not have helped. Well, some day he would have her, too.

But these were dreams for the future. The problem now was the Manhattan Opera House. What was to be done with this costly white elephant? There were two obvious alternatives. He could sell some of his remaining Harlem property or one of his Harlem theaters to keep the Manhattan going, but this would be sacrificing the profitable to maintain the unprofitable. He could sell the Manhattan—not easy to do with a house too large for ordinary drama—at a large financial loss. He did not mind that so much. What ruled it out

Built in 1883, the Metropolitan Opera House was gutted by fire in 1892. The theater's 1892–1893 season was cancelled while it was rebuilt. Photograph ca. 1905 (public domain).

was that it meant defeat, an inglorious withdrawal from his Napoleonic invasion of Broadway—a retreat from Moscow back to Harlem. No, at all costs he must retain a connection with this theater, keep at least a foothold in Broadway show business.

That meant one thing only. He must look for a partner. It must be a partner with a following in some form of show business who wanted his theater and his active participation. And that partner must be someone who needed him and his theater as much as he needed a partner. Was there any one at all, anywhere, who could meet such exacting specifications? Hammerstein gave the matter long and careful consideration and came to the decision that there was—the firm of Koster and Bial.

Koster and Bial. There was a name to conjure with, to all up visions of gay revelry, of twinkling toes and lilting tunes, of legs in tights and champagne drunk from dainty slippers in the fabulous Cork Room of the music hall on Twenty-Third Street. If the Gay Nineties were gay, Koster and Bial were more responsible for that fact than anyone else. From Park Row to Twenty-Third Street, they presided over an empire of wine, women and song. The Manhattan Opera House with its numerous boxes would be easily convertible into a gigantic music hall dedicated to light hearted and light headed revelry. Hammerstein decided an alliance with the Koster and Bial empire was, for the time being, the strategic salvation of his own halted Napoleonic campaign.

Although the empire of Koster and Bial stood for gaiety, frothy and unconfined, there was nothing frothy or gay about its rulers. John Koster and Albert Bial were solid respectable citizens, serious and industrious. Like Hammerstein they were immigrants from Germany. Like him they had achieved success and were worth a million, and like him they were businessmen in the theater. But there all resemblance stopped. Unlike Hammerstein, they were in the theater not because of any deep passion for it but only because it increased their business, and their business was beer and wine. Basically they were high class saloon-keepers. They took wine, women and song as their province—but women and song existed solely to promote wine.

John Koster had arrived from Germany, a youth of nineteen, in the same year Hammerstein had come. Bial had preceded him by a year. Four years later, the two became partners in a small east side restaurant. They prospered and opened others in lower Manhattan. They were not slow in discovering that the most profitable part of a restaurant was the bar and with each succeeding establishment the bar became larger and more prominent, the role of food more and more that of inducement to drink. Their restaurant and bar in the Tribune Building became the resort of prominent politicians, journalists and brokers, men who knew their liquor and how to hold it. Within a few years they were also in the beer bottling business, distributing beers that George Ehret[2] brewed for them.

Now the partners sought about for some further inducement to drinking. To people bred in the Germanic tradition the answer was obvious—music. This was the underlying principle of the German beer-garden. The amiable flow of music from an orchestra or band set in motion an equally amiable and steady flow of beer.

So it came about that in 1879 they opened a German-style concert hall and open air garden on Twenty-Third Street west of Sixth Avenue. Neither the genial Koster nor the more forceful Bial had any special interest in music but Bial had a brother, Rudolph, who was a well-known popular composer and conductor in Germany. He brought him over and installed him with a sizeable orchestra as the main attraction, supplemented by distinguished soloists. The new resort became even more popular in 1881, when the orchestra was replaced by the band led by Patrick Gilmore, the reputed composer of "When Johnny Comes Marching Home" and the most famous band leader in America until the rise of Sousa.

This engagement lasted six months and was so successful that the partners decided to provide entertainment on a larger scale. They abandoned the concert hall and garden for the large hall adjoining it which they fitted up as a charming music hall seating twelve hundred, patterned after the famous music halls of London and Paris. It had many unique features. The stage had no drop curtain because a city ordinance prohibited a curtain in places operating under a concert license, and if a theater license was given the selling of liquor would be illegal (a law whose repeal was never even considered until 1953). The difficulty could be adjusted by some discreet graft to the local police but Koster and Bial employed a more original device—an enormous fan which rose up from the footlights to serve as a curtain. The front half of the hall contained seats, the rear tables and chairs. There was a balcony composed of thirty-three boxes, each curtained off on three sides for parties desiring privacy.

A permanent stage show was installed, presenting short burlesques under the musical direction of Fred Solomon, brother of the Edward Solomon who was one of Lillian Russell's several husbands. The rest of the program was a bill of variety acts, mostly imported from Europe. Among the featured starts were such celebrities as the demure-faced Marie Lloyd of London and the piquant Parisian, Eugenie Fougere, two music hall singers who, in completely different styles, sang ditties that were scandalously risqué.

Koster and Bial's Music Hall became the gayest night spot in New York and its fame soon spread from coast to coast. But the feature that made it most celebrated and most notorious was the famous Cork Room. Here only one beverage was uncorked—champagne—and the uncorking made into a pretty ceremony. The purchaser's name, or his lady's, was duly inscribed upon the cork and the cork itself then set into the ceiling as a permanent part of the room decorations. In due time the ceiling and walls were covered with thousands of corks formed into elaborate designs and hanging in gaily beribboned festoons.

All this was innocent gaiety. The notorious feature (to the soberer minded) was the fact that the Cork Room was directly off the stage and as the girls trooped off stage they passed through it and could accept invitations to drink with patrons known to the management. They were, of course, in their stage costumes and frequently in tights. It was the idea of gentlemen drinking with ladies of the stage who had their legs exposed that scandalized the respectable.

As a device to promote the buying of drinks, a pretty showgirl at the table has never been improved upon, a fact well known to nightclub owners today. Although the Parisian stars also served as inspiration when so inclined, the regular queens of the Cork Room were Madge Lessing and Josie Gregory of the permanent show, two of the prettiest and shapeliest young women in New York. Actually nothing overtly indecent or rowdy was ever permitted by the respectable owners and any overstepping of the proprieties was dealt with quickly and quietly by an efficient crew of bouncers. But the Cork Room stood for Parisian naughtiness to everyone, and for downright sinfulness to many. No visitors seeing the sights of New York ever missed the Cork Room, where they could ogle at the spectacle of gentlemen drinking with painted beauties of the stage, sip champagne themselves and be immortalized in the heaven of the Cork Room ceiling.

The season 1892–1893 was the twenty-fifth anniversary of the partnership of Koster and Bial. They now ruled an extensive empire. In addition to the music hall they owned four of the most sumptuous saloons in the city, although they preferred to call them "refreshment parlors." One of them, called "The Corner," was situated at the south west corner of Sixth Avenue and Twenty-Fourth Street. It contained an elegantly ornate barroom, a severer colonial type old tavern, sitting room and billiard hall. Its location was strategic. Then the music hall closed. Those disposed for a night of serious drinking merely repaired to the Corner around the block. Today it stands as the only remaining structure of the Koster and Bial empire, a forlorn four-story building, its ground floor divided between an umbrella shop and a delicatessen store. On the cornice the engraved name Koster and Biel, can still be seen, and sixty years after, a plaque one flight up still reads, Koster and Bial's The Corner. It is difficult to believe this dingy structure once housed one of New York's most elegant saloons. In addition to these establishments there was the Koster and Bial beer distributing business which sold its merchandise at a handsome profit to its largest and steadiest customer—Koster and Biel. A beer importing business had also been added, bringing Bohemian and Bavarian brews to those fastidious patrons to whom the thought of drinking anything domestic was unthinkable. All parts of the empire flourished mightily but the crown jewel in the imperial diadem was the music hall. Quite apart from the charms of the hall and Cork

Room the variety bills presented there (the term vaudeville was just beginning to be used) were first rate and excelled anything to be seen in the city.

Without quite realizing how it had happened, Koster and Bial found themselves successful theatrical magnates, saloonkeepers in show business. It was always a bit bewildering to John Koster, who managed the food and drinks. He used to say that it puzzled him to observe that those weeks when the stage bill was unusually good the food and drink receipts always fell. The observation was accurate. When the performance was routine people went out to drink; when it was absorbing they gave no thought to refreshment and many came solely for the performance.

It sometimes made him wonder if by being in show business they were not really working against themselves. But as long as the music hall prospered nothing mattered.

Biel, the more imaginative partner, took charge of the theatrical side. He made an annual trip abroad to secure top European talent, judged them by their reputation, looks, personality. He could appraise "the female form divine" as well as the next man and had no difficulty in determining when a pair of tights were properly filled. He developed a genuine flair for discovering first-rate acrobats and specialty performers in obscure travelling shows and exploiting them as stars, and he learned the knack of putting together vaudeville bills of variety and contrast.

Koster and Bial's Music Hall was filled nightly with a gay crowd, as the girls on the stage raised shapely legs and the audience at the tables raised flowing steins, all to an obligato of popping corks from the Cork Room. Koster and Bial were wealthy and successful. Yet their success was marred by two considerations over which they grieved in the midst of their hall of revelry.

What was mainly responsible for both causes of grief was a woman, a woman young, beautiful and fascinating. Her name was Carmen Dauset Moreno, better known as Carmencita, and she was a Spanish dancer whom Bial had engaged in Europe in 1890. New York had never seen dancing so fiery, so passionately tempestuous, yet so graceful. It would not see such dancing again for many years, not until the advent of La Argentina. The Music Hall audience did not applaud. It stood up and cheered. In the Cork Room many a toast was drunk to the lovely and fiery Carmencita. As a respectable married woman off the stage she did not drink with strange men (or friendly ones), but now and then she gladdened the hearts of college boys out on the town by sending them her slipper to drink from.

Carmencita packed the hall week after week. Out of curiosity a newspaper critic dropped in one night. The next morning he was doing handsprings in print. Other newsmen quickly made the trek to Twenty-Third Street. They came, they saw, and they cheered. And soon fashionable society folk were arriving to see the wonderful new dancer for themselves. There was the rub. These respectable people felt out of place in Koster and Bial's.

The Music Hall attracted a gay, roistering crowd of men about town. Situated in the heart of the Tenderloin its patrons included the local politicians and their hangers-on and these were frequently notorious Tenderloin characters trailing a strong odor of the underworld. To Messrs. Koster and Bial, two solid, respectable citizens, this had always been a source of annoyance. Now it caused them to grieve in earnest. Again and again new patrons came who insinuated they would gladly bring their wives but it would be awkward to take fastidious ladies to a place where such questionable persons were in evidence to say nothing of the dubious goings-on in the Cork Room.

The souls of Koster and Bial yearned for respectability as only the souls of saloonkeepers can yearn. Their ideal was a resort where joy could be unconfined yet never unrefined.

With the coming of Carmencita and the new respectable class she attracted the ideal was within their grasp if only they would act with resolution and dispatch. This they did. They shocked and saddened their old time patrons by announcing the abolition of the Cork Room. To soften the blow they made quite a ceremony of it. They invited its habitués to an all-night wake in the Cork Room where they could fittingly drown their sorrow at its demise. At the stroke of midnight each guest received a tiny black coffin in which reposed one of his own inscribed corks. By morning the Cork Room had passed into history. Privileged patrons might still be permitted to visit the actresses' dressing rooms, like any ordinary stage door Johnnies, but any eventualities would henceforth be conducted off the premises. The next step was to bar all notorious or objectionable persons. This took patience, firmness and tact but by the spring of 1893 the Tenderloin characters knew they were not welcome and stayed away. Koster and Bial could boast their hall was safe for the most respectable lady to visit without embarrassment.

But the other source of their grief remained, and it too was in large part due to Carmencita. Frequently, when the bill was very good the Music Hall had turned people away. With Carmencita the rage of the town, hundreds were unable to get in. What greater tragedy could befall two businessmen than nightly to have to turn away cash customers. The spirit was willing but the capacity inadequate—a pitiful 1200.

It became clear to the partners that what they needed was a larger house further uptown in the thirties, on or near the Broadway theater district, to remove any lingering traces of Tenderloin atmosphere. So it came to pass that in June 1893, the firm of Koster and Bial was looking for a site on which to build a large music hall. It would cost a fortune but they had the money and they would be enabled to take in more money. Their search for a building site was common knowledge in theatrical circles. It was of course, known to Hammerstein and it was this fact that led him to decide that Koster and Bial were ideally fitted to become his partners.

Having made his choice, Hammerstein set out to share them with speed and adroitness. He made no direct overtures but authorized a real estate broker to make the proposal to them on his own. Then he began a series of well publicized conferences with groups of capitalists. He told the reporters that since putting on the ballet *Versailles*, he had been deluged with propositions to convert the Manhattan Opera House into a music hall on the plan of the Empire and Alhambra in London, where the principal feature was a ballet. He announced the departure from London of two of the directors of the Empire and his plan to negotiate with them. He was open minded on all the proposals, he said, but whichever he chose he would not in any case relinquish the artistic management of his house. All these meetings may have served to explore some genuine possibilities but their chief purpose was to inform Koster and Bial they had better hurry before they lost out and found themselves with a new competitor to boot.

The strategy was effective. Koster and Bial came in haste. They looked over the theater and Hammerstein explained his plans for its conversion. They were enchanted—the house was the answer to all their dreams. They could have the newest and finest theater in the city by the fall and save all the time, uncertainty and vast expense of building. They must have Hammerstein's theater at all costs. As for his desire to produce ballets and other shows, why, they were delighted. With his artistic productions combined with their variety performances, they could have the greatest music hall in the world. They wanted him as a partner. He was a man of their own kidney, so they thought. Was he not, like them, an industrious German, a self-made man who had made fortunes in such solid fields as tobacco and real estate? Was he not a non-nonsense, feet-on-the-ground businessman in the theater, even as they were, and a real theatrical magnate operating not one but three theaters? And as for respectability, this was the best part of all. They would be associated with a theatrical man who had produced the highest type of entertainment, one who had given grand opera and upon whose stage the great Booth[3] himself had walked. As partners of such a man they would rise far above even the suspicion of anything low class. They pressed Hammerstein on the advantages of their proposition and gradually, bit by bit, he allowed himself to be persuaded.

July 18 the grand alliance was consummated. When the three men affixed their signatures to the documents none of them could have suspected what a fateful partnership they had formed. It was to be one of the most profitable and most disastrous in the history of theater. One of the partners would be dead within twenty months, another would die a ruined man within four years, and the year after the sole surviving member of the trio would be penniless.

The deal was complicated but what it boiled down to was that Koster and Biel bought a half interest in the property for $375,000, paid to Hammerstein in the form of a mortgage he would hold upon the theater. A new firm, Koster, Bial and Company, would operate the enterprise. The three men were to be the owners and directors, and Hammerstein was to own a half interest in the firm. He was to direct ballets and stage productions; they were to engage the specialty artists and control the front of the house. The theater would bear the name, Koster and Bial's Music Hall.

The alterations that Hammerstein had designed were commenced immediately. On the orchestra floor every other row of seats was removed, leaving seven-hundred extra-roomy seats. This was important because, in addition to being permitted to smoke in their seats, patrons could have refreshments brought to them if they did not care to go to the lounges. To the back of each seat was affixed a sturdy rack designed to hold steins of beer. Behind the boxes on the second floor a large cafe lounge and promenade was fitted up. Here people could lounge or stroll or sit at tables to eat or drink. Ten of the center boxes were removed so that the performance could be heard from there and patrons wishing to see the number in progress could step up to the wide opening and command a full view of the stage. The house was full of Hammerstein ideas and innovations, and all of them filled Koster and Bial with admiration and enthusiasm. Meanwhile Hammerstein was rehearsing his lovely ballet, *Versailles*, only recently closed with *The Talisman*. Then interpolated in that operetta, he had been forced to condense the ballet. Now he could present it full length and Clara Qualitz, his premier danseuse, could demonstrate the fullness of her powers.

Saturday night August twenty sixth saw another wake on Twenty-Third Street, the last performance in the hall which had seen so much boisterous revelry. The house was packed for a special program. A number of the old stars were brought back and Carmencita graced the occasion. Fred Solomon sang a specially written song about the old hall and, at midnight, the entire audience rose and sang "Auld Lang Syne." It was worse than the Cork Room wake. A landmark of joy was passing from the New York scene, and there were genuine tears in the eyes of many of the old-timers.

Monday night, August 28, 1893, Twenty-Third Street lay in forgotten gloom, but all was gaiety and brightness on Thirty-Fourth Street. As the heading in one newspaper put it: "Koster and Bial's is dead. Long live Koster and Bial's!" Thirty-Fourth Street was ablaze from the lights of the theater as the carriages rolled up disgorging society men and their wives, men about town and their women, theatrical people, politicians, and a huge crowd lined both sides of the street for half a block either way excitedly spotting arriving celebrities. The next morning's *New York World* was to note that 3000 managed to get in and hundreds were turned away to join the crowds outside.

The *New York Herald* said:

> It was nothing more than the opening of a new musical hall, but if a stranger chanced to pass through Thirty-Fourth Street last evening he must surely have thought that a meeting of the greatest moment.... Was about to take place... Never was a theatre more densely crowded and never did different conditions of men and women meet so thoroughly in that spirit which makes the whole world kin... the laughing, the talking and the guying that went on... It was more like a theatrical carnival.... An evening which for general hilarity and thorough *sans gene* has never been witnessed inside a local theatre.

All the papers commented on the beauty and spaciousness of the house, the roominess of the seats, the elegance of the lounges and promenades. The *New York Press* said of the opening that it "marks a new epoch in New York amusements, as it adds the beauty of a ballet to the attractions and variety of the vaudeville... None of the famous gardens of Paris surpass in glitter and glamour the new Koster and Bial's... all gay New York was out." If there was financial panic abroad in the land Thirty-Fourth Street knew it not.

Promotional poster for Koster and Bial's Music Hall, ca. 1895 (public domain).

The first night audience was not undiscriminating; it was reserved at the beginning. But the program had been artfully planned to unfold a succession of ever higher climaxes. There were the usual acrobatic and singing acts, some familiar, some new, and all of them first rate. A particularly successful newcomer was Senorita Tortajada, a strikingly handsome woman with a fine figure who sang and danced with her own supporting company. Then came an old favorite, Paquerette, the French singing comedienne, whose appearance brought shouts of delight and numerous encores. Then to a storm of applause the brilliant Carmencita "somewhat stouter than of yore, rushed upon the stage as full of verve and fire as ever" and brought the house to a high pitch of enthusiasm. Finally, after a short intermission, the curtain rose on the ballet *Versailles*, given for the first time in its entirety. The brilliance of the dancing, the beauty of the costumes and decor brought gasps of admiration. "Of its kind," said The World, "nothing handsomer has been seen on the New York stage. Clara Qualitz acquitted herself with splendid distinction and the first night… came to a triumphant conclusion."

Despite the late hour the audience refused to leave. There were shouts of "Hammerstein!" and the builder of the house and producer of the ballet was summoned before the curtain to take a bow. There were also calls for Koster and Bial but those gentlemen were too shy for a personal appearance. They remained in their box and received the congratulations of their friends for having been so astute as to select Hammerstein and his theater for their grand alliance. With faces wreathed in smiles they looked over the packed house. The steins in the beer racks were foaming, in the lounges the wine glasses were being filled and refilled, and their own cup of happiness was running over.

The man who should have been happiest of all was Oscar Hammerstein. The evening had been a personal triumph for him. Six weeks earlier he had been in a difficult position. He had extricated himself by a brilliant maneuver. Again he had turned a defeat into a victory. But though he bowed and smiled he was not happy about the whole affair. He did not like the idea of having partners. He had been forced to it, and he did not relish his association with Koster and Bial. They were not theatrical people, merely high class saloon-keepers, and he had intended this house for more glorious uses than a music hall. Not that he despised vaudeville—he loved the theater too much not to respect every form of it. But his sights had been set on the arts of drama and grand opera. To that extent this evening represented a defeat and this defeat too he was determined to turn into a victory. He would raise music hall performance to the highest artistic level. The ballet was but a beginning; he had many creative ideas and he would use them in developing a new kind of music hall. He was to have the opportunity for creative activity much sooner than he realized.

In his office the reporters surrounded him, wanting to know his comment on the reopening of the Manhattan. He reminded them, somewhat morosely, that it was now Koster and Bial's—the Manhattan Opera House no longer existed. Its life had begun and ended in a single season. And he gave them a wry summary of that brief career which they were soon quoting in their columns. He told them: "I began with Mme. Bernard Beere, tried to continue with Meyerbeer,[4] and ended with lager beer."

3

The Prisoner in the Gilsey House

The grand alliance pursued its triumphal march. The entire opening bill was held over a second week, then a third with only minor changes. Full houses were the rule, a rule fully justified by the quality of the bill—nine acts, everyone of which, whether acrobatic, singing, dancing or other specialty, would have been the headline act on any ordinary vaudeville bill. The price scale was comparable to that of the first class theaters. A general admission fee of fifty cents admitted to standing room or to the lounges. Seats varied with location from seventy-five cents in the balcony to a dollar and a half in the front orchestra, and from six to fifteen dollars for a box.

It was frequently said that the new Koster and Bial's never developed the intimate charm of the old hall on Twenty-Third Street. This was true, not only because of the great size of the house, but because the audience was more heterogeneous. It was in effect, two distinct audiences—the old music hall audience and a new theater audience. The new audience treated the house as a theater. It came to see the show and remained in its seats except for the intermission, only occasionally ordering a beer or two to be brought to a seat. This was not the way a music hall audience was expected to behave. The true music hall patron did not sit, he circulated. He was in his seat for only a featured act or so; the rest of his time he spent lounging, conversing, promenading, eating and drinking. He was still within earshot of the stage and if anything of special interest was on, he could easily get a view of it even from the lounge and cafe.

What the new audience lacked in the way of spending on food and drink it made up by filling the house at theater prices, and by its respectability. The sight of reputable men accompanied by their wives emboldened Koster and Bial to seek yet greater heights of respectability. Why not go one step further—respectable women unaccompanied? To encourage this, a new policy for the Saturday matinee was announced. During these afternoon performances smoking would be forbidden, no refreshments served and the lounge closed down.

Hammerstein threw himself into the operation of the music hall with his usual energy and enthusiasm. Koster, Bial, business manager and press representative Carver Cline, and the other executives remained in their offices while subordinates carried out their instructions. Hammerstein, despite having two other theaters to supervise, was everywhere—in the front offices, in the basement, back stage, throwing off ideas like sparks. Here he was suggesting a new arrangement of the lounge, there an improvement in the ventilating machinery. Now he was devising new mechanical gadgets for more rapid scene shifting, and, another time, preparing a program of overture pieces for the orchestra. And all the while he was rehearsing the ballet, rearranging scenes, introducing new effects and improvements. The theatrical reporters marveled at his protean activity. One reporter ribbed him, saying he did everything in the theater except perform on the stage. "Don't be so sure," Hammerstein quipped back, playfully, "I may appear on the stage in a specialty act before long. What will I do? A balancing act in full view of the audience. What will I balance? My bank account."

September 1893 saw the beginning of major changes in the Music Hall program. Carmencita and others departed and in the new few weeks the major additions to the bill included a number of American debuts. One was Edmee Lescot, "chanteuse cosmopolite," from Paris, another Ada Reeve, very young, very lovely and talented, whom Bial had secured in London at the very start of her music hall career.

(In 1953 a British motion picture about welfare workers and their clients in a British police court was shown in New York under the title, "I Believe In You." An old woman, obviously a crackpot, is always pestering a welfare worker to look at her album. To get rid of her he finally consents and finds, to his amazement, not a family album but a scrapbook filled with pictures of a lovely young woman in scanty stage costumes. He is stunned at the realization that she was once a music hall beauty. The role of that old woman was played by Ada Reeve, still a lively performer close on to eighty, and the scrapbook was her own.)

The most important event among the newcomers was the much advertised American debut of Harriett Vernon, the well known English burlesque performer and professional beauty whom Bial had imported from London at a salary of $600 a week. Although the star of the bill, built up as the English Lillian Russell, she did not arouse any great enthusiasm. A large woman with a pretty face and magnificent figure, her poses were statuesque and eye-filling but neither her voice, nor her songs, nor manner of singing them, possessed any special attraction. However, like most music hall singers, she sang her songs in costume, changing for each number, and her costumes were triumphs of design, color and finish that dazzled the audience and brought "ohs" and "ahs" from the women.

Hammerstein, who felt that singing and singers should come under his jurisdiction, disapproved of the Vernon engagement as poor theatrical judgment. He did not make any issue of it with his partners, neither did he conceal his low opinion of the high-priced star. To Cline, he held forth on the subject with considerable asperity.

They were paying $600 a week, he pointed out, for a second-rate performer who never received more than $75 in the London music halls. And for what were they paying this large sum? For the lady's voice, which was mediocre? For her singing, which was poor? Her songs, which were dull? Her face and figure, then? They, at least, were good. But, Hammerstein pointed out, half a dozen just as good could be found in any chorus line on Broadway. Her only really outstanding attractions were her costumes—that was what they were paying $600 for. But if that was the case, he concluded sarcastically, why bother transporting the lady across the ocean. They could have had her simply ship the costumes for exhibition upon the stage.

Cline had little sense of humor but an excellent sense of publicity. What Hammerstein said in sarcasm he saw as a great idea. Exhibit the costumes—what a wonderful thought! In a moment he was thanking Hammerstein profusely for so brilliant a suggestion, then running off to set it into operation. To Hammerstein's vast amusement, a notice of special interest to ladies was soon widely published. It announced that on Thursday afternoon, September 28, from two to four, the costumes of Harriett Vernon would be on exhibition at Koster and Bial's.

No stranger sight had ever been witnessed within the precincts of a music hall than was seen at Koster and Bial's that Thursday—hundreds of elegant matrons, many with their daughters, excitedly looking, touching, handling, examining and admiring masterpieces of textile technique and the dressmaker's art. Moving among them with refreshments, the hall's staff of waiters in full livery served the ladies—with tea. The theater was filled with the hubbub of feminine voices—refined voices, speaking in cultivated accents.

Koster and Bial's costume exhibit and tea for ladies was a well publicized event. Whatever emotions it inspired in the breasts of the Cork Room alumni were never publicly expressed. That an institution once given over to the champagne toasts of gilded youths and painted women should come to this must have evoked feelings too deep for tears. But the faces of Messrs. Koster and Bial were radiant as they stood, two beaming hosts, welcoming their feminine guests. This was the ultimate step. They had entered the saloonkeeper's seventh heaven of respectability. The ghosts of the Cork Room were exorcized forever.

English burlesque performer Harriet Vernon (1858–1923), in 1885 (public domain).

Yet the one man who would have enjoyed the occasion most—the inadvertent father of the event—was absent. He would not have missed it for anything. But that very afternoon, only a few blocks away, Oscar Hammerstein was a prisoner in a locked hotel room, undergoing the severest ordeal of his life.

It all began innocently enough in a hotel cafe. Hammerstein was seated at a table with a group of theatrical personalities. The noted German-born musician, composer and conductor of comic operas at the Casino, Gustave Kerker, was there with Charles Alfred Byrne, the drama critic and librettist. Henry Neagle, dramatic editor of the *New York Recorder* and Leander Richardson, the theatrical writer who would become New York's first Broadway columnist, were also there, as was playwright Louis Harrison. After the occasion became theatrical history, a hundred others would claim they were there. Most distinguished of all at the table was James Gibbons Huneker, the music critic who was to win even greater celebrity as a drama critic and literary figure. His account is responsible for the errors in later references to the famous affair, for, writing from memory a quarter of a century later, he managed to get all the major facts wrong.

Only recently, Kerker had been Hammerstein's conductor for *The Talisman*. Since then he had composed a comic opera, *Venus*, for which Byrne had written the book. Hammerstein, who had attended the opening, had found it so dull that he had walked out before the end. At the table, he made no secret of his low opinion of Kerker's latest effort. The composer was very much put out. With considerable bitterness he complained of the long labor required to compose a comic opera and of the ease with which critics and amateurs dismissed the results of arduous effort.

Hammerstein snorted with derision. One would think a Wagner's *Ring* or Mozart's *Don Giovanni* were at issue, he scoffed—such fuss about a mere comic opera. It was so easy to criticize, Kerker retorted with considerable heat, but let those who talk try to compose an opera. That set Hammerstein off in earnest on the subject of popular music. He pointed out, among other things, that he was no mere talker about music; he was a capable musician and he had composed popular music himself. "Why," he said, warming up to the subject, "I'm no professional composer but I'd bet $100 I could write a comic opera in two days, words and music, and have it produced in any theater in New York." Kerker promptly whipped out his wallet and counted out $100. "All right, you braggart," he said, "I'm taking you." Carried away by the ardor of controversy, Hammerstein had not expected anything like this, but pride quickly overcame consternation. Manfully, he drew out a $100 bill, saying quietly, "I said I could do it and I can do it."

With unconcealed glee the others pounced upon the opportunity. More than once they had been annoyed at Hammerstein's boastfulness. The man was always bragging about the beauty of the theater he was building, the originality of the productions he was planning. True, he had a disconcerting way of doing the things he boasted he would do, but this time he had let his enthusiasm run away with him. He had gotten himself way out on a limb and they would have a high old time sawing it off. On the spot Byrne was made chairman of a committee to be formed of well known theatrical men. They were to draw up a formal contract setting the precise conditions for the wager. Kerker and Hammerstein were ordered to meet the committee at Byrne's office to sign the contract at two o'clock the next day. To make certain that Hammerstein could not palm off some production he might have been working on, the committee would select a subject for the story of the comic opera.

On the morning of September 28, when Hammerstein was to begin his work, several newspapers already carried the story of the unique wager being arranged that day. When Hammerstein arrived at Byrne's office he found a committee including Louis Harrison, J.I.C. Clarke,[1] and the producer George W. Lederer, manager of the *Casino*, New York's leading comic opera theater, together with a battery of newspaper reporters standing by with pencils poised.

The proceedings were conducted with the greatest seriousness and formality. In the presence of Kerker, Hammerstein was informed of the subject selected for his opus—the Kohinoor diamond—a fabulous gem, indeed, but hardly the most promising topic for a libretto. He was left free to treat the subject in any way he saw fit. Hammerstein received this information with a smile. Byrne then proceeded to read the articles of agreement. The document, unique in the annals of the theater, was both formal and formidable:

> It is hereby agreed between Oscar Hammerstein and Gustave Kerker, the wager being $100 on each side, that Oscar Hammerstein, being given a subject, will conceive a plot in one act, design the costumes, also the scenery, write the libretto and lyrics and compose the music of an opera within forty-eight hours from the time that he is locked up in a room for that purpose. Should he succeed Gustave Kerker loses the wager. Should he fail Oscar Hammerstein must pay Kerker $100. The opera to play no less than one hour.

It is further understood that at the expiration of the forty-eight hours a competent musician is to immediately proceed to copy the music composed by Mr. Hammerstein, to put the same into such condition as to obtain a perfect piano score as well as to put the concerted music into legitimate form for orchestration. The work then to be submitted to the following committee: A. M. Palmer, Jesse Williams, Leander Richardson, and J.I.C. Clarke, who shall be the sole judges as to the merit of the work for acceptance and production in a first class New York theatre. If the Judges should decide that the work is not worthy of a metropolitan production the said Oscar Hammerstein shall forfeit the $100.

With a sinking heart, Hammerstein heard the conditions as they were unfolded. He felt, as he later admitted, a noose slowly tightening around his neck. Outwardly, however, he accepted each condition with a smile. There was a story in later years that someone wanted to insert a clause requiring him to write the opera with one hand tied behind his back and that only at this proposal did Hammerstein demur, insisting upon two hands or nothing. But that is the kind of fanciful embroidery with which Broadway legends become embellished.

The contract duly signed, sealed and witnessed, the entire party-principals, committee and reporters—repaired to the nearby Gilsey House. In the hotel, Kerker offered to treat Hammerstein to drinks. "Oh, no you don't ! I want that $100," laughed Hammerstein as he went to the desk to arrange for rooms. He wanted a room for himself, a second room connecting with it and a piano. The piano would have to be rented for the occasion, the clerk informed him; then connecting a piano with a boisterous party, he fixed a reproving eye upon Hammerstein and began to ask pointed questions about the occupant of the other room. "No, no," said Hammerstein, "it's not what you're thinking of. It's just an affair between gentlemen to settle a bet." The clerk looked even more startled. "No, it's not what you're thinking of now, either—it's not a prizefight. I am to do some work there," Hammerstein explained. A much relieved clerk assigned him numbers 48 and 50, third floor, on the Twenty-Ninth Street side of the hotel and messengers were dispatched for writing and music paper and a rented piano.

The whole crowd followed upstairs. Hammerstein chose number 50. Jack Hirsch was established in number 48 to act as custodian and to ensure that his charge would be kept incommunicado. A ceremonious search of Hammerstein's pockets was made and no contraband found. His friends wished him luck, the others looked gleeful, the door was locked by Lederer and the key handed to Hirsch. It was 3:20 p.m. Thursday. Hammerstein's ordeal had begun. It would last until 3:20 Saturday. As the door was being closed upon him he called out to Kerker, who stood snickering derisively: "You think you've got me, don't you? Well, you haven't, I'm going to win that $100 of yours."

Hammerstein was feeling far from confident. For several hours, as he admitted afterward, he could not think of a beginning for a plot. Having made the boast, he felt he would look ridiculous if he failed. His honor was at stake. "It was all begun in fun," he said later, "but I realized after they locked me up in that room that it was a terribly serious affair. I would have given $1,000 to be out of it." There was a time when he was close to despair. The rented piano arrived in the evening but it was not the only piano brought in. Suddenly, from the room above came the sounds of a piano banging out "Ta-Ra-Ra-Boom-De-Aye." Kerker was determined to add some obstacles not contemplated in the articles of agreement. He was being aided and abetted by Ariel Barney, Louis Harrison, John Russell[2] and others, great practical jokesters all, their sense of humor better developed than their sense of fair play. While Hammerstein held his hands to his ears in desperation, Hirsch sent up a note asking the pianist to cease and desist. A reply promised there would be no more playing of the piano. There was not. But soon, the tune of "Pickin' on the Old Ham Bone" was being loudly plucked on a banjo.

Musical composition out of the question, Hammerstein tried to evolve a plot and found the going discouragingly slow. Hirsch was supposed to bar all reporters but he made exceptions for a favored few. A *Sun* reporter was permitted a few words with the prisoner and found him with his spirits at their lowest ebb. Hammerstein revealed that the scene of the plot he was working on was the South African diamond fields, that he knew nothing about the place and that whenever confronted by a difficult situation he would introduce a ballet.

"I have already committed three murders," he said wearily, " and I don't know how many more I may have to commit, but it looks to me now as if the pleasantest thing I could do would be to drown myself in the bathtub."

Later that night, after the banjo playing finally stopped, Hammerstein thought better of it, decided to drown the South African story instead and to substitute a more suitable plot. Then he went to the piano and began to play. For a long time he wooed the muse with musical offerings while various hotel guests complained to the desk, demanding to know who was hammering a piano at that late hour. A diplomatic night clerk told them confidentially that Paderewski[3] had slipped into town incognito and was warming up his hands. Hammerstein's muse did not fail and he was in the throes of composition most of the night, alternately drumming the piano and writing down notes.

Friday morning all New York knew about the prisoner in the Gilsey House. The *Herald* headline read: "Writing Opera Against Time." The *World* story was headed: "Having Fun with Hammerstein." The *Sun* had it on the front page: "An Operetta in 48 Hours—Hammerstein Bets $100 He Can Compose It."

Every paper had its reporters at the hotel and Hirsch was issuing periodic bulletins on the prisoner's progress, gauged from sounds of piano and pen and sights viewed through the keyhole. But Hammerstein's ordeal was far from over.

Early in the morning the strains of a hand organ playing "Little Annie Rooney" floated clearly into room number 50. Hammerstein looked out of the window of his prison. On Twenty-Ninth Street, directly below, an Italian organ grinder was cranking passionately. He threw him some money and waved him away. The man continued to grind. Evidently he thought his efforts were being appreciated. Hammerstein made motions and gestures indicating plainly "Go away!" No result. At the next window Hirsch opened fire with a seltzer bottle. The sprinkling did no good. Hammerstein reappeared at his window and emptied the water pitcher, scoring a direct hit. The music was finally doused, but no—a second organ grinder was coming around the Broadway corner lustily playing "My Sweetheart's the Man in the Moon," and presently two others were coming from the other end of the block antiphonally grinding out "Daddy Wouldn't Buy Me a Bow-Wow." And Hammerstein knew the pranksters were having their fun again.

New York then had a large population of Italian organ grinders. Around the corner Kerker, Barney, Russell, et al., were going at it in earnest, hiring them in batches to play by the hour. Whatever their method of communication may have been, it was swift and sure and it demonstrated its efficiency that day. The word had gone out to every hurdy-gurdy virtuoso in the city—there was good pay for music on Twenty-Ninth Street. From the east side, west side, all around the town they converged on the Gilsey House block, some with monkeys in their red uniforms and little red hats, others without simian assistants, coming in twos and in threes and in dozens. Soon the block was filled with blaring and wheezing hand organs and Twenty-Ninth Street was a cacophonous bedlam. Windows went up all over the hotel. Water pitchers, wash basins and less decorous receptacles were being emptied on the musicians. A similar serial barrage was being aimed from office windows across the street. But for every drenched musician who retreated, Kerker and his confederates had two or three fresh replacements ready to enter the battle.

Meanwhile, Hammerstein had dispatched, via Hirsch, an urgent message to Byrne and Lederer. Its burden was: fun is fun and fair is fair. He had made a bet and he was trying to carry it out in good faith. The conditions were difficult enough without these added torments and he wanted his rooms changed at once. A cry for justice, it did not go unheeded. Permission granted, Hammerstein, Hirsch and piano were swiftly moved to number 255 and 257, inside rooms in the annex.

Outside, the battle of the hand-organs mounted in fury. Kerker and company were still paying out money, unaware that the intended victim of the attack had been evacuated. As for their Italian mercenaries, with them it was now a matter of principle. They were fighting stubbornly for the rights they had come to America to enjoy—the rights of free assembly in the street and the right freely to exercise their calling by making music for good pay on Twenty-Ninth Street.

The hotel management now mobilized its uniformed troops, its elite guard in red, sending out a phalanx of bell-hops in a headlong charge that was to clear the street of the enemy. Now there were uniformed cadets deployed by both hostile forces. New York had seen many a strange sight but never anything quite so bizarre as this contest, with bell-hops in "monkey suits" on one side and monkeys in bell-hop suits on the other. The newsmen, always ready to improve a good story, stood in the hotel entrance egging on all parties to greater effort, an idea immediately taken up by the large crowd that had gathered on Broadway and was now cheering all combatants impartially. The hotel forces were well organized but outnumbered. With the help of some men from the offices across the street they managed to drive many of the organ-grinders off the block, only to find fresh reinforcements had come up, set up their field pieces and were going full blast.

The joke had now begun to turn on its perpetrators. Kerker and his friends did not need nor have money to pay for any more organ-grinders. But, like the sorcerer's apprentice, they had unleashed forces they could no longer control. Organ-grinders were still coming from distant parts, drawn by the lure of work at high pay. Worse yet, the unleashed forces were beginning to turn against their masters. Bedraggled organ-grinders, forced out of the melee, were gesticulating at them, demanding compensation for torn and soaked clothing and for damage to persons and instruments. As the clamor increased Kerker and his associates threw courage to the winds and made good their escape before they were completely encircled. The battle of Twenty-Ninth Street might have raged all day but for the arrival of the police who finally cleared the street, their clubs convincing the stubbornest musician that, all reports to the contrary notwithstanding, there was no profit in playing Twenty-Ninth Street.

Secure in his inner room, Hammerstein had really hit his stride. Furiously, with the frenzy of creation white hot upon him, he worked far into the night. If he had been much sinned against before, now it was the nearby guests who suffered as he banged the piano and sang his choruses and solo parts, including the high soprano, in voice loud with confidence. Complaints that a wild man was howling and thumping reached the harassed hotel management, who made what reply they could and counted the hours that remained to the end of Hammerstein's ordeal—and theirs.

The committee was also becoming anxious. All expenses were to be charged against the loser's $100 and Hirsch had been given free rein. The prisoner, well fortified with his own cigars, drank strong coffee and ate sparingly, but the jailer had developed an alarming appetite for thick steaks and liquid refreshment. Already the charge account stood at $98 and they had neglected to put a "cost plus" clause into the agreement.

The morning papers kept the city properly informed of Hammerstein's progress and the past day's events, with differing versions of the battle of Twenty-Ninth Street. No reader was left ignorant of the fact that this day, Saturday, was the day. The deadline, he was told, was 3:20 p.m. Would Hammerstein make it? Bets were being taken on the outcome and the odds offered duly announced by the omniscient dailies. If he did make it, there was still the jury which would have to pass upon the merits of the work, a jury of prominent theatrical figures, all well known to the public. Of the four judges originally announced, Palmer was unavailable and it had been agreed to substitute Charles Hoyt, author and producer of successful farces.

The general public read the accounts and speculated upon the outcome. The wiseacres along Broadway, however, knew better. Many of them maintained the whole thing was a huge publicity hoax to puff some show that Hammerstein had bought and was about to produce. They explained, knowingly, exactly how it would turn out Hammerstein would palm off the show as his own composition and the jury would praise it to the skies. He would win the bet, mount the work and reap the profits. They failed to explain, however, just how he had managed to enlist the collaboration of so many distinguished theater people, including several rival managers, in a publicity stunt for his own benefit.

In the small hours of Saturday morning Hirsch was awakened by his prisoner's voice telling him he had finished a rough draft and would rest before beginning a revision. A short nap and breakfast and Hammerstein was busy again retouching, adding, erasing, playing chords and phrases on the piano with one hand, his pen busy in the other hand.

By 3 o'clock the next room was packed with people looking tensely at their watches as the deadline drew near. Suddenly the sounds from the other room ceased and then the doorknob was rattled sharply. The door was quickly flung open. Hammerstein stood collarless and tieless, unshaven, his hair rumpled, his suit looking as if it had been slept in. He leaned wearily against the doorpost. But his eyes were shining and he was smiling. "It is over," he said quietly.

After the handshaking and congratulations had subsided, the liberated prisoner's first request was that a typist be sent up to arrange the libretto. His brief conference with that functionary was followed by a longer session with C.A. Wernig, the musical director of Daly's Theatre, who was to transcribe the music into a piano and vocal score and do the full orchestration later. Typed libretto, piano score and original manuscript were to be placed under seal and turned over to the jury. That body would meet 1 p.m. Monday in the same room and render judgment.

There were yet other matters to detain a very tired Hammerstein before he could leave for home and bath. He was shown a sheaf of telegrams from managers, some from Philadelphia and Chicago, asking to book the already famous work sight unseen. He smiled and shook his head. He was not going to let any manager have it. He would produce it himself.

The reporters surrounded him, clamoring for details of the opera's plot. They would not let him go until he gave them at least the scenes and cast of characters. Hammerstein wrote out "The Kohinoor, Comic Opera in One Act. Text and Music by Oscar Hammerstein. Place, London. Time, early nineteenth century. Three scenes: 1. A square; 2. A street;

3. The Old Bailey (prison interior)." He listed a cast including such characters as a Lady Dunbar and her aunt, Duchess Mink; a Lord Belgrave and his uncle, Duke Piff; Kohn, a dealer in diamonds; Minzesheimer, his clerk; and various lesser roles. Heading the entire cast of characters was one listed as August Querker, Composer and Organ Grinder to Her Majesty the Queen. They could not get him to divulge the plot, but before he left he admitted that this character called Querker was the comic villain of the piece.

Readers of the next morning's Sunday *Herald* found a long article headed, "Wrote His Opera Ahead of Time—Hand Organs Didn't Stop Him—Judgment Tomorrow." The *Sun*'s heading merely announced "The Kohinoor Is Done" and the world headline ran "Querker, Organ-Grinder—Dreadful Satire by Hammerstein."

One o'clock Monday at the Gilsey House found the same rooms which had been the scene of Hammerstein's agony jammed once again with theatrical people and reporters. Now behind the closed door the judges were deliberating. A professional pianist was with them to play the score. Lederer had been added to the original four and each had been selected for his specialized knowledge—Hoyt to judge the lyrics, Richardson for the dialogue, Williams for the music and Clarke and Lederer to judge overall merit.

After more than an hour's deliberation, during which a bell-hop made numerous trips in and out with trays and glasses and things, the door opened, revealing the judges sitting solemnly behind a solid breastwork of bottles. Hammerstein and Kerker were called to the "bar of justice." Chairman Williams rose, looking very uncomfortable, and after fortifying himself with another drink, read from a document as follows:

> We the undersigned committee, appointed to decide a wager between Gustava Kerker and Oscar Hammerstein, agree that under the strict terms of the wager Mr. Hammerstein has lost.
>
> In so deciding, the committee unites to place on record its unanimous opinion that the feat performed by Mr. Hammerstein stands unparalleled in all known competition of its kind; that he actually did in the space of forty-eight hours construct, write and compose a work of art which, although deficient in meeting all the requirements of the wager, has shown versatility and ingenuity worthy of sincere admiration.

Hammerstein's shoulders sagged wearily. He made no effort to conceal his disappointment. Nor did he seem consoled when Hoyt rose and made a speech in explanation of the verdict. The decision, Hoyt stated, had turned solely on a few technical requirements of suitability for Broadway production as stipulated. He told Kerker he had come very close to winning. (It was revealed later that Hoyt and Richardson had long held out for judgment in favor of Hammerstein.) Hoyt summed up by saying, "It was a mighty good operetta but a might foolish bet."

At the first opportunity, Hoyt took Hammerstein aside and offered to produce *The Kohinoor* in his own theater, the composer to get fifty percent of the receipts. A little later Lederer made a similar bid for his theater. Hammerstein gave them both the same answer and repeated it again for the reporters. He said he did not understand. If the opera was good enough for these eminent producers to present, why had they given judgment against him? By their decision, they had stigmatized his work as unsuitable for production. Very well, since its own judges had condemned it he would never let it be seen on any stage. With the announcement that his effort had caused him the loss of $100 in cash and 7 pounds in weight, Hammerstein departed with his unsuccessful manuscript. But not before the reporters had managed to get a good look at it and had taken down the plot and many of the lines.

Tuesday's *Herald* told the news with headlines reading: "Called a Genius for His Opera—That Was All Oscar Hammerstein Secured—Bids Made for the Kohinoor," Other headlines were more matter of fact, as the *World*'s "Hammerstein Loses—Judges Praise Work But Say It Won't Do." But on its editorial page that paper quipped: "At all events, Oscar Hammerstein can comfort himself with the thought that, as an operatic composer, he knows how to beat time." A number of papers gave details of the opera's plot and lines.

Public reaction was a mixture of disappointment, amazement and amusement. The disappointment was at the decision. Most people felt Hammerstein was entitled to the award even if his work was only passable and he received letters from all sorts of people expressing indignation that he had been robbed of his just reward. Most disappointed of all were the Broadway know-it-alls who had so confidently predicted the outcome of the "publicity hoax." Public amazement at Hammerstein's feat was followed by amusement now that the plot of the opera was divulged.

Actually, the one-act piece had three separate plots, or embryo plotlets—a Kohinoor theft plot, a romantic plot and a satiric plot, all interwoven together. Kohn, a diamond merchant and money lender has the Kohinoor for sale. There is a scene in the vein of traditional "Hebrew comedy" in which Kohn twits his clerk on his accent. The clerk pleads for time in which to improve it, is told he will be charged interest on his account and is threatened with foreclosure, after which Kohn sings a sprightly song in praise of himself. The first verse runs:

> In stocks and bonds I also dabble
> For only six percent I fight
> I shrink away from common rabble
> And never buy on Shabbas night
>
> Chorus—He never buys on Shabbas night

Lady Dunbar and Lord Belgrave have been promised in marriage by their families but are total strangers to each other. Each conceives the notion of purchasing the Kohinoor as an engagement gift for the other. Accompanied respectively by a stern aunt and a genial uncle, they arrive simultaneously in their coaches before Kohn's shop. There is a dispute over procedure between the coachmen, the four aristocrats sing a quartet and the young pair are smitten with each other. The news comes that the Kohinoor has been stolen. The police arrive, arrest everyone in sight, clerks, aristocrats, beggars, passers-by, and the scene ends with the entire crowd being carted off to the Old Bailey.

The second scene is really an intermezzo. The thieves are attempting to escape disguised as organ-grinders. A crowd of students forces them to stop and play while they dance in the street.

The final scene is laid in the interior of the Old Bailey. The evening before, August Querker, composer and organ grinder to the Queen, had presented his comic opera *Venus* at the Drury Lane. It was so atrocious that the audience had risen in its wrath and precipitated a riot. The police have arrested Querker, his performers and members of the audience for disturbing the peace and l have been brought to the Old Bailey, where the two crowds now mingle in prison. Various characters are brought out of the cells and sing solos and concerted numbers. Querker is mocked and ridiculed and Lady Dunbar and Lord Belgrave lament their seemingly hopeless love in a duet "It Might Have Been." The opera ends with the news that the diamond has been recovered; the noble couple discover each other's identities and embrace rapturously and there is general rejoicing for all except Querker, who is sentenced to two years for having committed a public nuisance.

The papers were so full of Hammerstein's opera that Tuesday as to quite cast in the shade the report of the new London farce which had opened at the Standard Theatre the night before. It was only a slight farce, to be sure, but it proved a hardy one, for, in one form or another, as play, movie or musical, "Charley's Aunt" would be around for the next half century.

It was with feelings of disappointment and defeat that Hammerstein had left the Gilsey House on Monday. Now, as he read the papers and received a flood of congratulatory messages he found himself one of the most famous men in New York and, for the time, certainly the most talked about. Hammerstein was the hero of the day and everyone was laughing at Kerker. Once again a defeat had been turned into a victory.

There were hurried conferences at Koster and Bial's. Manager Cline thought it foolish to allow all this magnificent publicity to go to waste. Whatever its merits, the forty-eight hour opera could be counted on to pack the house for a week, if only with curiosity seekers. Koster and Bial agreed and Hammerstein was soon persuaded. Within the week the Music Hall announced that *The Kohinoor* would be produced for a week's trial beginning October 30. Hammerstein issued a statement to the effect that he had changed his mind, that he would appeal the judges' verdict to the higher court of New York public opinion and that he was engaging his cast.

It was considered too risky to substitute the opera for the ballet; *The Kohinoor* might prove a failure. Instead Hammerstein condensed *Versailles* into a single scene. He was soon very much occupied re-rehearsing the ballet, casting and rehearsing the one-act opera, for which he had obtained a full scale production with specially created costumes and scenery designed by its composer.

A reporter who dropped in at Koster and Bial's on the afternoon of the 27th to chronicle a rehearsal of *The Kohinoor* heard Hammerstein explaining to F. O'Neill, who was cast as Querker, how he wanted the part played: "You must burlesque the part—not play it straight. Nobody ever takes seriously the original, who bet me I couldn't write this opera. Remember?"

The production was rounding nicely into shape. But things were not running so smoothly the following day. Hammerstein had scheduled a dress rehearsal for his singing and dancing chorus. They were awaiting his arrival when Harriett Vernon had an idea for a new song. She thought it would make a nice effect if the chorus could be stationed in the wings to join unseen in the refrain. She communicated her desire to Bial, who immediately had Hammerstein's chorus set about rehearsing her song. A little later Hammerstein arrived and after listening incredulously, asked what in thunder his chorus was doing. "Mr. Bial's orders," he was told. "Who's running this chorus?" Hammerstein exploded. Then, dismissing them all for the day, he headed straight for the office of his partners. There was a lively row between Hammerstein and Bial. Koster tried to make peace unsuccessfully and only the best diplomacy of Carver Cline finally managed to soothe ruffled feelings.

It was the first open flare-up between the partners. Trivial though it was, yet it was a perfect indication of the misalliance the grand alliance really was. As a man of the theater, Hammerstein would have been outraged at the disruption of any rehearsal, let alone one for a production of his own creation. Bial, on the other hand, thought Hammerstein utterly unreasonable. Vernon was the star of the bill and wasn't anyone getting $600 a week entitled to have her requests granted? Nor could he understand why anyone should be so concerned about a mere rehearsal, one that didn't even involve principals, only a lowly chorus.

On opening night, Koster and Bial's was packed to the doors. The enormous bill of top-flight acrobats, comedians, song and dance and ballet stars was itself enough to attract a huge audience. It included Ada Reeve, Harriett Vernon and the condensed *Versailles*. But when the number seven was displayed on the panels there was a perceptible stir and it was evident that his was the number—*The Kohinoor*—that had brought the crowd. The work was already famous enough, but many believed it was only a joke and would be played for laughs. There was a short wait, an air of expectancy, then the curtains parted slightly and Hammerstein appeared before the audience.

"I know it is contrary to custom," he said, "for an author to come before the curtain before his work has been heard, but—it is safer." After the laugh subsided Hammerstein became very serious. He sketched briefly the circumstances leading to the composition of the work and admitted frankly it was a rash wager made in the heat of an argument. But he was earnest in emphasizing that he did not want the piece to be judged as a freak but on its merits irrespective of the time in which it was created. He said he had done as well as he was capable of doing and would probably do no better in forty-eight days or weeks and concluded by reading a sworn statement by the orchestrator that no changes had been made in the score as originally written within the contracted time.

After the brief overture the opening scene revealed an elaborate production with many original touches. The curtain rose upon a night scene before the house of Kohn, with laborers, beggars and vagabonds sleeping in the street, some of them snoring loudly. The two thieves who have stolen the Kohinoor enter and as they sing of their exploit the snores begin to harmonize and form a chorus to their song. The thieves escape, day breaks, the sleepers wake and are joined by pretty flower girls and others, and Kohn and his clerk come out for their comedy scene and duet.

The action and stage business flowed swiftly and smoothly as a succession of solos, duets, quartets, waltzes and marches bubbled gaily through the three scenes of the work until the final curtain touched off salvos of enthusiastic applause. There was a volley of calls for Hammerstein, in which the rasping voice of playwright-producer Hoyt could be heard above all the rest. Hammerstein came out smiling. "I knew you'd like it," he said, and invited anyone who wished to do so to examine privately his original piano score and manuscript.

"On appeal the public has reversed the verdict in the case of Hammerstein versus Kerker," said the World next morning. "The audience was large. It came to scoff, it remained to approve… Well acted… well sung… well costumed and well staged, The Kohinoor pleased everyone."

There were some differences of critical opinion about the lines and lyrics. The *Herald* thought them trivial, the *World* found them without merit. On the other hand the *Press* thought the libretto no more silly than the average comic opera story and the *Sun* found many of the stanzas amusing. About the music there was little difference of opinion, although some found it uneven and showing signs of haste. "… a good deal of pretty music," said the *Herald*, singling out especially Kohn and the clerk's "clever duet with a catchy refrain" and the noble couple's "very pretty duet, 'It Might Have Been.'" The *World*, noting the score's "decided popular quality," said "The Kohinoor is but a musical jest, but it puts to shame many a serious effort."

"The Kohinoor has … made a bit," said the *Press*. "The audience that assembled… to treat the production as a huge joke were agreeably disappointed, as it held their respectful attention. The music is original, bright and catchy. Several charming waltzes, notably the finale of the first scene and the waltz which is alternately sung and whistled in the third scene, deserve special attention. They have a catchy quality that is sure to make them very popular. The quartet in the first scene... a duet between Belgrave and Lady Dunbar in the third and the latter's solo are creditable and tuneful compositions."

The only really adverse criticism was in the professional theatrical paper, the *Dramatic Mirror*. It took the position that bet and opera were a publicity hoax and refused to consider the work seriously.

Quite different was the opinion of another professional paper, *The Spirit of the Times*, which wrote: "The music is bright and catchy and much more original than that of more pretentious operas... Mr. Hammerstein evidently meant to satirize the fuss which the compilers of the present class of comic operas make about their fakements." The paper went on to say: "Neither in London nor Paris is there a music hall which presents on the same programme an original opera, a grand ballet, song and dance people, acrobats and comedians, and Koster and Bial thus verify the promises... made... when they removed... to the magnificent Manhattan Opera House."

All week *Kohinoor* drew packed houses and every night the Music Hall resounded with applause for Number Seven. The announcement had already gone out that it would be held over a second week. And still the wonder grew. People came who had never set foot in a music hall. Many were professional musicians, a group not given to looking kindly upon the efforts of amateurs. Like others of the skeptical they came to scoff and remained to praise. They remained also to find the enormous bill of fare of variety entertainment a surprisingly satisfying repast.

The Sunday newspaper reviews of the theatrical week revealed that *Kohinoor* had been an outstanding event in a week of notable events. The illustrations on the dramatic page of the Sunday *Press* featured Harriett Vernon starring at Koster and Bial's, Ellie Milton in "Charley's Aunt," Henry Irving and Ellen Terry in Tennyson's "Becket." Topping them all were two portrait of the week's outstanding composers. One was Reginald de Koven, then the country's foremost composer of light opera. His *Robin Hood* was already a classic and his "Oh Promise Me" already part of the American wedding ritual. His latest opera, *The Algerian*, with Marie Tempest, had opened at the Garden Theatre. The other portrait was of Oscar Hammerstein.

The Sunday edition of the *Sun* quoted an experienced musician's comment at the close of a performance at Koster and Bial's: "Well, I came here expecting to find something remarkably bad, and I went to the Garden Theatre expecting something wonderfully good. In both cases I was disappointed, but I have no hesitation in saying that I find Hammerstein's piece more amusing and melodious than de Koven's."

Hammerstein was supremely happy—a vindicated man. Nightly he was called out to bow his thanks amid scenes of enthusiasm. The brain child he had fathered in his prison in the Gilsey House was alive and lusty, and it seemed that everybody who was anybody in New York was coming to see it. Carver Cline was happy as the box office receipts swelled and "standing room only" was the rule. The entire bill was held over a third week unchanged and then for yet a fourth week, after which Hammerstein took it uptown for a week at his Harlem Opera House.

But now the situation at the opening of the house, a few months earlier, was reversed. Only Messrs. Koster and Bial, who should have been filed with unalloyed joy, were not happy. They were naturally gratified at the sold out houses, the tremendous publicity and the new class of patrons attracted, all of the highest respectability. Yet they were assailed by doubts and forebodings.

Hammerstein was not turning out to be the man they had taken him for. They had thought he was one of them, a businessman, that he was interested in the theater, as they were, because it was a profitable business. Now they saw that he was interested in the theater for its own sake. He was actually one of those who, for some unaccountable reason, wanted to produce, to create for the sheer love of it—an artist! And now the disconcerting thought came to them that they had a genius for a partner. It made them profoundly uneasy. In their saloon-keeper souls there was a deep sense of dismay and foreboding of danger ahead. Whatever else might be said of them, in this their instincts were sound.

4

Glorifying the Human Form

Although the 1893–1894 season saw national depression[1] spread over the country, Broadway was gay.

The Metropolitan Opera House, the temple dedicated to the rituals of lavish social display, was even more festive than usual. When the season began on November 27, after a year without any Metropolitan Opera, it was the second grand opening of the house and it ushered in a new era. The house itself having been reduced to a shell by a disastrous fire, the interior was now completely rebuilt and refurnished. The company had been completely reorganized, the box-owning stockholders reduced from seventy to a more exclusive thirty-five, exactly the number that could fit into the first tier of boxes, henceforth to be the Diamond Horseshoe.

Managers Henry Abbey and Maurice Grau—great impresarios both—after their one experimental season, were now in charge of the new operatic order. The Golden Age of great singers was launched. The opening cast in *Faust* was itself the first of the famous "all-star casts," containing four ranking stars—Emma Eames as Marguerite, Jean de Reszke as Faust, Edouard de Reske as Mephisto, and Jean Lasalle as Valentine. But the season was to see two new artists add even greater luster to the company.

Two days after the opening, the great French singer, Emma Calve, appeared as Santuzza in *Cavalleria Rusticana*, the fiery little opera that Hammerstein had introduced to New York two years before. She gave New Yorkers a taste of what dramatic operatic acting combined with impassioned singing could be like.

Five days later, the other new artist made her debut in *Lucia*. She was, of all things, Australian and her name was Nellie Melba, the singer Hammerstein had contracted to present to America the year before and who might have saved his opera season if Mapleson had lived up to his end of the contract. It must have given Hammerstein somewhat rueful satisfaction to read the *Tribune* critic's tribute to her as "the finest exponent of vocalization since Sembrich" who received "a superb greeting." Perhaps it only increased his determination that someday this great star would shine upon his stage.

The season was equally brilliant and much gayer on the level of operetta and comic opera. At Daly's Theatre, dainty Marie Tempest was delighting her admirers in de Koven's *The Algerian*. The Casino, New York's home of musical gayety, was presenting *The Princess Nicotine*, a new comic opera by composer William Wallace Furst and librettists Charles Alfred Byrne and Louis Harrison, starring the one actress who represented American beauty incarnate—Lillian Russell.

Most successful of all was the show now at the Garden Theatre called *1492*, produced by E. E. Rice, the grand old man of musical comedy. Like most of Rice's shows it was a hodgepodge of musical comedy, burlesque, revue, specialty numbers and novelties. It made use of a technique Rice had first formulated in the fabulously long run and numerous revivals of his record breaking *Evangeline*. This was the constant introduction of new special features so that people could come to the show again and again. The most successful parts would still be there to be enjoyed over again and the new features would be fresh and novel. Among the novelties which crowded *1492* was one intended especially for the ladies—the "Daily Hints from Paris" by department store magnate R. H. Macy and Company—a feature the enterprising producer probably obtained gratis. *1492* came close to being a gay variety bill, but the gayest show of all was the true variety show at Koster and Bial's in which the bills were constantly changing.

The grand alliance marched gaily from one triumph to another in the house on Thirty-Fourth Street, but not without stresses and strains between the allies. The *Kohinoor* could have had a longer run than four weeks but at the end of November Koster and Bial decided to discontinue both the opera and the ballet and to maintain henceforth a policy of straight vaudeville.

Perhaps the most famous French female opera singer of La Belle Époque, Emma Calve (1858–1942), ca. 1885.

This was a real blow to Hammerstein. There may have been some doubt if singers came under his purview but there was no question that musical productions and ballet were his province. Had not Koster and Bial maintained that a chief reason for the merger was their desire to combine their vaudeville with his ballet? And had not his opera and ballet been a highly popular feature of the bills and certainly the most artistic? Most infuriating of all, there was no way he could force the firm to produce ballets or other productions. His half interest was in fact ownership of forty-nine percent of the stock and they could outvote him with their fifty-one percent. The reason for their action was that opera and ballet were expensive requiring a standing corps de ballet and chorus. They felt they could substitute two or three additional acts at a fraction of the cost without too serious loss in drawing power.

This change of policy would certainly have resulted in an open rupture among the allies but for two ways in which Koster and Bial mollified their partner. For one thing, although they abolished the ballet they retained the ballerina, Clara Qualitz, for a dance act that would be Hammerstein's presentation and under his exclusive direction. The other appeasement was even more important. The firm had managed to secure one of the greatest living celebrities for a three-month engagement and Hammerstein was asked to take charge of developing the format of the act and to supervise its presentation. With these new opportunities for creative showmanship offered him, Hammerstein was wiling to forego the ballet for the time being.

In later years, the acquisition of a certain celebrity was attributed sometimes to Hammerstein and sometimes to Bial. Actually, neither had anything to do with it. The man responsible was the celebrity himself. Early in November a handsome, mild-mannered man walked into the offices of Koster and Bial and announced himself as Eugen Sandow. He said he was open for an engagement if they cared to negotiate with him. They stared, incredulous at such an opportunity. This was the great Sandow, a German bodybuilder internationally celebrated as both the strongest man in the world and the world's most perfectly developed physical specimen of manhood. Even his famous chest expansion was insufficient to hold all the medals he had collected at international competitions of strength and physique. He had appeared before all the crowned heads of Europe and was friend and personal advisor on physical training to more than one royal personage. His feats of muscular strength and control were legendary. Even today the devotees of physical culture speak his name in tones of awe.

Among the most famous singers and actresses of the era, Lillian Russell (1860/61–1922) worked in theater and operettas for four decades (public domain).

Sandow's American tour had been under the management of Abbey, whose firm presented grand opera at the Metropolitan Opera House as one of its farflung activities. For some reason, however, Sandow's tour had not been well handled. It had received comparatively little attention and the presentation was poorly arranged. He had broken off with Abbey and allowed himself to be persuaded to take on as his manager a youngster with practically no theatrical experience.

This lad's father was the distinguished Professor Florenz Ziegfeld, Sr., founder and president of the Chicago College of Music. His stage-struck son yearned to be a theatrical manager and Sandow was his first big opportunity. Perhaps it was because he was uncertain about his inexperienced manager that Sandow had gone himself to Koster and Bial's, where he was engaged on the spot at his own price—a whopping $1,000 a week. But he soon discovered there was no need to doubt the energy and enterprise of the professor's son, for young Florenz Ziegfeld, Jr., was on his way to managerial fame, and the career that now began with the glorification of masculine strength was to reach its height with the glorification of feminine beauty in the Ziegfeld Follies.

Hammerstein was delighted to work with this genial Hercules on the presentation of an act that would bring out his unique qualities to the fullest. Sandow was easy to work with, a quiet, gentlemanly fellow, fully conscious of his remarkable powers without seeming to boast of them. "Here," he would say with a smile, "is a trick my friend, the Emperor of Russia, who is a very powerful man, once did in my presence." And he would calmly take a deck of cards and tear it in half. "Here," he would continue, still smiling, "is a trick my friend, the Emperor of Russia, did not do." And he would place two packs of cards together and tear them apart.

In presenting Sandow it was decided to give most of the act over to poses illustrating his phenomenal muscular development and control rather than to the usual strength stunts of such acts. Those feats would be left to the end to provide a sensational finish. The major portion of the presentation would be partly a scientific lecture-demonstration and partly an aesthetic demonstration of classic posing. The exhibition would be lifted to a level far above ordinary strongman acts. For the feats of strength themselves some original ideas were developed.

December 11 was the opening night of the huge new bill headed by Sandow, "The Perfect Man." Thirteen acts were presented, the final act being a production by itself, entitled "The Athlete of the Century—Sandow, Physically Perfect." The program announced a standing offer of $10,000 and Sandow's own gold championship belt to any athlete able to duplicate his performance, and introduced a sequence of eight anatomical demonstrations with the statement: "History does not record of the great gladiators of ancient Rome such wonderful muscular development as Mr. Sandow possesses."

The curtain rose upon a darkened stage. In the center was a small brilliantly lighted enclosure within which, posed upon a pedestal against a black background, was the great athlete, his torso almost bare in a skimpy white leotard. The first of the demonstration poses was listed in the program as "Muscular Repose—all muscles relaxed." Sandow's torso was a symphony of flowing lines. Next was "Muscular Tension—all muscles firm as steel." The strongest man in the world bulged impressively. The silent lecture on anatomy and plastic beauty continued, exhibiting in succession the biceps, triceps, deltoids, abdominal and other muscles, and chest expansion (the program claimed a 47-inch chest measurement and a 14-inch expansion).

The anatomy lesson concluded, the mighty man of brawn stepped down from his pedestal to demonstrate the power of those muscles in a series of feats, such as performing somersaults and barrel jumps while holding a 56-pound dumbbell in each hand or nonchalantly lifting 300 pound weights above his head.

At length the smashing finale. Sandow bent backward till his body formed a bridge resting on his hands and feet. A wooden platform 5 feet by 10 feet was placed to rest upon his chest and

Strongman Eugen Sandow (1867–1925), billed by Hammerstein and company as "The Perfect Man," performed both demonstrations of classic bodybuilder posing and prodigious feats of strength (photograph ca. 1890s).

knees. A grand piano was wheeled out and six husky men placed stout poles under it and lifted it to the platform, still holding on to the poles. A step ladder was placed alongside and out marched five men in flamboyant costume whom the audience recognized as the Hungarian Band that played in the promenade during intermission. One by one they climbed the ladder and stood on top of the piano, after which a pianist crawled up and seated himself at the piano and the band struck up a wild Hungarian arrangement of "Yankee Doodle," played with a special wildness induced by the cramped and precarious position. The men still holding the poles supporting the piano now pulled them out, leaving piano, pianist, band and music supported solely by Sandow. The house rang with cheers as the curtain descended slowly upon what the *New York Herald* called "the greatest musico-athletic feat… ever witnessed in this city." A moment later Sandow, looking perfectly fresh and debonair was before the curtain acknowledging the applause.

Hammerstein had given Koster and Bial's another sensation—a strongman exhibition as unusual in presentation as it was unique in execution. Again "standing room only" was the rule. Especially remarkable was the increase in the number of women in the audience. What non-smoking and non-drinking matinees had not been able to do was accomplished every evening by the fascination women seemed to have with the anatomy of Sandow. There was even a wholly new phenomenon—the stage door Jenny. At 11 p.m. each night, Sandow held a reception in his dressing room for a small invited group to whom he gave a personally illustrated lecture on the muscular system. The women usually followed the subject with more avid interest than their escorts and many went to great trouble to wangle invitations to these exclusive and intimate audiences.

Although education was being stressed in the new feature at Koster and Bial's, elsewhere that week art and culture also received their due in new presentations. The week saw the first American production of Oscar Wilde's play, *A Woman of No Importance*, with the distinguished actress, Rose Coghlan, and two important musical premieres.

The Philharmonic Orchestra's concert at Carnegie Hall was a notable event. In the huge new concert hall uptown, under the baton of the Anton Seidl, the first New York hearing of Dvořák's *New World* symphony was received with tumultuous acclaim. The occasion meant a good deal more than the entry of a very popular symphony into the orchestral repertory, for this work, regarded as the fruit of the composer's stay in America, was to be influential in turning the attention of American musicians to the utilization of native folk music, especially the negro spirituals. Not that the symphony was anything but pure Dvořák and, despite the famous Largo, wholly Bohemian in spirit; but the mere fact that a noted European composer found the despised "slave music" a rich and worthy musical treasure helped to bring about a new attitude toward the spirituals and other American folk music.

And on the same night that Koster and Bial's first presented Sandow, the Metropolitan Opera gave its first presentation of the new opera by Leoncavallo that was to become as popular as *Cavalleria Rusticana*—the famous *I Pagliacci*. Indeed *Cavalleria* and *Pagliacci* were destined to become the inseparable twins of the standard operatic double bill. At the great opera house, Melba was the first Nedda, Ancona the first baritone to sing Tonio's celebrated prologue and De Lucia the first tenor to beat a bass drum and to sing Canio's tortured cry, "Ridi, pagliaccio!" (Laugh, clown!).

The following week at Koster and Bial's the strong bill headed by Sandow was strengthened further by the addition of another star performer when Bessie Bellwood, a London music hall star, made her American debut. She was more than a singer, she was a personality, brown eyed, vivacious, very much the gamine.

Her voice and diction were first rate and her style distinctive. She did not sing her songs, rather she sang, talked, laughed, danced and romped through them. Between stanzas she would make impromptu remarks, talking to the audience in a confidential, bantering manner. She had a way of tossing off the most risqué remarks that made them seem hilarious rather than salacious. On the other hand, she could reverse the process and make a chorus of innocent nonsense syllables, such as "Hey, diddle diddle dum," seem wickedly suggestive.

In London she was famous for the devastating repartee with which she handled any fresh remarks from an unruly audience, and she was equally noted for her gamine behavior off stage. A lawsuit against the Duke of Manchester had brought her considerable notoriety. Among her other accomplishments she was also an expert boxer. She once thrashed a man who displeased her and, after flattening him, cheerfully paid a three guinea fine for assault and battery.

On one of her trips over, an Indian prince on shipboard became very much interested in her. The second night of her music hall engagement he attracted a great deal of attention sitting in a box in full regalia and a huge white turban. At the singer's appearance he tossed her a large bouquet of roses. She looked up, exclaiming to the audience, "Ah! There he is! Isn't he a prime lot?" Then, confidentially, "Me mother always told me I'd marry well and I believe she was right."

The audience at Koster and Bial's found her exhilarating. She went over big, dividing the honors with the great Sandow. One night there occurred an incident of unruly behavior—something now rare at Koster and Bial's respectable place. In one of the boxes a group of college boys became boisterous and began to shower coins upon Bellwood during a song. Finding this great sport, they continued to throw silver with increasing vigor. The singer received a silver dollar squarely on her eye, lost her composure and left the stage abruptly but returned at once to apologize to the audience. Then, putting up her fists, she turned to the offenders and dared them to come around to the stage door.

The week that saw Bellwood's debut also saw a new burlesque on the program of the Imperial Music Hall, a small rival venue. This merry medley of gags and music bore the title "Hamminstein in Distress." Its chief character was a composer named "Hosscar Hamminstein," its two scenes laid respectively in a room at "The Quiltsey House" and on the stage of "The White Elephant Music Hall." The actors' makeup gave them striking resemblances to Gustav Kerker, Charles Hoyt, Albert Bial and others.

The reviewers found the piece clever, although some of its satire and gags required inside theatrical knowledge to be fully appreciated. The chief actor gave a remarkably good caricature and his impersonation drew much laughter and applause. One night particularly vigorous applause came from one of the boxes. "Hosscar" looked up, then excitedly drew attention to where the original Oscar sat beaming with delight, and the audience promptly gave an ovation. It was Hammerstein's first experience of seeing himself caricatured on the stage. For the next twenty years it would be a commonplace. A Hammerstein impersonation would become a stock item in any act featuring mimicry of well-known figures.

This was also the week that introduced to New York one of the greatest impersonations in the history of grand opera—Calve as Carmen. The Frenchwoman's portrayal of the tempestuous Gypsy as a creature passionate and voluptuous, proud and capricious, electrified the Metropolitan audience. The sensational combination of luscious-voiced, expressive singing with a magnetic stage personality produced a personal triumph for Calve that almost obscured the phenomenal nature of the rest of the cast. Polish tenor Jean de Reszke was Jose, and the small part of Micaela was played by renowned American soprano Emme Eames, an example of prodigality that prompted Eames to say in wonder, "You must be a very rich man, Mr. Grau, to pay me $300 to sing Micaela." Later the even more expensive Melba was alternated with Eames in the role.

But Grau knew his business. *Carmen* became the opera season's biggest moneymaker with a record-breaking twelve performances, plus three more in a supplementary season. Although he once came close to it, Grau himself was never able to duplicate this record, not even with Calve, and it was finally considered impossible of repetition. Not until thirteen years later would another impresario surpass that record by presenting *Carmen* nineteen times in a single season. But now Oscar Hammerstein was busily engaged with two ex-saloonkeepers exhibiting a strongman at a music hall.

For all of Hammerstein's concern with Koster and Bial's, he did not neglect his Harlem interests. Although his own brother-in-law, Henry Rosenberg, was manager of the Harlem Opera House, he maintained constant personal supervision. Perhaps the high quality of the legitimate attractions he presented there consoled him for the less elevated atmosphere of beer and wine on Thirty-Fourth Street. The Columbus Theatre Hammerstein found less interesting and accordingly devoted to it only the most general supervision. He had made his son Willie business manager and the young man was learning his trade well.

Hammerstein managed to divide his time. If something of special importance was on uptown, he began the evening in his Harlem Opera House office, then came down to Koster and Bial's and stayed at a hotel for the night. Normally he began the evening on Thirty-Fourth Street, then looked in at his Harlem house before going home.

One night in January, he was at Koster and Bial's when he received an emergency message from the Harlem Opera House. The attraction there that week was a notable one. No less a personage than Mrs. John Drew, the grand old lady of the American stage, was appearing in *The Road to Ruin*. The veteran actress was always in her dressing room well ahead of time This night curtain time was approaching. No sign of Mrs. Drew and no word from her.

Hammerstein got in touch with the Oriental Hotel Yes and was told Mrs. Drew had left in a cab at the usual time, accompanied as usual by her dog, Flitters, and by her grandson, barely sixteen but already trying his fledgling wings in a tiny part in the play. After communicating with the police, who at once began a citywide alarm and search, Hammerstein jumped into a hansom cab, spurring horse and driver into a mad dash for Harlem and a waiting audience impatient for a missing star.

It was an anxious Hammerstein who rushed to the curb when Mrs. Drew's cab arrived at the theater one hour late. The explanation turned out to be simple enough: Mrs. Drew, as was her custom, had taken a nap during the ride. She had awakened to find the cab motionless in Central Park and a tired cabman and his tired horse all sound asleep. But the grandson—hadn't he noticed something amiss, Hammerstein wanted to know. The boy, it seemed, had dozed off too. Even the dog was asleep.

Mrs. Drew's first concern was about the audience—was it still in the house? Gallantly Hammerstein assured her any audience would wait half the night for so great a lady of the stage, as he offered her his arm and escorted her to the stage door. Behind them, looking somewhat sheepish as he carried Flitters in his arms, young Lionel Barrymore followed them into the theater.

Meanwhile at the music hall the variety combinations headed by Sandow and Bellwood continued their successful run. As a special thrill for the growing legion of Sandow's admiring female students of physical culture, the Koster and Bial press staff—no doubt hand-in-glove with their opposite numbers at the Casino—put out a story linking the name of Lillian Russell with that of the handsome strongman. An impending engagement was strongly implied. Nor could any number of denials suffice to overcome the irresistible logic of pairing the physically most perfect man with the woman of most perfect beauty.

One day in March, the Koster and Bial staff took Sandow out to the East Orange laboratory of Thomas Edison. There he exhibited for posterity his phenomenal physique for Mr. Edison's latest invention, the Kinetograph, a camera designed to "to represent by the medium of rapid photography, and a subsequent display of plates, with incredible quickness of succession, the movements of a person or of any number of persons in a scene."

For all the sensational success of Sandow's prodigious feats and Bessie Bellwood's clever ad-libs, the star duo within a few weeks found themselves making room for a third sensation, the aerialist Alcide Capitaine—a girl of eighteen who gave a startling performance on the flying trapeze. Young, pretty and graceful, she was as much a marvel of muscular development as Sandow.

Like Sandow, she concluded her act with a spectacular feat. While a long drum roll swelled and the audience held its collective breath, she hurled herself from one moving trapeze to another in a tremendous leap of thirty-eight feet and caught herself on by her knees. No sooner had she concluded this feat on her opening night than it became immediately apparent that she had performed an even more remarkable feat—she had stolen the show from Eugen Sandow and Bessie Bellwood.

Sandow, Bellwood, Capitaine—the triumvirate continued its triumphal march while lesser performers entered the bill and left. In any other show, many of these lesser acts would have been the headliners. All sorts of performers appeared in the course of the season. Not only were marvels of physical perfection exhibited but also their opposites, marvels of physical imperfection—freaks. One of these was Carl Unthan, the armless wonder who did more with his feet and toes than others do with hands and fingers, such as shooting out the markings on playing cards with a rifle, playing the cornet and violin and writing letters in an elegant "hand." Of a totally different order of freaks was Giacomo Inaudi, "the mathematical enigma." His was a "lightning calculator" act in which he solved the most complicated arithmetical problems correctly and instantly.

Of the more usual types of acts some were by performers of established reputation and some by artists just beginning their rise to the top. There was Maggie Cline, "The Irish Queen." one of the most popular singing comediennes in vaudeville. Leather-lunged, 173 pounds of dynamic vitality and geniality, her personality was indissolubly bound up with the song that made her fame as she made its. No audience would have dreamed of letting Maggie Cline go before she had given her exuberant rendition of "Throw Him Down, McCloskey!"

Another well known performer was Bonnie Thornton. Much admired as an excellent singing comedienne with a distinctive style of delivery, she was especially loved and admired by theater folk as the ever-faithful wife of Jim Thornton, noted comedian, singer and composer of hit songs. Within the profession she represented the ideal of wifely love. Jim Thornton was also Broadway's most lovable drunk and the favorite drinking companion of heavyweight champion boxer John L. Sullivan. Winsome Bonnie plugged his songs, managed his bookings and collected his pay when he was in no condition to, searched for him patiently when he disappeared and nursed him in sickness and in hangover with unswerving devotion. She once broke all records by remaining six months at Tony Pastor's Music

Hall, during which engagement she popularized Jim's song, "My Sweetheart's the Man in the Moon" and boosted it into a nation-wide hit.

Another top-flight artist was the high-wire performer Juan Caicedo, whose international reputation fully justified his billing, "King of the Wire."

Of the comparatively unknown artists who appeared during the season, two were young women destined to go far in the theater. One was the attractive singer Josephine Sabel, whose talents were to make her a favorite on both sides of the ocean. The other was the captivating dancer Josie Cohan, daughter of a veteran vaudeville team. With the addition of daughter and son the team was to become "The Four Cohans" and achieve top billing, partly because of Josie's marvelously graceful dancing and partly because of the talents of her brother as song and dance man, writer of skits and composer of songs—talents that were to make George M. Cohan one of Broadway's commanding figures.

The week of March 12 marked the high-water mark of Koster and Bial's star-studded bills headed by sensational performers. This was the last week of Sandow's engagement and of Capitaine's, Bellwood's having already closed. To the lover of vaudeville who today fondly remembers bills with one-star performer, plus several second and third-class acts, this bill of thirteen numbers will be a source of wonder.

The program included club swingers The Rawsons (long the top act of this type); Bonnie Thornton, singer and comedienne; Mlles. Qualitz and Neumann (Hammerstein's star ballerinas from his *Versailles* ballet); and Mlle. Bertoldi, contortionist (for years the world's leading performer in this specialty).

There was nothing wrong with the bills in the weeks that followed except that they were composed of nothing but first-rate performers. There were no sensational acts, like Sandow's. The house was well filled each evening but the S.R.O. sign was no longer in evidence. The resourcefulness of Hammerstein was soon to remedy this situation.

At the Garden Theatre, Rice's burlesque extravaganza *1492* was still running merrily, with novel features constantly introduced. On the night of March 21, a new feature debuted between the second and third acts, launching a craze that was to sweep over New York, and eventually across the country.

Edouard von Kilanyi's Living Pictures (*tableaux vivants*), which had just created a furor in London, presented reproductions of well-known classical and modern figure paintings, posed by live models against painted backgrounds and stage properties, within a huge gold frame—three-dimensional pictures.

Each time the curtains of the frame parted a new picture was revealed, the use of a turntable behind the frame making possible the showing of eighteen pictures in fifteen minutes. The subjects were all feminine, mostly in scant draperies and many were nude figures. (Actually there was no nudity, but flesh-colored tights and skillful lighting created a startlingly perfect illusion of bare flesh.) The tableaux were remarkably faithful copies of the original paintings and included several representations of sculpture, one of them, the Venus de Milo.

Among the pictures especially admired was Kilanyi's own Aphrodite, "wherein the beautiful goddess is seen rising from a shell in a mist of spray which glistens upon her rosy flesh with beautiful effect." The young woman with the breathtaking figure who posed as Aphrodite was listed as May Hamilton. Had her real name been known the sensation would have been far greater, but this was not to be ferreted out until several years later, after her engagement at Hammerstein's theater.

Only then did an enterprising reporter discover that this lovely model came from one of the most distinguished families in America. This was news at a time when it was said that actresses sometimes happened in the best families, and when many still thought the stage a fate worse than death for a respectable girl. For such a girl to pose in the "altogether" as Venus on the half shell was sensational.

The eye-filling young goddess' real name was Mamie Stevenson, and while she displayed her undraped figure nightly in New York, her distinguished uncle, Adlai Stevenson, was cutting a figure in Washington as vice-president of the United States. At the time, however, no one suspected that his niece was the much talked about model in the daring new living pictures. No more would anyone have suspected that his grandson and namesake would some day receive twenty-seven million votes as candidate for the presidency of the United States.

The living pictures became the talk of New York as *1492* reached its 300th performance going stronger than ever. Many were coming to the theater at 10 p.m. solely to see this feature. Most audiences and critics alike found the effect ravishing and sensational. The *Herald* called the exhibition highly artistic and found the realism, though startling, in no way offensive. A new art form had been created. There were those who found it shocking and one newspaper pronounced it "disgraceful, pernicious and wanton," to which the distinguished editor of the *Dramatic Mirror* made emphatic reply, calling it one of the most educational representations New York had ever seen. Even the clergy were divided, some denouncing the exhibition as indecent, others defending it as art.

Hammerstein was enthusiastic about the novelty and was an interested visitor backstage at the Garden Theatre to examine its construction. Even as he watched the performance, he was thinking of a hundred ways in which the idea could be improved upon both in the presentation and in the mechanism. He disclosed his enthusiasm to his partners and managed to persuade them, then went to work to devise a series of living pictures. He was certain he could extend Kilanyi's methods in size, scope and variety.

Kilanyi had brought with him from Europe his sets and several highly trained models as the nucleus of his group. Hammerstein had to start with nothing, to build and paint the sets, construct the stage machinery and train models who had never posed before, while himself learning by doing—all within five weeks, the time he gave himself to do it.

He discarded Kilanyi's turntable as too confining for his pictures, which were larger and included far more figures. Instead, he put his sets on wheeled platforms moving on rails and tracked the stage with loops, sidings and switches until it resembled the marshaling yards of a railroad freight terminal.

To increase the variety and satisfy more diverse tastes, the pictures were not limited to classical and sentimental subjects but included historical, biographical and patriotic themes. One of these inconveniences accompanying the original living pictures was that effective showing required a darkened theater, and spectators curious to learn the names of pictures were always striking matches to consult their programs. Hammerstein solved this difficulty by a simple device—he used the curtain covering the picture frame as a screen and had a stereopticon project the title upon it before it was drawn.

The Kilanyi pictures were shown in silence. Hammerstein selected appropriate music and sound effects to suit the mood and heighten the effect of each picture, and had the orchestra leader work out special arrangements. Only pressure of time kept him from composing the music himself.

Continually he found it necessary to spend much time arguing with his partners, obtaining their reluctant approval for each added item of equipment and material, for the engagement of more models or the requisitioning of additional stage hands. For five weeks Hammerstein was working morning, noon and night. He had not been so happy since the production of the *Kohinoor*—he was being creative.

From New York's preoccupation with gay musicals and living pictures, it would have been difficult to deduce the fact that the country was just then going through an acute attack of jitters. A year of soup kitchens in cities, depression and populism on the farms produced, among other radical recovery plans, the public works program, advocated by an Ohio businessman named Jacob S. Coxey. He planned to lead an army of 100,000 unemployed to Washington to petition Congress on May Day. There were wild rumors of insurrectionary masses converging from every part of the country for the march upon the capital. Panicky citizens feared the imminent overthrow of the government.

On May 1 "Coxey's Army" arrived in Washington, a full 500 strong. Cheered by a huge crowd the "Army" marched to the Capital, where a police force twice as large barred the way. When Coxey tried to mount the Capitol steps to read his petition the police became panicky, and in the ensuing scrimmage, "Army" and spectators were clubbed indiscriminately. The march on Washington ended with the arrest of Coxey and his aides, who were sentenced to twenty days for carrying banners and fined $5 for walking on the grass. The security of the federal government assured, cautious men of property breathed easily once more. The republic was safe.

Nicely timed for the passing of this national crisis was the May 7 date scheduled for the opening of Hammerstein's living pictures. He would have made the deadline he had set for himself but for a personal crisis. Just then, his young daughter[2] was stricken with appendicitis. An emergency operation was performed, there was an anguished interval before the distraught father was assured that all danger was past and the premiere of the Hammerstein Living Pictures was postponed three days.

The event had been well publicized, and the house packed to the doors. The bill was a typically gigantic 13-act Koster and Bial bill of variegated performers, ranging from Mlle. Lalo (Electric Lady Bicyclist) to Adrienne Larie (Chanteuse Excentrique), and from Leslie's Dog Circus to Caicedo (King of the Wire), with sundry singers and comedians interspersed between. Number 13, the closing act, was billed as "First Series of Living Pictures Devised and Executed by Oscar Hammerstein."

There were 19 pictures in all and their diversity, far beyond Kilanyi's, was sufficient to satisfy all tastes. For those of literary and romantic inclination, there were such paintings as Moulon's *Romeo and Juliet* and Knille's *Tannhauser and Venus*, of which the *Herald* wrote the next morning: "The voluptuous splendor of the original was represented with remarkable and most artistic fidelity."

There were "cute" subjects as "L'Orchestre d'Amour," which struck the audience as all the more delightful when the little fellow who posed as the cherub-conductor changed his position with complete nonchalance. For the sober minded there were such pictures as Millet's *The Angelus*, and for the students of human anatomy, once again Koster and Bial's was presenting perfect specimens, this time female, in such pictures as Fedro's *Truth* (appropriately naked), or *Nymph of the Wave*, or Tojetti's *The Three Graces*, which, one newspaper reported, "were greeted with wild applause."

Here too, Hammerstein had outreached Kilanyi. At the Garden Theatre the nude figures were never wholly unadorned. As a concession to propriety, there was always about three-fourths of a yard of ribbon strategically draped on each figure. Hammerstein insisted upon high fidelity reproduction of the original works of art. Not a piece of ribbon was permitted to break the long line or interrupt the flowing rhythms of feminine beauty. He believed firmly that where the nude was concerned, the audience was interested in the display of woman, not millinery, and the audience sustained his judgment affirmatively. Never before on any New York stage had the female form been so completely revealed and the admirers of beauty were enthralled.

But in diversifying the exhibit Hammerstein had also been imminently correct in his judgment that man does not live by beauty alone. Actually, the picture arousing the wildest enthusiasm was his own production called "General Grant at the Battle of the Wilderness," shown to the strains of stirring patriotic music. The audience gave it a genuine ovation.

Audience and critics agreed, the Hammerstein pictures were just as artistic as Kilanyi's, but larger, more elaborate, more diversified and more sensational. Kilanyi's pictures continued to be popular but now it was the Hammerstein pictures that all New York was talking about. Koster and Bial discovered, somewhat to their surprise, that they had another sensation to replace Sandow. Outside the box-office the S.R.O. sign was up again and it was staying up week after week.

By June the living picture craze had engulfed New York and was spreading into the heartland. Every music hall and vaudeville house in New York was showing inferior imitations of Kilanyi's and Hammerstein's creations, some of them quite crude artistically and technically.

The fever spread to the amateurs. A Fordham young ladies' club put on living pictures for a charity benefit and created a sensation by reproducing some of the same paintings being done on Broadway. For self-expression it was far ahead of ordinary amateur theatricals. Any young woman with a shapely figure could display it fully in the service of art, with no talent required beyond the ability to remain motionless half a minute or so. Even schoolgirls caught the fever, when the girls of the Patterson High School posed as living pictures in their commencement exercises. And once again, from scores of scandalized pulpits the stage was being denounced as responsible for the corruption of youth.

The week after the living picture premiere, Hammerstein refused to permit himself to be becalmed again in the doldrums of creative inactivity. Half ownership of the greatest music hall in America, plus ownership and supervision of two theaters—these were but his standards, routine activities. He had a piano put into his office at Koster and Bial's and began work on the composition of a new operetta. An inquiring reporter, watching his vigorous attack upon music paper with a pencil wielded in one hand and a large rubber eraser in the other, was told he wore out these implements in the ratio of two erasers to one pencil, and that when completed he would produce the opera in a Broadway theater. He knew his partners had no interest in producing any more musical shows.

Indeed, those gentlemen regarded his composing as unseemly in a business executive. To their ears the sound of a piano coming from his office grated intrudingly upon the familiar click of typewriters from the press room and the welcome click of coin from the box office. They persuaded him to undertake the preparation of a new series of living pictures. This was now their greatest attraction of the season, but Kilanyi was bringing out a new series, copying some of Hammerstein's innovations and already announcing that one picture would contain a dozen figures. They counted on their partner to stay a few jumps ahead.

Somewhat reluctantly, Hammerstein stopped work on his composition and began work on a second series of pictures. He worked at it steadily through the hot summer weather. For those hot summer nights, the firm provided its patrons with a comfortable roof garden. Although the roof was equipped with a stage and a number of vine-covered bamboo boxes, it was used only as a cooler promenade, provided with a restaurant and music, the orchestra playing of the roof being the same Hungarian Band that had once played on Sandow.

In the matter of size, Hammerstein's new pictures were a dozen jumps ahead of Kilanyi's. He was now using a gigantic frame, taking almost the entire proscenium opening so as to make possible reproductions of large-scale panoramic pictures. Sixty years later, another kind of living pictures—the motion pictures—would be preoccupied with the very kind of problems Kilanyi and Hammerstein were wrestling with—three dimensional pictures and wide screens framing large panoramic scenes.

The enormous scaffoldings required backstage for the new Hammerstein pictures took weeks of work and an enlarged crew of stage carpenters. In Makart's *Diane a la Chasse* there were fifteen female figures; Gerome's *Le Gladiateur* required some thirty persons to portray the arena and stadium spectators. The greatest problem was finding intelligent models in sufficient number. Hammerstein had a difficult time training some of his girls. A reporter found him at his wits trying to get a model into a difficult pose as Helen of Troy. In desperation he had strapped one of her legs to a pillar to make it easier to get the other leg into the desired position.

"Can't you throw that leg out?" he cried.

"Which leg?" asked the girl, completely confused.

"Your third leg!" he answered through clenched teeth. Then, throwing up his hands, he scratched the picture from the list.

The night of August 20 was the premier of the new second series and Hammerstein said it was his most trying ordeal since his imprisonment in the Gilsey House. Everything that could go wrong backstage did. The carpenters had used poor material. Dresses were caught and torn on nails and splinters. Some of the scaffolding was so rickety the models were in mortal fear of its collapse and everyone was having jitters. Fortunately, only two of the many contretemps were discernable to the audience. The orchestra got its music tangled and accompanied the picture, *The Lost Chord*, with a hornpipe, and in the picture, *Elaine*, the Lily Maid was seen hurriedly scrambling into her coffin, the curtains having been opened too soon. But apart from these vagaries all went well when seen from the front and the packed house voiced its enthusiasm.

It was evident that the S.R.O. sign would remain indefinitely and the same week work was begun on alterations designed to make the house hold more patrons for the fall season beginning September 10. The lounges were enlarged, and sixteen additional boxes constructed, bringing the total number to sixty.

That week also saw a small announcement in the theatrical news to the effect that Maurice Barrymore's daughter Ethel would make her professional debut on Friday as Lucy in *The Rivals* at the Long Branch Casino. This summer would see another fledgling emerge from the Drew-Barrymore nest.

The season which had seen the grand alliance inaugurated on Thirty-Fourth Street also saw the establishment of a new theatrical institution that was to be important for the artistic life of New York and have important consequences for Hammerstein. This despite the fact that it was not part of the regular Broadway theater but of that flourishing but peripheral German theater in which Hammerstein had begun his career in showmanship.

The central figure in this new development was Heinrich Conried, the actor and stage manager whom Hammerstein and conductor Adolph Neuendorff had brought to America fifteen years before. This was the Conried who, a year later, had tried unsuccessfully to form a German repertory company of his own and then had joined in the formation of the rival house that had finally forced Hammerstein and Neuendorff to discontinue their Germania Theatre. And this was the same Conried who, in addition to his theatrical rivalry, had been at one time Hammerstein's rival in love, although there they had both yielded the prize to Neuendorff.

In the years between, their paths had met occasionally when both men entered the mainstream of the English-speaking theater. Hammerstein had presented Conried's operetta company in his theaters, and once they found themselves crossing swords again when Conried, at the Casino, staged Aronson's rival production of *Cavalleria Rusticana* in opposition to Hammerstein's.

All though his years as stage director at the Casino, as actor and manager of concerts and operetta companies Conried had never given up his connection with the German stage. Nor had he ever given up his dream of having a German repertory theater of his own in which the best classic and modern European plays, especially the German, would be acted by a stock company equally capable of presenting farce, comedy, comic opera, serious drama and tragedy.

Now Conried had finally attained his cherished ambition by taking over the Amberg Theatre on Irving Place, for some years the chief home of the German theater in New York. Renaming it the Irving Place Theatre and hiring a completely new company, he had begun his season on October 2, the same day on which a certain committee had sat in judgment upon Hammerstein's *Kohinoor*. When he closed the season, he had given effective productions of forty-nine plays and operettas, including a dozen new works.

Conried had launched a new theatrical institution. He had made an artistic success. But beyond succeeding in remaining solvent he had not made any money. For he was immediately confronted with the kind of bitter rivalry he had once helped to create for Hammerstein and Neuendorff's Germania Theatre. The actors of the Amberg Theatre, whom he had replaced with his own choices and left jobless, had formed a rival company and taken over the old Aberle's Theatre (once a church) on 8th Street, renaming it—an ironic stroke of poetic justice for Conried—the Germania Theatre.

After competing with Conried in the same type repertory this group produced a local musical farce of their own called *Der Corner Grocer aus der Avenue A* and found they had created a smash hit. They had also created a new theatrical genre, German-American farce (as Harrigan had created Irish-American farce in his Mulligan plays) and they exploited the formula with a successful series of sequels beginning with *Der Pawnbroker von der East Side*. For some years to come there would be a German theater on Irving Place receiving artistic attention ad critical kudos and just keeping out of the red, and a German-American theater on 8th Street which received neither praise nor prestige but made money consistently.

Whatever his financial disappointment, Conried closed the season happy in the realization that he had his long-sought theater. He had indeed established a noteworthy institution. Classic and modern European plays which could never be seen on Broadway were to be given careful and effective production by a highly competent stock company, with occasional guest appearances of distinguished visiting artists from Europe.

The artistic and intellectual fame of the Irving Place Theatre was to grow. Conried would not gather wealth but he was to gather numerous citations and honorary degrees from leading universities. In ten years, his reputation would lift him into a commanding position in the theatrical and musical life of New York and the nation. He was to attain the great post of director of the Metropolitan Opera House, a position of such exalted dominance that no manager would be able successfully to challenge it—that is, no manager except Oscar Hammerstein, when the long duel between the two men would finally reach its climax.

The official close of the 1893–1894 season was a time of stock-taking for the partners in the grand alliance. For Messrs. Koster and Bial the merger had been a success beyond their fondest dreams. They were finding their partner somewhat difficult and somewhat incompressible but his contributions to the season's success were undeniable. They were well satisfied with the venture's profits, on all its features—admission, food, drink. Even the printed program had become a profitable advertising medium. If there was any proof needed that Koster and Bial's was a respectable place frequented by respectable ladies it could be found in the program item advertising and goods sold by a store on Sixth Avenue and 14th Street: "We sell goods cheaper than any house in the world, but for cash only—R. H. Macy and Co." That this item should appear in the Koster and Bial program was prophetic in a way no one could be aware of at the time. Another continuous and more appropriate item in the printed program was the advertisement of Kessler, Behringer and Co.: "Sole U.S. Agents for Moet and Chandon White Seal Champagne." This item, too, was prophetic of things to come and to come very soon.

For Hammerstein, too, the season should have been counted a huge success, yet he was profoundly dissatisfied. The Columbus Theatre season was, as always, highly profitable with its popular comedies and melodramas, in one of which—"Gentleman Jack"—the mighty hero was no less a person than James J. Corbett, heavyweight champion of the world and a quite competent actor. The season's bills here had also included some of the top minstrel and variety shows, as Primrose and West's Minstrels, Docksteder's minstrels, and Tony Pastor's Company. The trouble with this theater, from Hammerstein's point of view, had always been that it practically ran itself.

Now the Harlem Opera House, which for the first time had shown a fair profit, was developing the same trouble. Its reputation as New York's finest combination house was now so well established that it became the recognized rule for a successful Broadway presentation, whether comic opera or Shakespearean repertory, upon completion of its downtown run to go straight to the Harlem Opera House for a week before going out on tour. By this rule Rosenberg could now run the house with very little supervision. It was no longer necessary to look for bookings, only to select from among those offered.

Here, as usual, the season had presented the best seen on Broadway. The musicals had included Chauncey Olcott in *Mavourneen*, Marie Tempest in *The Algerian*, De Wolfe Hopper in *Panjandrum*, Lillian Russell in *The Princess Nicotine*, the Bostonians in their immortal *Robin Hood*, and Hammerstein's own *Kohinoor*. Among the outstanding actors and dramatic presentations had been the Kendalls in a repertory including the strong new Pinero play, *The Second Mrs. Tangueray*, which New York had found a "shocker," Marie Wainwright in *Camille*, once a "shocker" in its time, Mrs. John Drew, Alexander Salvini, Charles Frohman's Comedians in "Lady Windermere's Fan," Rose Coghlan in *A Woman of No Importance*, and E. H. Sothern in *Sheridan*.

The chief sphere of Hammerstein's activity had been Koster and Bial's. Bial's bills were of very high quality and would have attracted good houses, but the high points of the season with potent drawing power were all identified in some way with Hammerstein. The sensation of the early part of the season had not been Bial's star, Harriet Vernon, who aroused no enthusiasm, but Hammerstein's ballet and his *Kohinoor*. In the middle of the season the great sensation had been Sandow, for whose engagement no one could take credit, but for whose success Hammerstein's presentation was in large part responsible.

The sensation of the late season and summer and still going strong were the Hammerstein Living Pictures.

Instead of swelling with pride at this record, Hammerstein was chafing like a caged lion. His opportunities for showmanship were too few and too restricted, and under the policies of his partners the prospect was for less and less opportunity in the future. They had assigned him ballet and musical productions as his department and then abolished the department. The suspicion was growing that they had merely used his ballet to launch the new house on a higher artistic level and once well established were content to revert to vaudeville—first-rate vaudeville, to be sure, but vaudeville pure and simple.

Koster and Bial regarded singers as specialty acts, not musical performers, and refused to give Hammerstein a voice in their selection. When he inquired just what there would be for him to do, their only suggestion was a third series of living pictures and after that a fourth. Hammerstein was undoubtedly thinking of living pictures and his partners when he made his much-quoted remark: "Theatrical managers are like sheep. When one of them hits on a novel idea, the entire flock race after the same thing. Result, the idea is soon worn out and the public tired out with it."

Developing and improving the living picture idea had been fun, but by now it was a bore. The town was flooded with such exhibits and he knew, if his unimaginative partners did not, that within a few months the thing would be a drag on the market. What would be left for him then? When would these saloonkeepers understand that he could never be satisfied just to sit back and partake of the profits? He must have a theatrical outlet for his creative energies—anything else was suffocation.

As the opening of the new season approached, relations between the partners grew more tense. Outwardly all was calm but it was the calm before the storm.

5

Gala Performance—Unscheduled

Monday afternoon, September 10, Bial, Koster, Hammerstein and other officials of the firm sat in the empty music hall watching the rehearsal of the new bill that would inaugurate the season that night. Bial had imported a number of European artists and novelties to launch the 1894–1895 season with a huge four-hour show.

Next in the rehearsal was the star of the bill, the "chanteuse internationale," Mlle. Marietta Di Dio, whom Bial had brought from Vienna at $300 a week and whose American debut he confidently expected would create a sensation. The publicity department had been puffing her for weeks as the toast of Vienna and Paris, celebrated for her beauty, her elegant 17th and 18th century costumes, her gorgeous jewels and her many admirers. The public had been made privy to her Custom House declaration, where, upon arriving, she had valued her costumes at $50,000, her jewels at $80,000.

An actress's jewels are always good publicity, and actresses have always contrived to lose them or have them stolen, an event bound to insure a newspaper story. For the possession of valuable jewelry by a beautiful woman raises intriguing speculations as to the manner in which she obtained them. In Di Dio's case she had already attained considerable notoriety in Vienna, where she displayed her jewels like trophies.

Four years earlier she and her jewels had figured in an affair that became an international incident. A young Romanian prince, a member of the Bacaresco family and the son of the Romanian ambassador in Vienna, became her devoted admirer. Every afternoon he was seen driving in the park with her, every evening she sat bediamonded in his box at the opera until it was time to leave for the second-rate music hall in which she was then appearing.

The affair was becoming scandalous. For a prince to carry on with an actress was merely "Lèse-majesté." In gay circles it was even considered "de rigueur." But to flaunt it quite so openly was a bit "de trop." One evening the lady appeared entirely denuded of jewelry and the scandalous story was soon all over Vienna. The young man, finding himself in financial embarrassment, had borrowed her jewels to pawn. To bestow diamonds upon a mistress was one thing, to borrow them from one's mistress quite another and very definitely a "faux pas."

Court circles frowned their disapproval. When Prince Reuss, the German ambassador, gave his next diplomatic ball, the Romanian ambassador was invited, his son was not. His social standing at stake, the young prince came anyway, nonchalantly telling his hostess there must have been an oversight. The host promptly informed him point blank there had been no oversight—he was not welcome—whereupon both the ambassador and his son left without a word.

The next morning Prince Reuss received the father's challenge to a duel and all the chancelleries of Europe were aflutter. A duel between two ambassadors! An international crisis had been precipitated. Telegraph wires were busy across Europe, special couriers were hastily dispatched. There was intervention at the highest levels. The duel was averted. The pawned jewels were returned to the lady, the young prince to his native land. Di Dio became a celebrity and war between Germany and Roumaine was postponed for 25 years until the more serious international incident at Sarajevo.

The small group of men in the darkened theater expected something very striking when Di Dio walked out on the stage. They were not disappointed. Her appearance was startling. She was indeed a beautiful woman, placid featured, with brown hair drawn back pompadour fashion, and violet eyes. Her figure was stately and voluptuous, her manner ultra-refined, very much the grande dame.

What made her startling was her elaborate Parisian gown and her ornaments which consisted solely of diamonds of largest size and bluest water. Both earrings contained two brilliant stones, each the size of a nickel. Her necklace, like a shield protecting her bosom, was a solid mass of diamonds. Her bracelets, the rosettes that caught her train and the edging of her bodice were composed entirely of diamonds. She was wearing a good $75,000 worth of dazzling jewels.

The glittering Viennese chanteuse sang three songs, one in French, two in German. There was nothing striking about the songs. She sang them with very little voice, no vocal style and hardly any animation. She was so much the reserved grande dame that her eyes and face were almost expressionless, her gestures stiff and formal, her manner dull and lifeless, devoid of charm.

"She's no good," said Hammerstein, turning to Bial. "Cancel her engagement and send her back." Bial was outraged. This woman was a continental celebrity, a great star, he asserted, and she would make a sensation in New York.

"Take my advice," Hammerstein admonished his partner. "I understand singing and you don't. She's another Vernon—a singer who can't sing and tries to get by on looks, costumes, jewels and notoriety. You can't fool New York. She'll be a failure. I'm a partner in this firm and I don't want my money wasted. Exhibit her costumes and jewels if you want to but take her off the program. Send her away, I tell you."

Bial turned a deaf ear. He insisted the Viennese was a great artist and a great attraction. He had engaged her for six weeks and she would play six weeks. He did not need any advice from Hammerstein nor was he asking for any.

This was not the only act to which Hammerstein had raised objections. Earlier in the rehearsal had come the act second only to the star among the new presentations—the Nilsson Aerial Ballet. Hammerstein thought it a good novelty, but it involved difficult stage devices intricately synchronized with complicated light affects and it was obvious that the stage and electrical crew were unsure of their cues. He suggested to Bial that since this act depended upon illusion for its effect it had better be withheld from the bill until further rehearsed, and he reminded him that as a ballet it should have been under his own direction. Bial denied it was a ballet. It was a specialty act, he had said, and it would work fine by the evening performance. Hammerstein had no fault to find with the rest of the bill, which included some old favorites, and as for the acrobatic and animal acts, here Bial's taste was sure.

That night the opening of the new season found the house packed with an expectant audience. The old favorite, Eugénie Fougère,[1] was welcomed warmly, but she was suffering noticeably from the effects of Koster and Bial's new passion for respectability. Her gown, usually outrageously décolleté, was almost prudish and actually had sleeves. Her songs, too, had been toned down from their usually scandalous character. But despite these handicaps her normal Parisian diablerie asserted itself. The Hammerstein Living Pictures which closed the performance were received with the usual enthusiasm.

Of the new acts the most successful were the Martinetti Brothers, two acrobats who performed remarkable feats with the seeming strength of a Sandow and the grace and dash of a Carmencita. They received an ovation. Next in popularity came Tschernoff and his trained dogs who performed difficult and novel tricks, including a serpentine dance performed in costume under a spotlight by one of the talented animals.

The much-advertised feature acts did not fare so well. The elegant Mlle. Di Dio came before her expectant audience in her rich and dazzling costume which included white elbow-length gloves. By some lapse in fitting or dressing, one of these gloves was about two inches off her fingers, yet she persisted in using that hand for elegant gestures during her songs. With each gesture the flapping of two inches of kid looked more ridiculous than elegant and there were some titters.

The singer's lack of vitality and magnetism of any kind was disappointing. There was applause—any beautiful woman received applause at Koster and Bial's—but it was perfunctory, and the usher was forced to spring down the aisle with the basket of flowers to reach the orchestra rail before the last handclap died away. While an occasional reviewer, as the *New York World*'s, was impressed by Di Dio's air of refinement, others, as the *New York Sun*'s, were quite adverse, and there was general agreement that the much-puffed singer's debut was not a success.

The Aerial Ballet came a cropper at its debut. This was an expensive act in which five serpentine dancers, performing in a darkened stage and auditorium under colored spotlights illuminating their drapers, danced first upon the boards and then while lifted and suspended in mid-air. The intention was the illusion of disembodied color and movement floating in air, but the strong lights at the musicians' desks in the pit spoiled the effect and the spotlight movements were so bungled as to reveal all the mechanical devices, supposed to be invisible, and converted illusion into disillusion. Bial withdrew the act from the bill after the first night—an ignominious failure. To Hammerstein this was further evidence of artistic mismanagement. All the ballet needed to succeed was adequate rehearsing; it was Di Dio who should have been withdrawn.

It was a galling situation for Hammerstein. He not only understood and appreciated voices; he had a deep and abiding love for good singing. He saw no reason why music hall singing should be inferior. There were vaudeville singers who were first-rate artists of their kind. Indeed, he saw no reason why music hall audiences should not hear the best singing of any kind. They would recognize what was good, if not always immediately, very soon. But if they were given third-rate stuff how would they learn to like what was really fine?

Hammerstein managed to keep himself remarkably well informed of new developments abroad. When Bial had been leaving for his annual trip to engage performers, Hammerstein had spoken to his partner about the great new music hall star who had arisen in Paris. Her name was Yvette Guilbert and critics and public alike were hailing her as a supreme artist, a "singer-diseuse" who had created a new style of vocal art. She would make a fitting importation for the greatest music hall in America. He urged Bial to try to obtain her and his partner had promised to look into it.

Upon his return Bial's report had been wholly negative. He had been told that this Guilbert woman wanted the ridiculous sum of something like $1,000 a week to come to

America—the salary of a world-renowned grand opera star. More, he had seen the woman's photographs—she was plain of feature and her figure thin and angular. Imagine, Bial had laughed, a music hall singer who was not even pretty. It was preposterous. Reputation or no, he wouldn't offer her $100 a week. But he had found a really sensational star. He had secured Di Dio!

The more Hammerstein thought about the artistic judgment and policies of the partners with whom he was allied the angrier he became. He realized the futility of protesting. If his protest were to have any effect in forcing them to give him an adequate voice in the artistic direction it would have to be made in some more open manner. Even if it failed to budge these stodgy partners it would, at least, openly attest his own disapproval of their policy. Accordingly, he planned his maneuver for Thursday, the 13th, the fourth night of the new program.

It was always a matter of some surprise that so many reporters were in Koster and Bial's on a Thursday night to recount what happened and to disagree with each other upon the details. Hammerstein had allowed it to get out quietly, that there might be a story for the newspapers that night. There would be for he intended to provide it, but he had no idea of how good a story it was going to be.

Hammerstein sat alone in a center box on the promenade tier of the theater he had built. He was, of course, a celebrity known to the general public beyond the theater world ever since his victory in Harlem. Since the building of the magnificent Manhattan and the celebrated feat in the Gilsey House, he was now one of New York's fabulous personalities.

Unknown to Hammerstein, fate had willed it that in the adjoining box on his left there should be sitting that night another of New York's fabulous characters—George Kessler. Tall, handsome, athletic, he was one of the half dozen men in the city who constituted a race set apart to live seemingly charmed and charming lives. Like the others he was a professional man about town. Every night he passed through the most fashionable restaurants, bars, hotels and music halls, often with a beautiful actress or dancer at his side, driving from one to another in a showy carriage with liveried footmen. He was present at every first night at the theaters and known equally for giving enormous formal dinner parties and small, intimate late suppers with feminine company. He was a familiar figure at the gambling tables of the great clubs and at the racetracks. Summertime found him entertaining parties on his private yacht. And living on this scale cost him nothing. He was paid to do it, receiving an expense account said to be more than $50,000 a year.

Kessler was one of New York's champagne agents, a member of that fabulous profession which flourished in the Gay Nineties and did so much to keep them gay. The agent's mission was to promote the brand of champagne he represented by living on an opulent scale, ordering that brand in public and serving it in private. Once the identification of the man and the brand was thoroughly established anything that advertised the former thereby advertised the latter, and the agents vied with each other in ostentation.

None of them displayed much originality and whatever one did was immediately copied by all. In this they followed the pattern set by high society—ostentation without imagination. So when a rival agent drove down Fifth Avenue in a hansom cab drawn by a team of horses, everyone talked about this startling innovation. No one had ever hitched two horses to a hansom before and the name of the agent (inseparable from the name of his champagne) was all over town. Within the week Kessler was driving a hansom with a spanking team and driving it further and faster to the glory of Moet and Chandon's White Seal Champagne. Kessler, who was not dependent upon sales commissions (having his own distributing business, Kessler, Behringer and Co.), was one of the wealthiest and most successful of the New York agents.

In sporting circles, they were still talking about the clambake Kessler had given in the betting ring of the Saratoga race track a month before. He had turned the ring into a huge dining hall for his six hundred guests. All the prominent turfmen were there. The big feature was the dessert. A hundred colored waiters marched in, each carrying a large watermelon into which a bottle of champagne had been poured. The bottles (Moet and Chandon, of course) were standing neck-down in the melons.

The violence of Kessler's temper was as well known as his extravagance and he had been involved in a number of rows. Not long ago, at a gambling club, he had made a scene that was typical of him when he walked up to the roulette table demanding a couple of stacks of chips. The croupier gave him two stacks of red chips. Kessler asked the value of each chip. When told it was $5 he angrily flung the chips on the floor shouting, "Do you take me for a grocery boy?" He got a stack more befitting his exalted station, lost $6,000 within a few minutes and left. Only a few weeks ago, at the U.S. Club in Saratoga, he had lost $18,000 at baccarat in a single night.

At Koster and Bial's, George Kessler was both a friend and a fixture. The printed program regularly carried the advertisement of his company and brand and the firm did business with him, buying his merchandise in quantity. He was himself a constant and free spending frequenter of the place and had been one of the chief ornaments of the old Cork Room. He never bothered to purchase admission but was passed in as a friend of the management and he was one of those who had special stage door privileges and was always introduced to the imported actresses. Kessler was not a man to stoop to anything less expensive than a star and it was said that he was taking a great deal of interest in the current star from Vienna.

This was quite apparent when Mlle. Di Dio performed that Thursday night. The applause, as usual, was polite but perfunctory, except for one box where George Kessler and several friends applauded enthusiastically. Suddenly a sharp, sibilant sound was heard. Someone was hissing the star—vigorously. Such expression of disapproval was almost unknown at Koster and Bial's, where the audience sometimes received performers with complete indifference. Certainly a beautiful woman had never been hissed at Koster and Bial's. Necks were craned and heads turned. It seemed, incredibly, to be coming from Hammerstein's box. Kessler and his friends clapped more loudly, as if in answer, the hissing increased in vigor and intensity. It was Hammerstein. He was standing up now at the front of his box making gestures of disapproval. The audience was buzzing now. It was still incredible—a manager hissing the star of his own show! Di Dio hesitated, then retired in confusion.

Kessler strode to the rail at the front of his box, his tall figure leaned forward into Hammerstein's box, his face flushed.

"How dare you insult a lady by hissing like that," he demanded, towering over the manager.

"She's no good," was Hammerstein's loud reply, "and if you understood anything you wouldn't applaud."

"Well, you can't insult this lady," the agent persisted.

"Who says so?" demanded the manager aggressively. "This is my theatre and I'll do as I please!"

"You're a coward and a cad!" Kessler shouted.

"Oh, you'd like a chance to be her champion," Hammerstein shouted back. "Well, I'll tell you where you can go."

The whole house heard him tell Kessler where to go, after which the two men fell to exchanging epithets vigorously and colorfully. There was a commotion among some women in the box on the other side. A man ran into Hammerstein's box crying out for the two men to desist from their language—his wife was hysterical. The irate man turned to him and both told him where to go. There was a scream followed by a thud. The man, crying "My wife—she's fainted!" ran back to his spouse and the two belligerents resumed cursing each other.

In the orchestra, the audience had risen in their seats and were looking up at the two men. The whole house was now in an uproar of excitement. From their box Koster and Bial could not see the principals. Their anguish was acute. A common brawl in their respectable precinct! And such shocking language! This had never happened even on Twenty-Third Street. Where were the bouncers? Who was the ruffian who had hissed? Who was the other man? They could not believe their ears when told the one was their own partner, the other their friend and favorite patron.

Bial rushed out in a rage. He found Hammerstein and Kessler now in the promenade, still cursing each other, surrounded by an excited crowd. Hammerstein was ordering the agent out of the theater. Kessler was defying him to put him out and Hammerstein was calling for the policeman on duty. Unable to … break through the crowd, the usually quiet Bial shook his fist and shouted over their heads, "You should be the one put out, Hammerstein, you … you"—he hurled the worst epithet in the vocabulary of a German businessman—"you loafer!"

At this point police officer Petrosini, detailed at the door, shouldered his way through the crowd to the two quarreling men. Hammerstein demanded he eject the wine agent for disorderly conduct. Kessler drew himself up to his six feet plus, looking the picture of injured dignity. The policeman knew Hammerstein was an owner and manager but he also knew that Kessler was a friend of the management and a privileged customer. He said he found no grounds for disorderly conduct and refused to eject anyone. But the crowd, he said, was blocking the passage and creating a hazard. He began to disperse the bystanders, shooing them back to their seats with firmness. Officer Petrosini was a remarkable man, as an Italian had to be to get on a then practically one hundred percent Irish police force. Kessler disappeared in the crowd. Hammerstein went downstairs. The officer went upstairs to the roof garden. The trouble was over. Or so it seemed.

No two accounts agreed on exactly what followed a few minutes later. Hammerstein claimed Kessler accosted him and began to push him around. Kessler alleged Hammerstein waylaid him. At any rate, there were the two men again, standing in the lobby exchanging epithets not meant to be heard in polite society. Another crowd quickly gathered around them.

Suddenly Hammerstein struck the wine agent on the jaw and the big man went down. When he got up Hammerstein rushed at him again, but this time Kessler, an expert boxer, met him with a straight left and now Hammerstein went down. Picking himself up, Hammerstein rushed again. Another straight arm sent him sprawling a second time. Determined to close with his larger antagonist, the belligerent manager tried again only to be floored a third time. There was a cut near his eye as he rose, as full of fight as ever, when a flying wedge of house attaches intervened between the combatants. Hammerstein was still trying to get at the wine agent as they pulled him away into Cline's office off the lobby.

Kessler disappeared against just as officer Petrosini appeared too late to do anything but disperse the crowd once more. Peace and tranquility again restored, Messrs. Koster and Bial retired to their office upstairs in anger, shame and genuine bewilderment.

A number of friends went up to Koster and Bial's office to sympathize and commiserate with the partners in their hour of humiliation. Bial declaimed stoutly: "Such conduct by a manager of this house cannot and will not be tolerated by his partners. Miss Di Dio is an artist of rare ability and there is no reason why Hammerstein should have hissed her." Koster expostulated: "Why, it is unheard of. I cannot understand it. Hammerstein never drinks; he must be crazy." The discussion was soon cut short. Someone rushed in crying: "Come down quickly—it's starting all over again!"

There was no doubt as to who was responsible for starting matters this time. Mlle. Di Dio, straight from her dressing room, gown, jewelry, personal maid and all, had come tearing into the lobby in search of Hammerstein. The critic who complained of the dull expression of her eyes should have seen then now—they were ablaze.

She tracked the manager down in Cline's office and stormed into the room, her high-pitched denunciations in German proving to all within earshot that hell hath no fury like a woman hissed. She opened up on Hammerstein with a remonstrance of classic elegance: "You dog! You are no gentleman!" She continued to upbraid him with mounting vehemence. "Never have I been so insulted before. You bring me from my home to this country and then hiss me upon your own stage!"

A *World* reporter described her performance as "a dressing down that would do credit to a Viennese fish-wife." It was a transformation act that fascinated even Hammerstein as he watched the grande dame vanish, the air of elegant refinement and reserve dissolve in the accents and epithets of a patois straight out of the gutters of Vienna. Between torrents of abuse, she told Hammerstein she was a great artist who had sung before better people than him and his line, that she had appeared before crowned heads and no one had insulted her like this.

When he had the chance to get in a word, Hammerstein told her quietly that his head was not crowned but it did have eyes and ears, that he knew a good thing when he saw it, also the opposite. "Now go away, lady, and don't bother me" he pleaded. All this accomplished was to send Di Dio into another shrieking tirade.

At this moment the door opened and in strutted Kessler, who then stood dramatically against the door and made the most incredible speech of a whole evening of incredible events.

"It seems," he declaimed, "that I have arrived in time. I returned fearing that a man who could hiss a woman and a stranger might even strike her."

It might have come straight out of one of the melodramas Hammerstein presented at his Columbus Theatre. It probably did.

Hammerstein cursed the wine agent and ordered him to be put out. Kessler hurled a few choice epithets of his own, which seemed amateurish to those who understood German and had heard Di Dio. He turned to the singer and told her to slap Hammerstein's face. She hesitated, standing between the big man who was urging her on and the little manager who was looking fighting mad. Verbal abuse was one thing; slapping this peppery fellow might be tempting fate. She noticed also that Kessler was not at her side but standing behind her, none of which accorded with her sense of the fitness of things. The lady took a quick step to one side. His field of vision clean, Hammerstein immediately hurled himself at the enemy.

Kessler had no time for fancy boxing. He found himself pinned to the door, where the two grappled, Di Dio shrieking encouragement to her champion. Locked together, the men lurched about the room, knocking over furniture. Then both fell heavily to the floor, where they rolled pummeling each other while Di Dio screamed.

For weeks the subject of Di Dio's singing voice was debated pro and con. About her screaming voice there was never a question—in volume, altitude and intensity it was unsurpassed. It filled the lobby, it pierced into the auditorium, bringing out an excited crowd. It brought officer Petrosini, who came bursting in, separated the antagonists and jerked them to their feet. Each man charged the other with assault and disorderly conduct. With the wisdom of a Solomon, the officer accepted both versions and arrested both men.

They went quietly as he marched them out of the lobby and into a cab for the West Thirtieth Street Police Station. Koster, Di Dio, and her maid piled into another cab and followed, Bial remaining to restore order in the house. Several reporters commandeered the remaining cabs and dashed off after them. A few more reporters, manager Cline and other officials set out on foot for the station house. Almost immediately this rearguard found itself a vanguard. The entire theater had emptied out on the street and had fallen in behind them in a gay procession. They had come to see a good show. They were getting a better one than they had dreamt of and the next act would go on at the station. Bial, who had been standing in the lobby trying to persuade people back into the theater, was engulfed in the surging tide of outgoing humanity, swept out of the lobby, and left stranded on the sidewalk to watch forlorn the last of his audience disappearing down the street.

Inside, true to the traditions of the stage, the orchestra was missing and an act was being performed half-heartedly to empty rows of seats—even the ushers had gone—till a merciful stage manager put them out of their misery. Ringing down the curtain, he told everyone backstage to call it a night and go home.

At the station house, Sergeant Lane was in charge of the desk for what seemed a routine night until officer Petrosini brought in two irate men in evening dress who charged each other with disorderly conduct and assault. At their heels came something even more unusual at the Tenderloin police station: a third man, equally irate and in similar formal attire, accompanied by a beautiful woman in a rich costume dazzling with jewels that lighted up the gloomy precinct. Entering close behind them came several reporters. The sergeant had hardly finished booking the names and complaints before the station house was invaded by several hundred excited persons in evening clothes who crowded every inch of space. Outside, hundreds more were milling about in the street. Sergeant Lane looked on in amazement. This was no ordinary case of disorderly conduct.

The beautiful Di Dio went straight to the side of her protector. Koster, pointing a trembling finger at his partner, said: "Never speak to me again. You have disgraced the name of Koster and Bial."

Hammerstein hooted his scorn at this, making sarcastic references to Kessler's relations with actresses and accusing Koster of running a disorderly house. This sent Koster shaking with apoplectic rage. He pounded the sergeant's desk demanding the right to make a formal charge against Hammerstein for this insult but was at a loss just what to charge him with. His friends finally dissuaded him and calmed him down sufficiently to cease spluttering and announce that he and Bial would have nothing more to do with Hammerstein.

Normally, the sergeant would have set bail in such a case at $100 but the presence of so many elegantly dressed people made him cautious. Something of great moment might be involved here. He set bail at $500, the case to come up next morning in Jefferson Market Court. Neither Hammerstein nor the extravagant Kessler had that much cash with him.

Koster promptly furnished bail for Kessler and left triumphantly with the wine agent and Di Dio, leaving his partner to languish in jail. Most of the crowd began to leave. Hammerstein sent a message to Bial asking to be bailed out and received a flat refusal. They would teach him a lesson, Bial had said. Hammerstein dispatched another messenger to find George Bullwinkle, proprietor of the Aulic Hotel at Broadway and Thirty-Fifth.

Before he was locked up the reporters got a few words of his side of the night's story. He told them he had used his prerogative in disapproving a performance, as any member of the audience had a right to do. "This Di Dio woman is no good," he said, "and her songs are indecent. When I saw her at rehearsal I knew she would be a failure. I told my partners to discharge her and they refused. Of course I hissed. Why not? It was my own theatre." There was a public issue at stake, he said—a man's right to publicly express disapproval of a performance, especially a performance taking place on his own property. Asked if Koster and Bial could force him out, he scoffed, telling them he held a $300,000 mortgage on the theater and could foreclose on them if he wanted to, but he would not discuss his plans now.

It was after midnight when Bullwinkle arrived to bail out the imprisoned manager. Hammerstein had been locked in a cell for more than an hour. His planned protest had worked out more effectively than he could have foreseen but he was furious at his partners now. So they wanted to teach him a lesson? He was not a man to be given lessons by such as they. He would teach them a few things and he would not be satisfied to show only them, he was going to show New York what he was capable of accomplishing. For during that hour in a cell a dream first began to take shape in Hammerstein's mind—the dream of Olympia.

It was in September of the previous year that the erstwhile prisoner in the station house had been the prisoner in the Gilsey House and in the headlines of every New York paper. Another September had come and now, once more Hammerstein's name was in every paper and on every tongue. The front page of the *World* shouted the headlines: "He Punched Oscar Hammerstein—Club Man at Koster and Bial's Objects to Manager Hissing Marietta Di Dio." The three-column story in the *Herald* was headed: "Hit Hammerstein—Hissed Singer in His Own Theatre, Then Fought with George Kessler—Both Arrested." The *Sun*'s captions told the public: "Oscar Hammerstein Hisses a Performer—Owner of Concert Hall Building Raises a Lively Rumpus in His Own House."

There was vast public amusement at the episode and there was also a good deal of discussion of the issue Hammerstein had raised. What about the right to hiss? Editorially the *World* quipped: "Oscar Hammerstein seems determined to maintain his right to hiss and 'his'n.'"

That morning Jefferson Market Court was full of reporters detailed to inform New York of the aftermath of the spectacular clash between two of its most fabulous characters. Kessler arrived in typical style in a magnificently equipped brougham with two liveried footmen, from which he stepped in all his sartorial magnificence. Less magnificent were his three companions in the vehicle, Koster, Bial, and Issac Fromme, his lawyer and theirs. Hammerstein came with his lawyer, Morris Wise, looking chipper despite a small piece or two of sticking plaster on his face. The principals had drawn a full house, including many of the theatrical profession and many merely of the curious.

Justice Voorhis presiding disposed of a number of routine cases and came to the main event—mutual charges of disorderly conduct and assault by Oscar Hammerstein and George Kessler. He heard Hammerstein's side first and it was clear this was no routine case of the kind. Hammerstein said he had hissed an actress in his theater whose performance had not pleased him. He said a matter of public policy was involved—the right of a spectator to hiss a performance, as well as the question of his right as a proprietor to express his displeasure on his own premises. He claimed these rights. Kessler, whom he referred to as a "professional loafer," had interfered with his legitimate exercise of them and he charged him with disorderly conduct. "What about the other charge of assault?" the judge asked. "Never mind, Your Honor," said Hammerstein, "I am not injured. Let the assault pass."

Kessler's story was more routine. He asserted Hammerstein had created a disturbance and had attacked him when he protested. Koster and Bial stood ready to corroborate his version.

The judge was appreciative of the fact that the manager had raised some genuine issues. He was a sincere upholder of individual rights of self-expression and an equally strong supporter of the rights of private property. He had, also, a sense of humor.

"Well," he said, "I will discharge both of you, at the same time warning each to behave properly in the future. As to this hissing business, I must say that in his own theatre or anywhere else a man has the right to so express disapproval. Good day, gentlemen."

Hammerstein looked pleased, Kessler nonchalant, Koster and Bial disappointed. And now the reporters swarmed about the principals, seeking and obtaining statements. They got the judge to amplify his opinion about the right to hiss. He told them: "The right to applaud carries with it the right to disapprove. But in both cases individuals should not interfere with the rights of others who have paid for an evening's enjoyment."

Hammerstein's statement gave the reporters plenty of copy, most of it new and opening up fresh angles. "I hissed," he said, "because of my objection to the Koster and Bial method of bringing to this country a lot of foreign women whose stock in trade is indecency. This Di Dio sings objectionable verses and should not be tolerated. The trouble dates back to my first protest against importing these foreign women. They all proved dismal failures. There was Harriett Vernon, for instance, who received $600 a week and who did not draw 600 cents. People did not care for these foreigners except when they wanted something indecent. It was expected that they would draw on their reputation of having had trouble with dukes and other celebrities. We lost money whenever these people appeared."

Pointedly, Hammerstein noted the house made its greatest profits from Sandow and from his own living pictures. He went on to say: "This Kessler is a big loafer whom Koster and Bial gave the run of the house. He never paid to come in. He sponged on the house and acted as if the foreign women were brought over for his benefit. There are serious questions to be settled between me and Koster and Bial outside the one in hand. I have instructed my attorney to begin suit for dissolution of partnership. Koster and Bial can buy my interest if they choose, but I shall have nothing more to do with them."

Kessler gave his statement while brushing his silk hat and smoothing his gloves before being driven away in his brougham. "You see," he told the newsman, "this fellow Hammerstein is crazy, crazy as a loon. Think of a man hissing one of his own performers. Why, I might as well go around declaring my wine is no good. He says Mlle. Di Dio's songs are risqué. Why, my mother and sister can listen to any song she sings. The only reason she is not a greater success is that she is so eminently respectable. Now you must understand that I never saw this lady before last night. I happened in there by chance. When I remonstrated with Hammerstein he used the most frightful language. It is not true that he knocked me down. He never touched me. Now he's talking of closing a mortgage for $300,000. Koster and Bial can come to my office any minute and get a check for the amount of it."

The most unique statement of all came later in the day in the inimitable English of Mlle. Di Dio. "I have been treated never so before," said the grande dame. "The chanson is a good chanson. It is tres modest. You would not sing it in church, no. Maia, it is not mauvais. All the kleine kinder sing it on the streets of Vienna."

In the courthouse the reporters were still pressing questions upon Hammerstein. He stopped them short. There were some urgent matters on Thirty-Fourth Street, he said, that he must attend to at once. They watched him go into action, striding out of the court, hailing a cab, directing the driver to Koster and Bial's as fast as you can, and driving off at a fast clip.

Something was up. The reporters promptly gave chase and they were hard on his heels when he sailed through the stage door of the theater. A moment later he had summoned the stage manager and stage crew. Standing in the center of the stage, he struck a mock-dramatic pose and announced: "I leave this place forever and you must get along as best you can. No more living pictures for me. I shake the dust off my sandals and git."

Marshaling six stagehands, Hammerstein led them through the darkened theater to his handsomely furnished private office on the second floor. Soon the furnishings were being carried out of the building. Quite a crowd, including a number of theater officials, gathered to watch as desks, chairs, tables, a piano, pictures, curtains, books, papers and opera scores were deposited on the sidewalk. A moving van arrived presently, and everything was piled into it for carting away to the Harlem Opera House. Hammerstein followed in a cab. As it started off he waved his hand toward the great house he had built and called out to the group standing at the entrance: "Goodbye, I'm going and I won't be back. You can run this thing yourself. I won't interfere."

Messrs. Koster and Bial were incredulous when told their partner had cleared out, lock, stock and barrel, without so much as an effort to negotiate their differences. "Come and see for yourselves," they were told. They went to Hammerstein's office. The scene that met their eyes was bewildering; it was as though a tornado had passed through the room Papers, trash and debris of all kinds littered the floor, except for one place. In the very center of the room a space had been cleared. There, reposing upon a box, was a package, neatly labeled and tied with ribbons—the original manuscript of the *Kohinoor*, the parting legacy of genius to saloon keeping. It was a typical Hammerstein touch.

All of these events were set forth in the newspapers with loving care and detail for the delectation of their readers. The *Herald* even furnished, as one of its illustrations, a drawing captioned "Present Condition of Hammerstein's office."

The weekend was filled with conferences between Koster and Bial and their advisers. As they surveyed the trend of public opinion, the two men were bewildered at the unexpected turn taken by the affair. There was something here they simply could not fathom. They had expected that, publicly disgraced, a contrite and chastened Hammerstein would offer no further trouble. Having taught him a lesson, they were prepared to be magnanimous and to forgive his trespasses upon suitable assurances of good behavior.

By every expectation their partner should now be in disgrace. He had violated every rule. Had he not publicly insulted a lady—committed the unpardonable sin of hissing a beautiful woman—and had not his ungentlemanly behavior been properly rebuked by outraged masculine gallantry? Had he not engaged in a vulgar brawl and suffered the ignominy of arrest and arraignment in a police station? He had not even had a particularly good press. In two papers, the *World* and *Herald*, accounts had put him wholly in the wrong and Kessler in a favorable light, although in fairness they had made it clear that Kessler was not known for the sweetness of his temper or for any aversion to creating scenes.

Yet, somehow, Hammerstein had emerged the hero of the affair. He had even gotten off scot-free in court, without so much as a fine. Here were common charges of disorderly conduct and assault, and here were Koster and Bial ready to substantiate the charges against him, and by some legerdemain he had turned the whole matter into a public issue of the right to hiss and the judge had supported him. What should have been an inglorious defeat had become a victory. Had Koster and Bial been familiar with their partner's history or divined his future career, they would have known that turning defeat into victory was his most notable characteristic—and the more tremendous the defeat the more glorious the victory.

There were several considerations that turned public reaction in Hammerstein's favor. One of them was his own adroitness in presenting himself as the champion of the right of public expression of disapproval as well as the defender of native virtue against foreign indecency. Another was admiration for Hammerstein's pluck in taking on a man whom all accounts made clear was not only a head taller but also heavier, younger, and a trained athlete. The very fact that some accounts painted Hammerstein the aggressor throughout only made his physical courage more remarkable. But what called out the greatest admiration was the man's artistic and moral courage. The idea of a manager hissing his own star performer in his own theater stuck the public imagination. This was a man of principles and convictions.

In many ways the general public was more discerning in its appraisal of Hammerstein than were many of his associates of the theater world. Within the profession there were two opposing theories to explain his behavior and these diametrically differing views of his personality would continue throughout his career. In the present instance Koster and Bial, like Kessler, were certain that Hammerstein was crazy. All their forebodings, they felt, had now been fully justified. This is what came of taking a genius into partnership. These geniuses were all screwballs, likely to go out of their minds without warning at any time. This view, then and later, was shared by many in one form or another. To some it meant the impulsive idealism of the artist, to others the temperamental eccentricities of genius. For the two ex-saloonkeepers it meant merely being crazy.

A smaller number held steadfastly to the view that Hammerstein never did anything on impulse, that all his seemingly emotional outbursts were shrewdly calculated effects carried out with cold-blooded rationality. In this case, they said, he had deliberately planned the hissing and the disturbance.

Both views were wrong and both were right. Oscar Hammerstein was a man of strong emotions but almost always his feelings were disciplined by an intellect equally strong. Rarely were head and heart more inextricably intertwined in one man. He lost his temper frequently and would fly into a rage. But it was never an ungovernable rage. Even as he stormed, he was fully conscious of the effect he was making and could shorten or prolong the duration of his rage as the dictates of reason prompted.

Of course, Hammerstein's hissing had been no sudden impulse. It was a planned protest. He had hoped thereby to force his partners to heed his views. If it accomplished nothing else it would publicly dissociate him from their policies. He had tried valiantly to raise the artistic standard of the variety performances and they were frustrating all his efforts. At least he could air his frustration.

He knew that this dramatic method of protesting would be effective and sensational. He did not know that Kessler would be in the next box to play the gallant in defense of Di Dio. There was nothing planned about his fight with the champagne agent. His rage was genuine and spontaneous. He was not a man to brook interference at any time or place, but when an outsider tried to interfere with him in his own theater Hammerstein saw red. But if Hammerstein was seeing red, he was also seeing how beautifully this fitted into his plan, making it even more dramatic and sensational. He had only to give himself free reign and let his nature take its course. That course had led straight to the police station.

At the station house another unforeseen event turned Hammerstein's planned protest into a final break. When his partners gave support and hail to Kessler, leaving him to be locked up, this was the crowning insult that turned his attitude toward them from frustration and contempt to cold fury. And in his fury, he realized that here was a heaven-sent opportunity to free himself from this unendurable partnership. The grand alliance had come to an end in a police station, and during his hour's stay in a jail cell Hammerstein formulated the dream of his next venture, one dwarfing all the things he had ever done in a single enterprise whose boldness and grandeur would amaze New York.

Neither Koster nor Bial believed that Hammerstein would be crazy enough to break up so profitable an alliance, but the public rift was bad publicity for the house and they concluded that a truce was essential. They called a directors' meeting for the next Thursday at which the three partners could talk things over. They would have to find some way to pacify their bellicose partner.

Worst of all, Hammerstein's hissing of Di Dio had been taken up as a fashion. Every night now there were hisses. People came to judge for themselves the singer who had aroused the ire of Hammerstein. Many concluded he was right and gave vent to their critical opinion in hearty hissing. Others applauded the lady because they liked her singing or her looks or merely in gallant defense of a persecuted woman. At every performance the audience divided into pro–Di Dio's and anti–Di Dio's. The star's applause was longer perfunctory, it was now vigorous but purchased at the humiliating price of enthusiastic hissing. It was equally humiliating for Koster and Bial. They protested that it was shameful, scandalous. But there was nothing they could do. Had not a judge proclaimed the right of everyman to hiss? It made them all the more anxious to bring this unpredictable Hammerstein back into the fold before he did some other crazy stunt to disrupt and demoralize their respectable theater.

If Koster, Bial, Kessler and others thought Hammerstein an erratic genius who had gone crazy that Thursday night, and if others thought the hissing episode had been a wholly calculated piece of play-acting, there were five men in New York who had a third theory of their own. They, too, thought the whole thing an act, planned for its effect, but not of Hammerstein's planning. They were unalterably convinced it was all a publicity stunt for Moet and Chandon's White Seal Champagne.

No less than three of the wine agents called upon Hammerstein over the week and with practically identical business propositions, embodying a single and simple thought. They offered the most liberal inducements. All they wanted in return was an arrangement to be punched in the face by Oscar Hammerstein at some fashionable and crowded resort.

6

Lawmen, Showmen and Shysters

The newspapers devoted so much space to the war clouds gathering in the management of New York's great music hall as to leave comparatively little room for discussion of war and rumors of war abroad. Tension between England and France over Madagascar had created a war scare. This was sufficiently absurd to deserve no more attention than maneuverers in a music hall. But in a far-off corner of the world, in a land most Americans had never heard of, a real war had begun and that very weekend its first great battle had been gouth. At Pingyang in Korea the invading Japanese had routed a Chinese army in a decisive battle whose highlight was a fantastic charge by 300 Manchurian cavalry on white horses with pennoned lances leveled against Japanese riflemen and artillery. With brilliant and relentless strategy, the Japanese were already landing troops on the coast in the enemy's rear to cut off their retreat to the Yalu River. No one would have then believed that in less than 60 years American armies would be fighting in the same spot and an American general would be using the same strategy.

The newspaper readers of New York did not take much interest in foreign affairs. They found the war on Thirty-Fourth Street vastly more entertaining. Most of the communiqués were coming from Hammerstein's side. His lawyer, Morris Wise, had advised him against disrupting so profitable a partnership and on Sunday issued a statement to the effect that Hammerstein would not take any legal steps to jeopardize the large interests involved. "He feels," said Wise, "he has sufficiently protested against what he regards as mismanagement of the house. His action in hissing Mlle. Di Dio, while unusual, was, he believes, perfectly justifiable as a protest against what he regarded as a disgracefully poor singer."

Wise was doing his best to cool off tempers and quiet down the whole affair. A sadly disappointed public brightened up again when it became apparent that Wise's client had other ideas. For, on Monday Hammerstein talked freely to the reporters, repeating his previous accusations against Koster and Bial and hinting broadly at some new ones. The reporters wanted to know about a rumor that Hammerstein would go before the Lexow Committee to charge Koster and Bial with keeping a disorderly house. This was the investigating committee that was making daily headlines, for New York was now in the throes of a tremendous anti–Tammany[1] drive to clean up vice and corruption in the city.

It had all begun when the crusading the Reverend Dr. Charles H. Parkhurst realized the futility of denouncing sin and graft from the pulpit without evidence that would stand up in court. Quietly he pursued his own undercover investigation, personally visiting brothers, gambling places, dens of every kind of vice and iniquity, all flourishing under political protection, and gave his sensational testimony to the public. The forces of decency were thoroughly aroused. With elections coming up, the state legislature intervened, and the investigation headed by Senator Clarence Lexow[2] was uncovering plenty of evidence. The crow now was—"Go higher up"—in the hope that if a clear trail could be followed all the way it would lead directly to the high police officials and into the mayor's office. It was known that Koster and Bial had close connections with Tammany Hall through their lawyers, Isaac Fromme, and the reporters pressed Hammerstein to find out if he intended to pursue this juicy angle. He told them, with a smile:

> You can hardly blame me for not wanting to fire off my ammunition in advance of the fight. But since you've brought up the subject, I will show you the kind of people my associates are. This man Kessler has had altogether too much to do with the running of this house, through his intimacy with Koster and Bial. He insisted upon being personally introduced to every singer who appeared on our stage, and Koster and Bial aided and abetted him. Of course, when invited to go on the roof garden with him, or even to attend little suppers afterward, the artists had to accept or fly in the face of the men who employed them. I don't want to give out now what my plans are, but I will say this—I have employed expert accountants who are now investigating the books of Koster and Bial and they are unearthing facts and methods of procedure which come to me in the way of astonishing revelations.

A hint to the press is sufficient. Tuesday's *Herald* carried the headline, "Hammerstein Will Fight—Hints at Financial Irregularities in Koster and Bial's." There were anguished denials from the two partners, wounded again in their vulnerable respectability, and they were even more determined that their belligerent associate must be brought back into the fold.

Tuesday's papers also carried another piece of theatrical news of considerable importance. But neither those who wrote the reviews of the new play offered by Mansfield the night before nor those who read them were aware of the importance of the event in theatrical history. Of the new generation of actors, Richard Mansfield was coming to the fore as the most brilliant and enterprising. In his repertory season at the Herald Square he was offering a new play from London that had several unusual features. For one thing, it was that interesting phenomenon—a play written by a critic. The author, unknown in New York, was a London literary and dramatic critic, although better known as a music critic. His name was Bernard Shaw, his play was called *Arms and the Man*, and Mansfield gave a brilliant performance in the role of Captain Bluntachli. The *Sun* said the play "proved a very entertaining piece of extravagance and offered a great deal that was genuinely witty along with bits that were unspeakably silly." The *World* review bore the heading, "Shaw's Play is Caviar." Through the next four decades New York would find this new playwright witty and silly, delightful and infuriating, and by the end of the period audiences would have developed a decided taste for caviar.

It was exactly one week after the now historic fracas that the three partners met for the director's conference that was to straighten out their differences. Wise and Fromme were there with their respective clients. For three hours the wrangle continued with Hammerstein doing most of the talking. Nothing was accomplished. Koster and Bial offered to sell out to their partner—for a princely sum. Hammerstein would have none of it but countered with an offer to sell them his interest. He named a figure which they promptly rejected.

The only decision reached was that Hammerstein would move back into the theater, not in a managerial capacity, but only as an office resident in order to protect his interest as a profit-sharing partner. He would be on the spot to check the receipts and books with his own accountant. But first he made the condition that he be given the office used by Manager Cline, letting that gentleman move into the large and handsomer room formerly his own. Several newspapers commented that the only outcome of a three-hour meeting was that

Hammerstein and Cline switched offices, and Koster, Bial and others offered Hammerstein's insistence on taking the inferior room as further evidence of his irrational behavior. Yet anyone with a rudimentary notion of theatrical effect would have understood his reason. He had made a dramatic departure from the theater. He was returning only because, for the time being, it was important for him to be on the premises. But after his symbolic exit from his office he could scarcely return to the same room. Hammerstein was too good a showman to cap a climax with an anti-climax.

The deadlock in the management did not prevent the performances continuing on their merry way. However parlous the artistic state of the music hall, its financial condition left little to be desired. The same bill continued to draw large houses. The Hammerstein Living Pictures remained a great attraction. Even the star, Di Dio, was now what she had never been before, a sensational attraction, succeeding nightly in dividing the audience into two applauding and hissing factions.

Toward the end of the month a sensational new performer was added to the bill—Mrs. Annie Abbott, "The Georgia Magnet."[3] Her act would have been even more effective had there been a Hammerstein to stage it, for the presentation lacked variety and climax. But the lady's feats were sensational enough. A slightly built woman, she lifted four persons on a chair and performed other stunts appropriate to a Sandow. Her most baffling feat was to permit husky men from the audience to come up and lift her, then to place herself in a different position, after which none of them could budge her, although they strained until they were blue in the face. Mrs. Abbott claimed she possessed mysterious magnetic powers of an occult and supernatural sort.

As part of Cline's build up in advance of her opening, Mrs. Abbott gave a demonstration at the offices of the *New York World*. The great Sandow was invited to participate and had been unable to lift her. At the theater the Georgia Magnet aroused the audience to wonder and applause. In the newspapers she evoked columns of discussion of her alleged mysterious and mystifying powers, the *Sunday Press*, for one, devoting a full page to the subject under the headline "Is Her Force Trick or True?"

Professor Hyslop of Columbia University visited Koster and Bial's to observe the performance and conduct an investigation of the new phenomenon. They show being gay and the beer excellent, the good professor required a number of visits before his research was sufficiently advanced to justify a conclusion. He announced that all of Mrs. Abbott's feats were tricks that could be performed by anyone with the necessary knowledge of mechanics and muscular effort. By that time, however, this fact was no longer news. It had been published in the *New York World* three weeks before, discovered by a woman, who, unlike the professor, had not only announced the conclusion but had demonstrated it.

She was the *World*'s own star reporter, Nellie Bly, the most famous woman reporter in America and the embodiment of all the resourcefulness, daring and enterprise of the "New American Woman." A few years later her paper was to send her on a solo trip around the world in eighty days in dramatic proof of the feasibility of the Jules Verne story. After watching Mrs. Abbott's original demonstration in the *World* offices, she claimed to have seen through the trick and that she could duplicate it. She invited Sandow and the others back for a second demonstration and proved herself equally resistant to all efforts made to lift her. All was duly spread before the public in a four-column article by Bly, together with a signed statement by Sandow which she had requested as a testimonial to her expose. Sandow did not relish being put in this position. That his physical development was a marvel of perfection was a matter of common knowledge. In his statement the great athlete also revealed that there was nothing puny about his mental development. He admitted that when Bly had placed herself in the same position that Mrs. Abbott, had he had found it just as impossible to move her. His statement concluded:

> I really do not know what powers Miss Abbott possesses. I really do not know what power Miss Bly possesses. So I will not try to explain it. I only know that it is lucky that every woman does not possess that power or whatever it is. It is already difficult enough to move a woman.

Although the Georgia Magnet continued to be a strong attraction at the music hall, this kind of publicity cut down considerably the magnetism of her drawing power. The most unkind cut of all came from the judicial bench. As the result of a dispute over rent, Abbott moved out of her lodgings and went to court with a complaint that her former landlady was holding her trunks. The case came up before the same Judge Voorhis who had presided over the Hammerstein-Kessler affair. "Well," asked His Honor slyly, "Why didn't you make use of your magnetic powers?"

The unsuccessful directors' conference had produced a truce between the embattled allies. Wise saw no reason why it could not be maintained indefinitely. All Hammerstein need concern himself about was drawing his share of the profits. Hammerstein thought otherwise. Clearly, his own lawyer did not understand his motivations. Hammerstein did not care how profitable the business was. He wanted to be rid of these saloonkeepers once and for all. He would force them to buy him out on terms satisfactory to him. They had broken faith with him when they discontinued the ballets. After that and the way they had treated him in the police station he felt he had no further obligation to them. He would harry and harass them in every way until they gave him what he wanted, and he intended to be ruthless in obtaining it.

For this he needed a different type of lawyer than Wise. It was Hammerstein's practice to choose his lawyers the way he chose the cast for a production. He first decided the legal role he wanted played then selected the lawyer best fitted to play it. At times he might have half a dozen legal performers acting for him separately, each performing a specified role in his elaborate legal drama. He now required someone as well connected politically as Fromme, someone who was brilliant, resourceful, and, when necessary, completely unscrupulous. For casting this role Hammerstein made an unerring choice, thus bringing on the scene another of New York's fabulous personalities, a figure incredible, fantastic—Abe Hummel of the famous and infamous firm of Hower and Hummel, the two most brilliant rascals in the city.

A New York celebrity, Hummel was a distinctive, even bizarre fixture in the metropolis. "Little Abe," as he was called, standing scarcely five feet high, his enormous head quite bald, always dressed in neat but somber black, was a familiar feature at every first night in the theater, at the racetracks and fancy restaurants. A free-spending bachelor, his big parties for stage and sporting people were the gayest in New York. He had personal charm, amiability and wit as well as extraordinary ability and craftiness.

Legally, he led a double life. On the one hand, he was a noted criminal lawyer. Howe and Hummel were the most notoriously successful criminal lawyers of the day, the mouthpieces of the underworld, counsel for the defense and the despair of prosecuting attorneys, masters of the art of concealing and producing clients and witnesses.

On the other hand, Hummel was the leading theatrical lawyer of the period. The Howe and Hummel clients included P.T. Barnum and Tony Pastor, Edwin Booth and Henry Irving, John Drew and the Frohmans. Hummel represented such diversely glamorous personalities as Modjeska and Lillian Russell, Fay Templeton, Lilly Langtry and Little Egypt. He was the outstanding authority on dramatic rights and contracts, and his briefs became part of modern theatrical law. Arranging divorces for actresses was one of his specialties and it was he who developed the scandalous techniques of perjured testimony, private detectives, professional co-respondents and collusion that were to become commonplace. He developed breach-of-promise actions into a flourishing legal blackmail racket.

The combination of criminal and theatrical law practice was not altogether incongruous, for in one sense the firm of Howe and Hummel was a producer of theatrical spectacles. As their biographer, Richard Rovere, points out, in the line of professional witnesses they "kept on call as many sweet-faced grannies, fond wives, doting children, …. Chin-choppered family doctors as any Broadway casting agency."

It was whispered that Little Abe led a double life in a more sinister sense. There were dark rumors that he was not only the mouthpiece for criminals but actually the mastermind behind many criminal enterprises. In his criminal, divorce and breach-of-promise practice, Hummel made regular use of blackmail, perjury and bribery, but, curiously, there was no corruption in his theatrical practice. He had a genuine love for the stage and its people and a sincere devotion to the interests of the theater.

The movement begun by Dr. Parkhurst did oust Tammany for a period, yet never touched Howe and Hummel. But a brilliant District Attorney—William Traverse Jerome, now winning his spurs as assistant counsel to the Lexow Committee—was eventually to bring about the firm's downfall and put Little Abe behind bars after an epic legal battle that would last four years.

Hummel and Hammerstein got along famously as they planned their strategy together. Although Hammerstein's accountant had not completed his investigation of the music hall's books, it was clear that he had struck pay-dirt already. The first week of October saw Hummel go into action with a sudden two-pronged attack. The truce was over.

On Monday, in behalf of Hammerstein as a stockholder, application was made in the Supreme Court for the appointment of a receiver for Koster, Bial and Co. Hummel gave the reporters a statement that whetted their appetite: "I can only state that an examination of the accounts has shown a most astounding state of affairs… the books show that Mr. Hammerstein is abundantly justified in applying for a receiver." Hammerstein's statement was even more terse. "I have had enough of this Koster and Bial business. I have done all the work while they have been getting all the perquisites."

Koster and Bial were still reeling from this sudden onslaught when they were struck from a wholly unexpected quarter. Late Wednesday they were served with papers in an entirely different action brought in Albany, giving them less than twenty-four hours to appear before the Attorney-General of the State of New York. Hummel's assistant, Steinhardt, who was given charge of this attack, was employing a rarely invoked legal procedure. When a stockholder's interests might be injured by the delays of an ordinary suit, or where a public interest was involved, the intervention of the State could be requested. Steinhardt was going to lay before the Attorney-General a request to have the Governor remove Koster and Bial as directors of the corporation and to appoint a receiver pending proceedings for annulment of the partnership and examination of the books.

Steinhardt was Howe and Hummel's most brilliant pupil. Under their expert tutelage he was capable of even more unusual legal maneuvers. On one occasion he was to arrange a lawsuit so that his firm represented both plaintiff and defendant, the victim of the collusion being no less a person than August Belmont.[4]

When the Albany express pulled out of New York Thursday morning, Hammerstein, Steinhardt and other legal counsel were in one car, Koster, Bial, Fromme and their entourage in another. The two parties did not speak to each other in passing. Before the Attorney-General, Steinhardt made his formal motion on the grounds that Koster and Bial had been guilty of malfeasance of office, of making improper charges against the corporation and of improper accounting of funds. He submitted the firm's expense account as evidence to support charges of blackmail paid to officials at City Hall and protection money paid regularly to the police.

The hearing was a heated one. Fromme, a pompous man, with a dignity easily ruffled and a temper quickly lost, jumped to his feet as soon as Steinhardt made his motion.

"This is scandalous," he cried. "We have received only a few hours notice of this application…. I ask for thirty days extension of time…"

"Yes," interposed Steinhardt, "while you are doing just as you please and keeping Mr. Hammerstein out of his rights."

"What do you mean?" shouted Fromme. "Hammerstein has made crazy accusations against us…. I cannot understand why with such a man as Morris Wise already retained, he has chosen to resort to a firm of criminal lawyers in this matter."

"That is a specimen of good taste to which it is scarcely necessary to reply," replied Steinhardt, adding icily: "However, it is better to be the criminal lawyer than the criminal."

There was a long wrangle. The Attorney-General finally granted a ten-day adjournment and all concerned took the evening train back.

The office of Howe and Hummel saw to it that the newspapers had all the details of the charges. Among the allegations published was one that Koster and Bial in their beer distributing firm charged Koster and Bial's Music Hall a higher price for beer than they charged other customers, thus diverting some of the music hall's profits, which they shared with Hammerstein, to their own pockets.

But the charges arousing the greatest interest were the mysterious items in the expense account that plainly pointed to graft and corruption. The papers spearheading the anti–Tammany drive pounced upon this aspect. The *New York World* summarized, and the *New York Press* printed in full the telltale expense account. Among the unexplained items was an amount for $3,000. Bial had told the accountant, it was said, that this had been paid to officials in the mayor's office to expedite the issuing of the hall's license. There were monthly items of $100 listed as commissions, which the accountant had been told were regular payments to the local police for "protection." The *World* ran an editorial calling Hammerstein's charges against his partners a fruitful line of investigation for the Lexow Committee and a promising lead for "going higher up."

Personally, Hammerstein was a man who would rather fight than pay graft. He had shown that in Harlem. But it is unlikely he was unaware that the Music Hall paid for protection or that he was shocked by it. All the music halls paid police tribute. The precinct captains had wide discretion in reporting a hall as respectable or disorderly and recommending approval or denial of a concert hall license. If necessary, they could invoke an old ordinance prohibiting concert halls within 200 feet of a church. That New York was not the most moral of cities was not due to any dearth of churches. The city was studded with houses of worship, many hard by the music halls. All of which made things easier and more lucrative for the police. Normally, all this would have been routine, but in the midst of a "clean up corruption" campaign in an election year, it made a wonderful club for Hammerstein to wield against his partners.

Koster and Bial were aghast when they saw the papers and met the inquiring reporters. Here was the entire city stirred up as never before with investigations, exposes, accusations, with daily denunciations of sin, corruption and Tammany before mass meetings of citizens. The city reverberated with the cry "Go higher up! Turn the rascals out!" And here, this crazy partner of theirs had put their theater—their respectable house—squarely in the middle of the whole hue and cry.

They faced the reporters with their backs to the wall. "It's a lie!" cried Bial. "I deny I ever said a word about $3,000 paid to the Mayor's office or money given for police protection." Fromme hastily interposed with the claim that he had received the $3,000 for special legal services. Between them no one could think of a good explanation for the monthly payments of $100.

The persistent reporters pursued the subject into the police station of the Tenderloin precinct in which the hall was located. Now they had its commander, the notorious Captain Schmittberger, backed against the wall. "I deny I ever received a cent for protection!" the Captain shouted. But this statement was now in the category of famous last words. The Lexow investigation had done its work well. The trail of policy gambling and other protected rackets had been followed straight into the precinct houses. Within a week, the Captain was publicly exposed as having shaken down shipping companies for large sums for waterfront protection.

It was on the Wednesday of the same week in which Hammerstein was launching his legal blitzkrieg that he called in the reporters. He had some news for them. They came expecting to find him breathing fire and smoke against his erstwhile allies. Instead, they found a Hammerstein genial but strangely subdued. His news had nothing to do with the strife in the music hall, it concerned his intimate family troubles, specifically, his won Willie.

The reporters pricked up their ears. They knew the young man had been business manager of the Columbus Theatre. They remembered also the mysterious announcement last February that Willie had gone to San Francisco on a business matter and had been replaced by his brother Harry. It would be a most unusual kind of business that could call a manager of a combination house 3,000 miles from his theater in the middle of a busy season. There had been a few intriguing rumors but all inquiries met with a wall of impenetrable silence. There was some mystery here. Hammerstein's son seemed to have vanished out of sight and out of mind. At long last the veil of secrecy was to be lifted.

The reporters now learned that Willie, then 20, had eloped with a girl barely 16. Her name was Alice Nimmo, she was Protestant, of Scotch-Irish stock, and had been living on 123rd Street a few blocks from the imposing Hammerstein mansion on 120th Street. She was pretty and a romance was progressing sweetly when the Nimmo family's removal to Westchester precipitated a crisis for young love. Willie took his destiny into his own hands. He decided to elope with his sweetheart without the consent and against the expressed wishes of his father.

Hammerstein did not tell all to the reporters, but he admitted frankly that he had been very angry, partly because of the couple's tender age and partly because of the girl's different religion and background. Nor did he conceal the fact that Willie had not even notified his father of the marriage. He understood the couple were now out somewhere with a traveling company his son was managing. He said jokingly that, being in the middle of a fight with Koster and Bial, he did not want to divide his enmity. Therefore, he had forgiven the boy and was waiting to hear from him to bestow his blessing.

There was obviously a good deal of feeling underneath his jocular manner and an amount of understatement not usual for Hammerstein. "Besides," he explained, "he did nothing more than I did when I got married. I did it without my parents' knowledge." From one who had run away from home to cross an ocean at 16 this was the most remarkable understatement of all. Hammerstein spoke as though the affair were quite recent, but the reporters knew Willie had been out of the Columbus eight months. One of them asked about rumors that Hammerstein had disinherited his son.

"That is not true," Hammerstein said quickly. "I may have said something about that when I first heard the news, but that has all passed. But it wouldn't worry Willie much if I did. He is able to take care of himself. Why, before he was 18 he began to earn his own living. But he can have all the money from me he needs." He added a final word: "He is a chip off the old block. He is just as good a manager as I am. Only he cannot compose operas yet."

The newsmen understood what was weighing on Hammerstein's mind. He was a father wanting a lost son back and this was his way of saying publicly: "Come home. All is forgiven." He did not need to say more, they sensed the rest.

There had been a terrible row between father and son. Willie was not as articulate as Oscar, but he had all his father's stubborn independence and the same sturdiness of spirit. He was not going to permit parental dictation of his personal life. The stormy scene of paternal wrath and filial defiance was played out to its melodramatic climax with the father ordering the son from his house. If Willie wanted to be on his own, he could henceforth be on his own, his father shouted. He never wanted to see him again. And after the boy left Hammerstein issued the strictest orders that Willie's name was never to be mentioned at home or in any of his theaters.

Willie disappeared completely and as the months went by Hammerstein was disturbed by feelings of guilt and remorse. It was not difficult to surmise what he was thinking. He was clearly horrified at the realization that he was repeating the pattern of his own father, the father against whom he had rebelled and from whose tyranny he had run away. Willie had reacted as he had once done himself. And he had not even given him the chance to run away. He had himself driven him away. Hammerstein did not allow himself the comfort of discussing his feelings until the day he partially relieved his mind by talking to the reporters. But after the public announcement of forgiveness, the weeks were to pass with no tangible result.

George Blumenthal was the new treasurer at the Harlem Opera House that season. He was to become one of Hammerstein's most devoted associates. When he had arrived in September one circumstance puzzled him. He was constantly meeting three of the four Hammerstein sons, but no one ever mentioned the fourth whom he knew had but recently managed the Columbus. He soon sensed a deep estrangement.

One evening when Blumenthal was in the box office a young man, shabbily dressed, haggard looking, came to the window, asking, "Do you know me?" Blumenthal did not. Furtively the stranger whispered, "Is anyone around?" There was not. Blumenthal was prepared to face a hold up when the man identified himself as Willie Hammerstein. He wanted to know if his father ever spoke of him. He had been having a rough time of it, barely keeping his head above water, and he looked it. His need was obvious when he said he would appreciate a few dollars. Blumenthal gave him five dollars and promised to tell his father the boy would be back the next evening.

When Hammerstein came in later Blumenthal went to his office, saying he had some news. He stood there awkwardly, trying to think of a tactful way to begin. Before he could say anything, Hammerstein had jumped up and seized his arm with an eager "Was it Willie?" Told it was, he breathed a fervent "Thank God!" followed by a flood of questions: where was he now, how did he look, how was he dressed, would he come again? Blumenthal gave him the answers and Hammerstein said, simply, "I'm glad you took care of him. Here's your five and ten more to give him when he comes back. He'll need it to spruce up before he comes home."

For the rest of his life Willie was Hammerstein's favorite son. In large part this was because of his respect for Willie's ability, for he rated him above the others. But in some measure, it was also his way of making amends to the son he had once driven out of his house. It was quite fitting that when his first son was born the following July 12, Willie should name him for his own father. Among the numerous Hammerstein children and grandchildren there were to be many who were gifted. Yet it seems perhaps most fitting of all that it should have been Willie's son, Oscar Hammerstein II, the future author of *Show Boat* and *Oklahoma*, in whom the genius of Oscar the First would reveal itself most fully.

During that same crowded first week of October there occurred also two literary events of note. The early part of the week saw the arrival of one of the most widely read of British authors—A. Conan Doyle, the popular creator of Sherlock Holmes—for the inevitable American lecture tour. The end of the week saw a more somber literary event, the death in Boston of the celebrated Dr. Oliver Wendell Holmes at 85. The Autocrat of the Breakfast Table had gone to a statelier mansion. Among the distinguished friends at the funeral service—Dr. Eliot of Hayward, Julia Ward Howe, William Lloyd Garrison, and the others—it is doubtful if any of them guessed that the dead man's son and namesake, already a judge, would outstrip the father both in the number of his years and in the greatness of his fame.

Under Hammerstein's legal attacks all during that week, Koster and Bial could only take defensive measures. They interposed as many obstacles as they could to Hammerstein's examination of the books, and they barred him from access to the theater except for his office. And they began to discharge all employees hired by their partner, or known to be friendly to him, in deadly fear of possible subversion in their midst. If they thought in this way to gain a respite from Hammerstein's harrying tactics they were quickly disillusioned.

Hammerstein opened the next week with a wholly new legal attack. Monday morning he was in court with Abe Hummel and secured from Judge Gildersleeve an injunction restraining Koster and Bial from interfering with him in the management of the business, in his examination of the books, and in the performance of his duties as a director of the corporation The defendants were ordered to show cause Thursday why the injunction should not be made permanent and a receiver appointed to wind up the affairs of the company. The charges of malfeasance, misconduct and misappropriation of funds were repeated and expanded.

When the injunction notice was served upon them, Koster and Bial were thrown into consternation. A number of special deputies were hastily sworn in to protect the premises until the music hall resembled a beleaguered fortress—a flurry of activity which did not pass unnoticed by the reporters assigned to keep track of the merry war on thirty-fourth street. And now Hammerstein prepared to follow up the legal maneuver of the morning with a test assault upon the citadel itself.

Hammerstein had always had charge of the hall's stage crew and orchestra. On Saturday his stage carpenter had been fired. The man had gone to his union and there were threats of a strike of all the stagehands. Thus Hammerstein's interest as a stockholder was now concerned as well as the interest of an employee.

At 8 p.m. that evening, accompanied by C. C. Siegmund, his accountant and personal representative, Hammerstein brought his stage carpenter to the stage door. A special deputy-sheriff barred his way. Hammerstein went around to the front and through the lobby. At the door another special deputy was stationed. The manager ordered him away in language that was vigorous and picturesque. As the man quailed before the storm, Isaac Fromme came up to block the way, pompously advising Hammerstein not to enter the theater. Hammerstein asked what business he had being there and ordered him out of the house. Fromme stood his ground. Drawing himself up, he said he was present to advise his clients how to obey the injunction served upon them. The manager started to brush past him, and the lawyer put out a hand seeking to restrain him. This is what Hammerstein had been waiting for. Calmly he stepped back, took aim and struck Fromme squarely on the jaw. The lawyer let out a howl of anguish, then began to shout "Help! Help! Police!" The policeman in the lobby ran up and promptly placed Hammerstein under arrest.

Ten minutes later, at the desk of the West Thirtieth Street Police Station, Sergeant Lane looked up and blinked. An officer was bringing in a gentleman in evening clothes. Oscar Hammerstein was charged with assault and battery. Behind him came John Koster and several reporters. It seemed almost a repeat performance—but not quite. There was no lady in dazzling jewels and the gentleman preferring the charge was Isaac Fromme, the well-known lawyer. Probably the rest of the crowd would be along shortly. Hammerstein wanted Fromme charged with disorderly conduct and when the Sergeant could not see his way clear to entertaining this charge the manager excoriated him fluently.

Bail was set at $500 for appearance in Jefferson Market Court next day. Sergeant Lane noted another variation. This time Hammerstein had Siegmund on hand to provide bail. Koster and Fromme had left by the time the bond was signed. As Hammerstein left, he announced loudly enough to carry to the desk that he was going right back to the theater and that this time he was going to break Fromme into small pieces. This had its intended effect. Sergeant Lane hurried out to the back and ordered out the riot squad.

What followed was pure farce straight out of Mack Sennett.[5] As Hammerstein entered a cab at the front entrance of the station house, at the back entrance six of the burliest men on the force were piling into a patrol wagon. The speeding wagon passed Hammerstein's cab en route to Thirty-Fourth Street and dashed up to the music hall. In a moment policemen were jumping out and running into the building bent upon the prevention of bloodshed. When Hammerstein alighted at the theater, he could scarcely keep a straight face at the sight of six helmeted and blue-coated stalwarts drawn up in the lobby in formidable array. Nevertheless, he went through the options of demanding his rights while the line of police maneuvered to keep a nervous Fromme behind a cordon. After a few minutes of warlike marches and demarches the doughty manager retired to his private office and talked to the reporters.

"I did this thing on purpose," he said, "to see just how far these people would go. I am going to have Koster, Bial and Fromme up for contempt of court in violating the injunction. These men had no right to have deputy sheriffs around to deprive me of the rights which the injunction gives me." Then, looking at his watch, he observed that the night was still young and took his departure.

A new farce by Hoyt was opening that night in Hoyt's own theater on Fifth Avenue. A typical Hoyt concoction, one reviewer described "A Milk White Flag" as a mixture of good humor and bad taste, with plenty of songs, dances and specialties. Hillary Bell, the brilliant and independent drama critic of the *Press* was coming into the theater foyer for the second intermission when his eye caught sight of Hammerstein, looking radiantly serene. Bell was more than a distinguished critic; he was too good a newspaperman to overlook a celebrity. And he was one of Hammerstein's most enthusiastic admirers. He engaged the manager in conversation with results duly reported to his readers as follows:

> Mr. Hammerstein came up smilingly in the foyer. "You look happy," said I, "is Di Dio gone?" "No," said he, "It isn't Di Dio this time. It's Fromme." "What about Fromme?" said I. "I gave him one," said he, "I was arrested again." "Out on bail?" said I. "Yes," said he, "just come from the station house. Thought I'd drop in to see Hoyt's new piece," and thus he chatted gaily until the curtain went up. It is only people who do not appreciate the humor of Hammerstein that fail to get along with him. Koster and Bial are grave, serious men. Fromme has no fun in his nature…. Abe Hummel, on the contrary, is of a merry wit, and he would rather crack jokes than pates with Hammerstein. So the lively little lawyer and his impulsive little client assault the enemy instead of each other.

Tuesday's newspapers brought joy to the hearts of a public that had been following the communiqués from the civil war in the great music hall. Once again all was as it should be in gay New York. Legal maneuvering had given way to direct action. Again there was high comedy and low farce, excitement, color and drama. Once more there were Hammersteinian fireworks, a flaring temper, a swinging fist and a prominent face to intercept it. And Oscar Hammerstein was back on the front page like a fresh breeze blowing through the sordid news of the election campaign.

The headlines on page one of the *Press* shouted: "Hit Lawyer Fromme—Hammerstein Used Fists and Was Arrested—Koster and Bial Restrained—Injunction Secured by Their Dissatisfied Associate." The front page of the *World* proclaimed: "Hammerstein is Hot Yet—This Time Goes for Isaac Fromme—A Test Case, Says the Manager—Extra Police Called to Quell the Bellicose Oscar." On its editorial page the *World* quipped: "Oscar Hammerstein can create an operetta in much less time than he can compose himself." One group of readers alone read the news with pangs of disappointment—the audience at the Music Hall the night before. Except for a very few early arrivers they had missed the real show.

But when the curtain rose upon the next act of the comedy-drama Tuesday morning at Jefferson Market Court there was "standing room only" in the courtroom. There was a flavor of old home week about it. There was Judge Voorhis again and there before him were the familiar actors, Hammerstein, Koster, Bial and Fromme, the prominent lawyer this time in the role of complainant. The only new actor was Hammerstein's counsel, the brilliant theatrical-criminal lawyer Hummel, a notable addition to the cast.

Fromme, as the first witness, gave his version of Hammerstein's assault, corroborated by several witnesses, including Koster. Fromme took his seat between Koster and Bial and Hammerstein was called to give his testimony.

"I went into the lobby," he said, "and found a stranger to me refusing admittance to my stage carpenter. I expostulated and suddenly that shyster rushed up and shouted to this man, whom I afterward discovered to be a deputy sheriff appointed by Koster and Bial in defiance of my injunction, 'Don't you mind that man; he has no business to give orders here.' Then I asked that shyster—"

Fromme, his face flushed, jumped to his feet, shouting in a rage: "What shyster? What system?" Hammerstein turned, deliberately pointed at the man standing up. "That shyster, Your Honor." Koster and Bial hastily pulled their choking counsel down into his seat while the courtroom roared with mirth. Judge Voorhis banged his gavel and Hammerstein calmly resumed: "I asked him what he was doing there and he butted me with his head. Then I caught him by the coat and I smote him."

Several witnesses corroborated Hammerstein's testimony and Hummel interjected:

"We admit that we smote him, but he was illegally interfering with my client's business in defiance of an injunction of the Supreme Court."

The Judge remarked that possibly the Supreme Court was itself quite able to punish those who flouted its injunctions. At any rate since Hammerstein had admitted striking Fromme he would have to held for trial. He reduced bail to $300 and paroled Hammerstein in custody of his lawyer, ringing down the curtain for the present. Fromme left for his office to begin a civil suit against Hammerstein for damage to his dignity and reputation; his clients left for their office and called a conference.

Koster and Bial were not noted for quick-wittedness but a great light was beginning to break into their consciousness. Hitherto they had clung to the theory that their former ally was crazy—an unpredictable screwball acting upon ungovernable and momentary impulse. It seemed the only way to explain the actions of a man seeking to injure a profitable business in which he owned a large share.

Now the awful truth began to dawn upon them. Hammerstein was doing these things deliberately, striking again and again at their most vulnerable spot—their hard-won respectability. Any day now they could expect to be punched in the face in their own theater by their own partner. It was not bodily harm they dreaded but the damage to their dignity and repute.

They had struggled long to attain this precious respectability, and in four weeks Hammerstein had made a shambles of it. He was not satisfied with public accusations of indecency, crookedness, bribery and corruption—he was out to make them utterly ridiculous. How proud they had always been that their hall had never seen a brawl, how they had boasted of their trained staff's ability to spot trouble before it started, to hustle drunks off the premises. Now the papers were full of details of disorderly conduct, assaults, arrests, of constant brawling and fighting, not among drunken patrons but among the owners of the house themselves.

Hammerstein was deliberately making them the laughingstock of New York and they could see the handwriting on the wall. They would have to get rid of him no matter what it cost to buy him out. They knew now their professional and business life was at stake. Their war with Hammerstein was a fight to the death. They would try to sell their lives as dearly as possible and they would try to buy their partner out as cheaply as possible.

However serious the matter for Koster and Bial, to the public it was a merry war, a lively comedy show in which Hammerstein was at the same time the showman who produced it and the chief protagonist who played in it. He was now providing a three-ring legal circus, with three actions running in three different courts, the spotlight shifting from one to the other. On Tuesday the focus had been upon the Jefferson Market Court; within forty-eight hours the spotlight shifted.

Time: Thursday. Place: The Supreme Court. Scene: The hearing on Hammerstein's injunction. The performance was well attended but curtailed. Koster and Bial were to show cause why the injunction should not be made permanent and a receiver appointed. But Fromme raised technical objections and requested a week's postponement. Hummel did not oppose the request and Judge Gildersleeve granted it, to the great disappointment of the audience.

At the Music Hall that evening there was another disappointed audience. The patrons noted the air of tension in the house, they observed the augmented number of police, deputies and special guards spread the theater and they thought with zestful anticipation what a terrible man this terrible Hammerstein must be. Never before had they seen so many exhibit so much alarm at just one single individual. All through the performance they listened hopefully for sounds from the lobby or backstage that hostilities had begun, but had to content themselves with hissing Di Dio, or applauding, as the case might be. The newspapermen were the most disappointed of all. And the *New York World* even commented on its editorial page: "Yesterday was very dull in this city. Oscar Hammerstein kept the peace."

Before another forty-eight hours had passed the spotlight had shifted again. Time: Saturday. Place: Albany. Scene: The hearing before the Attorney-General of the State of New York. Hammerstein was there with Steinhart and Bial with Fromme, flanked by a whole battery of associate counsel.

The Koster and Bial lawyers claimed Hammerstein was motivated solely by spite. They denied interference with his examination of the books or his functions as vice-president of the corporation. They did not mention that in the view of his partners he had no functions except to direct ballets which they had abolished.

Their chief argument was that state intervention and receivership would hurt a profitable business by damaging Koster and Bial's high reputation for moral and financial responsibility. They presented evidence that the firm had made a profit close to $70,000 a year on Twenty-Third Street and that the new corporation had made $15,000 net profit the very first month on Thirty-Fourth Street and maintained a high level ever since. On drinks alone their profits had averaged over 115 percent. (Koster and Bial wondered anxiously how this revelation would sit with their patrons.) They presented affidavits from businessmen attesting to their reputation for integrity.

Steinhardt then rose to suggest that perhaps the reputation of Messrs. Koster and Bial was not so spotless as to be injured by the Governor's intervention. As evidence of undeniable stain, he now exploded a bombshell of devastating effect by reading into the record the fact that they had once been convicted of keeping a disorderly house on Twenty-Third Street. For the next few minutes the entire Koster and Bial legal staff was strenuously engaged in holding their clients down in their seats.

This conviction, unearthed by pitiless legal research, probably dated from the time Koster and Bial had not yet learned the importance of paying for police protection and had been given an object lesson in the scope of police power to teach them what they needed protection from. They were being accused of bribing the police. Now they had flung at them the result of failure to do so. They were getting it both ways.

After the agonizing disclosures made in the hearing it was cold comfort to Koster and Bial to learn later in the day that they had won a legal victory. The Attorney-General had issued an opinion denying Hammerstein's request on the ground that his interests did not require the Governor's intervention. The corporation was financially prosperous. Hammerstein's redress was a court action to restrain any illegal acts and the action already begun in the Supreme Court should be concluded there. It is unlikely that Hammerstein and Hummel were either surprised or disappointed by the decision. The action had already served its purpose.

The following week of October 15 was crowded with theatrical and musical events. On Monday night a completely unknown young English actress made her American debut in a new play, *The Transgressor*, and became a sensational success overnight. The reviewers thought the play crude and the role immoral but they found Olga Nethersole a charming and expressive emotional actress with a rich voice, considerable power and irresistible allure. Their only criticism was that she needed to contain her volcanic temperament; her emotions were too intense, too sultry. She played the "other woman" to Wilton Leckaye's role of a man married to a wife hopelessly insane. The play was considered immoral because it justified the other woman and blamed archaic divorce laws.

There was a rash of controversy, discussions, interviews. Nethersole made a spirited defense of her role and the need for more liberal divorce. She was clearly more than just an actress. She was a personality and the debut was wholly typical of her, a foretaste of things to come. Discovering that the public found bad women more interesting on the stage than good women, she was to specialize in such roles and in controversial plays, creating numerous sensations in parts which she played up to the hilt for sin and sex, with a few extra twists to shock the respectable. Before long, people would be repeating a new version of the nursery jingle that ran:

> I love little Olga
> Her plays are so warm
> And if I don't see them
> T'will do me no harm.

The same night at which Olga Nethersole was making her leap into fame, an audience at Hammerstein's Columbus Theatre was paying homage to another and more literal leap into fame. There a play *On the Bowery* got a rousing reception from a packed house which had come to applaud not the performance but the mere appearance of a celebrity as a star. This bright luminary—Steve Brodie—was not an actor at all but a Bowery character who had become famous and his name a household word because he might or might not once have jumped off Brooklyn Bridge. Many accepted his claim to the feat. Just as many were convinced it was a hoax but accepted him as a celebrity nevertheless, if only for the daring of his imposture.

That same day in far off Vienna, the world was paying tribute to worldwide fame of long standing. The city of waltzes was waltzing as never before for it was dancing in honor of the Waltz King himself. It was the climax of the Johann Strauss jubilee celebrating fifty years of music making by the world's greatest dispenser of lilting tunes. Gifts and greetings poured in from every part of the globe. Rudolph Aronson had come all the way from New York to present a gigantic silver wreath in behalf of the host of admirers in America. The entire palace danced in the streets while distinguished figures from the worlds of government, theater and music graced the great reception, the representatives of music including the great Brahms himself. It was on this occasion that the great symphonic composer, when asked for an inscription in an autograph book, jotted down the first bar of "The Blue Danube" with the sentence, "alas, composed by—Johannes Brahms."

That week in New York, one wholly non-theatrical event cast a long shadow into the future. The first of the fast ironclad battleships in the new American navy anchored off Whitestone, Long Island, after a test run from New London in which her twin screw engines had been put to an all-out speed trial. The naval officials were elated at her top speed of 17.82 knots. They claimed the fastest battleship in the world. In the event of naval warfare, she would be a ship to remember. Four years later, in a Cuban harbor, she would indeed prove herself a ship to remember. The entire country was to ring with the cry: "Remember the Maine!"

But it was the theatrical warfare in America's greatest music hall that New York followed with greatest attention, for during that week the spotlight on Hammerstein's legal circus shifted back and forth with kaleidoscopic speed.

Time: Monday. Place: Court of Special Sessions. Scene: The Fromme-Hammerstein assault case. This time, Hummel being called away, Hammerstein requested a postponement which was granted over Fromme's strenuous protest. Fromme even offered to drop his civil suit for damages if Hammerstein would forego the postponement and was dumbfounded when the offer was spurned. Why, the man actually seemed to enjoy being sued. Fromme was even more obtuse than his clients. He still failed to realize that in increasing the number of lawsuits he was playing into Hammerstein's hands and giving his own clients more undesirable publicity.

Time: Thursday. Place: The Supreme Court. Scene: The postponed injunction hearing before Judge Gildersleeve. Fromme denied all the accusations, although in denying the charge that Hammerstein was not permitted to exercise his authority as a director, he was forced to admit that Koster and Bial had never intended him to have any authority. And he finally came up with an explanation of the monthly items of $100 carried on the books as commissions. These, he asserted, were actual commissions to the head waiter on sales of liquor, though he did not offer to explain how they always came to the same round sum.

Perhaps realizing the lameness of these explanations Fromme took refuge in various counterclaims and personal attacks upon Hammerstein and finally succeeded thereby in obtaining another adjournment for the submission of further affidavits. The tactics of the defense were now to fight delaying actions as long as possible.

Time: Friday. Place: Court of Special Sessions. Scene: Finale of the assault and battery case. Fromme, a principal in this action, made the serious tactical error of acting as his own lawyer and was not the first or last lawyer to regret it. As for the complainant bringing the charge he had to take the witness chair, giving Hummel the delightful opportunity to cross-examine the opposing counsel.

Hummel was fully aware of the pompous lawyer's low boiling point and took full advantage of it. Deliberately he baited his opponent until Fromme became excited and began to raise his voice. Whereupon Little Abe interposed icily with "I must ask you not to shout. Remember that this is a courtroom." At this Fromme boiled over and began to shout until the judge banged his gavel and called him to order. After several repetitions of this Hummel asked the witness to begin all over again and try to describe calmly how he came to be involved in the incident.

"I was there," shouted Fromme, "to look after the interests of Koster and Bial and…" Judge Grady interrupted: "You, as a lawyer, ought to know that you must confine yourself to the assault." "And you, as a judge," shouted Fromme, "ought to know that what I'm testifying to is evidence!" Bang! went the gavel.

After Hammerstein's testimony the judge announced his decision that an assault had taken place as admitted by the defendant. He said nothing to Hammerstein in remonstrance but merely fined him fifty dollars. Any elation Fromme may have felt was quickly dispelled when he saw Hammerstein's broadly smiling face as he paid the fine. It was the look of one who thought the item cheap and was seriously contemplating the purchase of a dozen. The spectators who had filled the courtroom left with the feeling that they too had gotten their money's worth. Fromme left determined to withdraw his damage suit and firmly resolved henceforth to leave the witness chair to his clients.

As October drew to a close, the election campaign in New York City and the state mounted to a climax. The Democratic National Administration made no attempt to aid Tammany but both the President and Vice President came to New York to help the Democratic state ticket, President Cleveland to confer with the state leaders, Vice President Stevenson to speak for Senator David B. Hill, the candidate for Governor. All was in vain. The same surging tide that swept Tammany out and installed William Lafayette Strong as mayor on a reform ticket also swept Republican candidate Levi P. Morton into the Governor's office. Tammany Hall leader Richard Welstead "Boss" Croker had found it convenient to go abroad. A number of exposed grafters were facing jail, and for the Herculean task of cleaning up the city's police force, former state assemblyman Theodore Roosevelt had been selected as head of the Board of Police Commissioners. The reform movement begun by the Reverend Dr. Parkhurst had scored a tremendous victory for clean government against sin and corruption.

In the theater world a triumph of comparable dimensions was scored by Olga Nethersole in *Camille*, her first appearance anywhere in the role of Dumas' hectic heroine. Supported by an able cast including Maurice Barrymore, her leading man in a stirring performance as Armand, her portrayal bowled over critics and public alike. Some reviews did not hesitate to rank her with the great Camilles—Helena Modjeska, Sarah Bernhardt, Elanora Duse—extraordinary praise for a young actress completely unknown two weeks before.

At the great music hall on Thirty-Fourth Street a different star now headed the bill. The wondrous Carmencita was back again in what was to be her last appearance in America. Di Dio's engagement had come to its close. The sound of hissing was heard no more in the great auditorium and Koster and Bial breathed sighs of relief that the time had come for their foreign star to gather up her diamonds and return to her native Vienna.

But the bejeweled singer surprised everyone by announcing instead her retirement from the stage with the disclosure that, the week before, she had been quietly married to Stephen Thorn, a young man of excellent family. About the financial status of the bridegroom, whom the *World* described as "an immature man-about-town," opinion was as sharply divided as over the merits of the bride's signing, some of his friends claiming he had an income, others equally certain he had nothing. There had been no church wedding. The marriage had been performed in the home of a clergyman, who turned out to be the fiery Reverend Dr. Parkhurst himself.

The crusading preacher had initiated and sparked to victory a reform movement of huge proportions. In bringing the Viennese beauty from the primrose path of the footlights into the sacred bonds of matrimony, he may well have felt he was encompassing an achievement of equal magnitude—the reform of a notorious woman.

7

Hammerstein's Folly

During the month of November things quieted down on Thirty-Fourth Street. Koster and Bial continued their delaying actions, and, for the time being, Hammerstein and Hummel were refraining from further legal pressure. Hammerstein himself was rarely seen in the usual managerial haunts along the Rialto. Instead, he was spending a great deal of time walking about Longacre Square—a strange place for a theater manager to be seen.

It was not a respectable section of the city and certainly not of any theatrical interest. For some years now the Broadway Rialto had its northern outpost at Thirty-Ninth to Fortieth streets, marked by the Metropolitan Opera House and the Casino, now joined by the new Empire Theatre. Even the electric light and power cables did not continue above Forty-Second Street where Longacre Square began. Further north, between Central Park and Riverside Drive, there was a thriving residential area of fine houses and apartments. But the Broadway area from Forty-Second along the square to Fifty-Seventh Street was run down and disreputable, frequently referred to as Thieves' Lair. Ill-lit and forbidding at night, respectable folk avoided it after dark.

Hammerstein was not there out of idle curiosity but in pursuit of a vision. The dream that had begun during the hour spent in a prison cell of the West Thirtieth Street Police Station some two months earlier was now coming into sharper focus and definition. Hammerstein the theatrical manager and Hammerstein the real estate expert were combining forces once more in the formulation of a daring plan of great magnitude.

Occasionally, Hammerstein could be seen standing motionless on Forty-Second Street at the spot where the New York Times Building now stands. He was silently gazing northward into the square where Broadway crossed Seventh Avenue, his body still, his thoughts racing, his inner vision peering into the future.

Here, he told himself, around this seedy square, there was something more than another residential area for future rehabilitation and development. Here were the natural crossroads of the city, its future focal point. And here was the logical future center for the Rialto. This was where he would make his next theatrical venture and make this square the hub about which the theatrical life of the city would eventually turn.

The city, too, was settling down into a period of relative quiet after the tumult of the election and political overturn. The big sensations in the news were now from abroad. That strange far-off war in the orient had developed swiftly to its climax as the Japanese overran Korea, invaded Manchuria, and now startled and shocked the world by the capture of Port Arthur, the wanton destruction of the city and the ruthless massacre of its population. It threw a wholly new light upon the quaint little people from the land of cherry blossoms and politeness.

The theatrical world had also been stirred by news from abroad. For several years reports had been trickling in of the phenomenal Parisian triumphs of Yvette Guilbert, the music hall singer Hammerstein had vainly urged Bial to secure. Now the reports were still coming of her electrifying triumph in London last spring at the Empire Music Hall. That a singer singing in French should have scored such a success with English speaking audiences indicated recognition of a transcendent art.

There had been doubt that the Parisian realism of the French chanteuse, especially in the matters of sex, would be acceptable outside of Paris. Yet the London critics and public had acclaimed her greatness. Even the staid *London Times* had admitted that "her songs are fairly rich in innuendos, but the effect of this is softened by the singer's artless humor, the simplicity of her dress and the limpidity of her enunciation."

One of the first English critics to recognize the new artist was Bernard Shaw, who had written in *The World* (British): "Another great artist has come.... It amuses her to tell interviewers that she cannot sing and has no gestures; but... there would be very little fun for her in that if she were not one of the best singers and pantomimists in Europe.... Technically Mlle. Guilbert is a highly accomplished artist. She makes all of her effects in the simplest way and with perfect judgment.... Her command of every form of expression is very remarkable, her tones ranging from the purest and sweetest pathos to the cockiest Parisian cynicism..."

Alerted by these reports all the New York managers were now eager to secure the great chanteuse. The singer whom Bial had not thought worth $100 a week had turned down offers of $500. Then Edmund Gerson offered her $700. She refused, pointing out she now earned that much in Paris. When she spurned another offer of $1,000, and finally Rudolf Aronson's sensational bid of $1,500, it was regretfully concluded that Yvette Guilbert was too expensive a luxury for profitable presentation in New York.

The lull in hostilities on Thirty-Fourth Street did not last long into December before Hammerstein and Hummel decided it was time to re-apply pressure. On December 5 they obtained a Supreme Court order requiring Koster and Bial to show cause why they should not be punished for contempt of court for refusing to allow Hammerstein's representative to inspect the books and check the box office receipts. It was a day of happy activity for Hammerstein. That evening he listened to the orchestra at the Harlem Opera House playing for the first time a new Hammerstein composition called "The Shenandoah," dedicated to playwright Bronson Howard.

Koster and Bial's first reaction to Hammerstein's legal pressure was one of peevish retaliation. At a new election of officers they ousted him from his position as vice-president of the firm, Bial taking the office in addition to that of treasurer, a wholly meaningless and futile action. Having thus given vent to their feelings they then bowed to the inevitable and did what Hammerstein's action was designed to force them to do—begin negotiations for the purchase of their partner's interest. Their variety bill that week took on added interest by the reappearance of Paul Cinquevalli, still the king of jugglers, and the presentation of a third series of living pictures.

The last week of December produced a brilliant event at the Metropolitan Opera House, a performance of *Les Huguenots* with the first of the tremendous all-star casts that were to make operatic history. Hammerstein was presenting seven (count them, seven) of his outstanding stars simultaneously in one performance, three women (Nellie Melba, Lillian Nordica, Sofia Scalchi) and four men (Jean and Edward de Reszke, Pol Henri Plançon, Victor Maurel). For such prodigal largesse the audience gladly paid the special rates advanced from the usual five dollars to seven dollars.

During the second week of January an announcement by Hammerstein created a sensation. It revealed that on January 2 he had purchased property on Longacre Square for the site of a new theatrical enterprise. Coming from one who had already built three theaters this revelation by itself would not have been so spectacular. It was the scope and magnitude of the plan that was breathtaking.

The plot was on the east side of the square between Forty-Fourth and Forty-Fifth Streets—not at the Forty-Fourth Street corner, nor at the Forty-Fifth Street corner, nor yet in the middle of the block. It took in the entire block front and had cost Hammerstein $850,000.

A whole block front for one theater? Not at all—for three theaters! Hammerstein intended to erect a single huge structure which would comprise three separate auditoriums—a theater, a concert hall and a music hall—furnishing concerts, light operas, ballets and vaudeville, and one general admission of fifty cents would admit to all. Later, another auditorium would be constructed upon the roof, making a total of four theaters in one colossal structure. The vast establishment was to be named Olympia and Hammerstein planned to have it ready by November. It would be, undoubtedly, the greatest structure devoted exclusively to theatrical entertainment anywhere in the world.

This was the dream of Olympia, the great new vision whose nebulous outline had first come to Hammerstein during the hour of his brief incarceration in a police station jail. In announcing his plan he had made only partial disclosure of the dream. The complete vision in all its fullness was never revealed to the public. What had been announced now was that portion of the dream Hammerstein planned to realize within the next few years. It was enough to provoke varied reactions and to set tongues wagging within and without the theatrical world.

The general public found the news exhilarating and received it without doubts or reservations. Hammerstein was the sort of man who, when he said he could write an opera in forty-eight hours, proceeded to write it. Therefore, if such a man said he intended to erect the greatest theatrical structure in the world in Longacre Square in ten months, obviously he would do so. The public had already formed the naive habit of expecting Hammerstein to do the impossible and Hammerstein was never to give them cause to change that habit.

Poor, naive public! Within informed circles of the theatrically sophisticated reactions were more realistic. They ranged from raised eyebrows to open derision. There were a few who thought Hammerstein's plans farsighted and who remembered how often before he had carried out plans which had seemed like unrealizable boasting. But for the most part the professionals were completely skeptical.

The location was all wrong, many were quick to say—too far north of the Rialto and not respectable. No fashionable theater audience would be seen in so disreputable an area. To build a theater in Longacre Square was foolhardy. To build a whole block of theaters was the sheerest folly, of which only one as crazy as Hammerstein would be capable. There were those who said the announcement was all a bluff, a dramatic gesture designed to frighten Koster and Bial. The vast project would never actually materialize. Many who did not question Hammerstein's serious intention ridiculed his time schedule. Such a huge construction project could not possibly be completed in ten months; two years was a more likely period. And some, noting the prominence of a music hall and vaudeville in the scheme, said knowingly the whole thing was a spite project, conceived for no reason but to spite and injure Koster and Bial.

The latter view was indeed taken on Thirty-Fourth Street, where the thought of a competing music hall came as a shock that filled Koster and Bial with alarm. Koster, who was feeling the strain of the civil war with their one-time ally, promptly fell ill and took to his bed. However, the music hall and beer magnates were soon persuaded that Hammerstein's announcement was not to be taken too seriously. Thus reassured, they felt they had nothing to fear and Koster was soon able to leave his bed.

Whatever the interpretation and despite the doubts, Hammerstein's announcement had given the theater world a dramatic sensation. And simultaneously he was providing Harlem with a dramatic sensation of the theatrical sort by presenting Olga Nethersole's tempestuous Camille at the Harlem Opera House.

But the most dramatic theatrical scene of all was being played upon a far-off stage at the Eeole Militaire in Paris, from which the foreign news brought a remarkable human interest story. A young French army captain had been court-martialed and found guilty of spying for another power. January 5 had been the day of his public degradation before 3,000 troops amid awesome drum rolls and trumpet blasts. The accounts described how the condemned man was stripped of his insignia of rank and honor, the epaulets, chevrons and brass buttons ripped from his jacket, his sword broken in two, and how at the end of the ordeal, his spirit unbroken he had cried out passionately: "I am innocent! Vive la France!" It was the tremendous opening scene of a drama called The Dreyfus Case that was to convulse a nation for five years and bring France to the verge of civil war. The depths of corruption in state and society were to be plumbed and yet there would also be revealed the noblest capabilities of the human spirit when idealistic political figures, journalists and literary men, as Emile Zola, Jean Jaures, George Clemencean, Anatole France, Leon Blum, rallied to the support of truth, justice and honor.

The week of January 21 saw the artistic high-water mark of the season at Koster and Bial's when the music hall launched the American career of one of the most amazingly versatile talents ever known. It was the American debut of a young English girl, still in her teens, with a dainty figure, large expressive eyes and saucy mouth, who did imitations of theatrical stars that were remarkable for realistic mimicry and subtle drollery. She was the star of the bill at $500 a week, a huge salary for a mimic.

It was only last season that young Cecelia Loftus, better known as Cissie had burst upon the London music halls and created a sensation with her wondrous imitations of Sarah Bernhardt, Yvette Guilbert and other celebrities. Overnight she became an idol of the music halls and the darling of the aristocracy who demanded her constantly as an entertainer for their drawing rooms. And she had given London more to talk about by her romantic elopement with the son of a distinguished historian and former member of Parliament, Justin Huntly McCarthy, himself on the threshold of a notable career as playwright and adapter of plays.

Before a fashionable first-night audience that packed Koster and Bial's, Cissie Loftus gave her witty imitations of Bernhardt, Guilbert, Beerbohm Tree, Vesta Tilley, Albert Chevalier and others. The audience was getting imitations of a number of great performers it had never actually seen, although the young mimic soon studied and added such native figures as Tony Pastor and Maggie Cline.

The artistry and cleverness of the newcomer's work received critical praise but Koster and Bial were keenly disappointed, even though the engagement served to restore some of the hall's battered respectability. They were completely unaware of how great a talent they had presented to New York. They knew only that after the premiere their star drew good houses but not packed houses, and that the audiences liked her but did not go wild over her.

They offered no return engagement and clearly intimated that they thought her subtle work was drawing room entertainment, out of place in a large theater. Cissie Loftus was to make that idea look very foolish indeed.

Koster and Bial had more to worry about that week than the failure of their new star to make the smashing popular success they had anticipated. Despite their delaying actions Hammerstein's suit to compel them to render an accounting of the corporation's finances was proceeding relentlessly with two Supreme Court hearings during the week. Koster and Bial were spurred to greater activity in the negotiations for the buying out of Hammerstein's interest.

In a few days the negotiations reached the final stage. Hammerstein had laid down the minimum price he would accept. Koster and Bial made an ultimate offer below that figure, stating it was the maximum above which they would not go. They reasoned that Hammerstein's court expenses were heavy and Hummel's fees high. The amount now at stake would not justify further legal costs. They had only to hold firm and Hammerstein would accept their offer.

For his part, Hammerstein divined their reasoning perfectly. He was even more anxious to end the partnership than they were and he was in urgent need of large amounts of cash for his great new venture. But he was determined to get his minimum figure and not a penny less. He decided upon a strategic shift to a radically different line of attack that would hurl the most terrible threat of all at his unwilling partners. He left them in perplexed suspense by making no reply whatever to their offer. Cautious feelers brought no response. Suddenly Hammerstein seemed to have lost all interest in the negotiations.

January passed into February. The first week of February passed and still no word from Hammerstein. This week, however, did not pass without making theatrical and musical history. For it contained the artistic event of the season at the Metropolitan Opera House, the first performance in North America, on February 12, of Verdi's *Falstaff* with Emma Eames, Salchi and Zélie de Lussan, with the title role taken by the great singer and actor who had originally created it—Victor Maurel.

Hard on its heels came the first performance in New York of Saint-Saens' *Samson and Delilah* as an opera (it had been heard in oratorio form). Despite the great Francesco Tamagno as Samson, the Metropolitan found the opera lacking in popular appeal and promptly put it on the shelf, not to be revived until 1915 as a vehicle for another great tenor—Caruso. By that time, *Samson* had become a highly popular opera as a result of its magnificent performances at the Manhattan Opera House. The builder and manager of this second Manhattan Opera House, constructed in 1906 was the same manager who had built the first Manhattan Opera House—which New Yorkers of 1895 called Koster and Bial's—and who was just now keeping the Koster and Bial management in a state of anxious suspense.

Not until the second week of February did Hammerstein have an announcement. Talking to a *Dramatic Mirror* reporter about his Olympia project, he said: "I have already started to clear away the rubbish on the site for my three new theatres. I have engaged J. B. McElfatrick and Son as architects and they will have the plans ready in two weeks to submit to the Building Department. I expect to open the houses in November."

In the McElfatricks, Hammerstein had again the finest theater construction firm in the country, but his reference to architects was of considerable, and, for him, of unusual, modesty. For Hammerstein was always his own architect, designing his theaters, despite his lack of any formal training in this field. What his architects did was to put his plans into technically correct form, a collaboration mutually profitable to all concerned. He always learned many technical points from them and they invariably got some original ideas from him.

When the reporter asked about the negotiations for the dissolution of his partnership with Koster and Bial, Hammerstein had his opportunity to unloose the threat he was holding in reserve. Nonchalantly he replied: "I have no intention to give up or to sell my interests in Koster and Bial's. I consider I have a good thing in my arrangement with them and I intend to stay. I get fifty cents of every dollar they make and I don't have to do a stroke of work. All the difficulties have been smoothed over and we are now on amicable terms."

This intelligence was soon conveyed to Thirty-Fourth Street, where the thought of being saddled with Hammerstein in perpetuity threw Koster and Bial into such panic that all their firm resolve dissolved into abject surrender. They sent word posthaste to Hammerstein, agreeing to his terms. He kept them on the hook another few days before accepting their offer and on February 23, an agreement was signed, including a stipulation for dismissal of the legal action against Koster and Bial.

By the terms of the agreement Hammerstein's stock in the corporation was purchased for $75,000 and Koster and Bial were to pay him the full amount of his $300,000 mortgage on the property when it became due in August. They also agreed to assume the obligation for the original $60,000 mortgage on the property, as well as all other outstanding obligations in the way of interest, taxes and insurance. In addition, there was an accounting of the profits during the one and a half years of the partnership and Hammerstein received as his share a sum reported as well over $100,000. Altogether, he received close to half a million for getting out.

Hammerstein was finally out of the music hall firm. The partnership was dissolved, the grand alliance terminated, to Hammerstein's unrestrained delight and to Koster and Bial's unspeakable relief. For them, getting rid of Hammerstein was expensive but well worth it. The quarrel with their partner had added to the gaiety of New York, but it had taken a great deal out of them. Koster, especially, had felt the strain of the last six months. Now their ordeal was over. They were done with this unpredictable genius—so they thought.

The ink on the partnership termination documents was scarcely dry before new announcements began coming from Hammerstein. "No," he told a newsman, "I do not contemplate a trip to Europe this summer. I shall engage all my attractions for the Olympia by cable. I think I shall astonish New Yorkers next year and show them what can be done in the way of a vaudeville entertainment. I have got several novelties up my sleeve, each a big thing in itself." More Hammerstein bluff and boasting, said the Broadway wiseacres, all this talk of attractions for a non-existent theater.

As a matter of fact, Hammerstein was not relying exclusively upon the trans-Atlantic cables. He did not reveal that he had quietly sent brother-in-law Rosenberg to Europe to act as his own personal representative on a very secret mission.

Within a week plans and estimates for Olympia were filed with the Building Department. It became known that Hammerstein had extended his site deeper into the block by purchasing the two houses adjoining the property on forty-fourth and Forty-Fifth Streets for $45,000 each, that they were already being torn down, and that the triple theater was expected to cost $600,000 for construction alone, not counting interior fittings and decoration. The exterior of the vast structure was to be chiefly stone in material and Renaissance in architecture.

Evidence that Hammerstein meant business continued to mount. The construction contracts had already been given out. The excavations were to be completed by the end of the month and work on laying the foundations was scheduled to follow immediately.

In mid–March an auction was held in the old Metropolitan Hotel at Broadway and

Prince Street. The building had been closed and sold in a property sale that included the historic Niblo's Theatre. The entire contents of the fine old hotel were being put up at auction, and the ornate banquet hall was filled with hotel and restaurant men attracted by the sale. The hall itself was famous for its seventeen glittering glass chandeliers, imported fifteen years before at a cost of $25,000 and regarded as the finest examples of crystal work in the country.

After disposal of various furnishings and equipment, the famed chandeliers themselves were put up for sale. The huge central fixture went on the block first. Down front a few well-known big hotel operators offered bids. A higher bid came from someone in the crowd of onlookers standing at the back—probably some big hotel man from outside the city. The outsider kept topping the other bids until the great chandelier was knocked down to him for $900. Everyone was trying to see who the unknown bidder could be. Only a very big operator could use such an item. Curiosity turned into astonishment when the outsider was recognized as a New York celebrity—the theatrical manager, Oscar Hammerstein. Was he a collector of crystal work on a vast scale?

The bidding for the sixteen smaller fixtures was spirited but the noted outsider could not be shaken off as the bids advanced until at the end the lot went to him for $2,630. Handling and transportation of the ornate chandeliers would cost an additional $2,500, but, as the new connoisseur of cut glass smilingly explained to the curious throng, he thought the items a bargain for his purpose, which was to remodel them for electrical wiring and installation in his new theater. The site for the Olympia was not yet cleared, but already its interior decorations could boast the most gorgeous crystal lighting fixtures of any theater in America.

But it was on March 18 that Hammerstein sprang his most sensational announcement when he called in the theatrical reporters. He was ready to tell them the name of the first great star he had engaged for the opening of the Olympia Theatre in November (Rosenberg had just cabled that the contracts had been signed). He would present, for the first time in America, the celebrated French chanteuse, Yvette Guilbert. He had engaged her for four weeks at a salary—here he told the reporters to hold their breath—a salary of $3,000 a week!

"She'll cost me more," he told them, "for I have agreed to pay first class fares to and from Europe for herself, maid and manager. But I don't regret the bargain. The American public is anxious to see Guilbert and I want to show the American public that the management of the new Olympia will stop at no expense to get the best attractions Europe affords I'm having trouble with Yvette, though. She cables that she won't sing at matinees nor on Sundays. I may arrange the matinees, but she is obstinate on the Sunday question. This is the first inkling I've had that Yvette is religious."

The reporters had a story. The American debut of Yvette Guilbert as the opening attraction for the Olympia was electrifying theatrical news, but that a music hall singer, or any entertainer, for that matter, should receive the astounding sum of $3,000 a week was a general news story without precedent.

There were a few grand opera singers—a very few—who received $1,000 a night and they rarely sang three nights in one week. There was, of course, Adelina Patti, who received $2,000, but singing an operatic role was an entire evening's exhausting task. Hammerstein was paying a singer $3,000 a week for a nightly fifteen-minute appearance to sing three songs! Even Patti never got $25 a minute. Not only was Hammerstein breaking all records; he was setting a record that would be unapproached for years. $3,000 a week would still be a star's salary in 1954 but the comparison would be wholly unfair: $3,000 in 1895 (more than $90,000 in 2019 dollars) and every one of them tax-free.

There were immediately, the "experts," pointing out how here was conclusive proof Hammerstein had again gone out of his mind. Erecting three theaters in a place like Longacre Square and then paying a performer $3,000 a week—why, he would lose his shirt in a month. Other "experts" continued to scoff at the idea that such a project as Olympia could possibly be ready any time next season, let alone November. But whatever the critics and skeptics were saying about "Hammerstein's Folly," the entire theatrical profession was sitting up and taking notice. Except for two of its members, cast down into deepest dejection.

Koster and Bial had allowed themselves to be persuaded that Hammerstein's grandiose plan was only talk, at any rate years off in realization. To raise the cash to buy him out they had liquidated the greater part of their empire of saloons and restaurants. They had put almost all their resources into the music hall, the greatest music hall in America. And now Hammerstein was out to ruin them by creating a triple-threat institution, including a rival establishment that he evidently intended to make the greatest music hall in the world. And they themselves had given him half a million to help him do it!

Four days later, John Koster, a man of fifty, was stricken with a fatal heart attack. The violent warfare that had made such merry reading for New York but which had become literally a life and death struggle for its participants had taken its toll of one of them. The following day both the Saturday matinee and the evening performance were cancelled, and the music hall kept dark for the first time since its inception.

Bial had always been made of sterner stuff than Koster. His chief trait was stubborn tenacity and the death of his partner seemed to act as a spur to his resolution. He girded his loins for battle. On Monday, March 25, Bial walked grimly as a pallbearer at Koster's funeral. On Thursday afternoon he stood smiling at the door of the theater, welcoming an audience despite the fact that none of them had paid for their tickets. They were distinguished guests invited to a special performance.

As part of the program of rehabilitating the dignity of the house, a special professional matinee had been scheduled and everyone of importance in the theater world was there. Attracted, no doubt, by the new star, Cissie Loftus, it was the most brilliant audience the music hall had seen. It included such actors as Henry E. Dixey, William Faversham and Henry Miller, such comic opera stars as Camille D'Arville and Adele Ritchie, managers, as Rudolph Aronson, and two dazzling foreign stars currently in New York—Lillie Langtry, the English actress and celebrated professional beauty and the lovely and distinguished French actress, Gabrielle Réjane.

Bial was stubbornly resolved to meet Hammerstein's challenge. After all, Koster and Bial's was a phenomenally successful music hall, its theater new and beautiful, its financial resources substantial and its credit standing excellent. Already Bial had cabled his agents abroad to comb the continent for top vaudeville talent. He instructed them to engage for next season every single European star available. They were not to leave a single performer of any reputation for Hammerstein to secure and they were to meet and top any offer he might make.

New York was going to have a new kind of theatrical war. It had known various merry wars between legitimate theaters, managers, and actors. It had known the great opera war between the new Metropolitan Opera House and the old Academy of Music. Now it would see the merriest war of all—a war between two great music halls. Next season New York would be a gay place indeed.

April was a month of interesting theatrical doings, including one resounding success and one complete failure. At the Garden Theatre a dramatization of the Du Maurier novel that was the current craze became a smash hit, with Virginia Harned starring in the title role of Trilby and Wilton Lackaye creating the stage realization of the character that added to the English language the name Svengali.

On the other hand, neither the prestige of a considerable run in London, nor the excellent playing of a cast led by Viola Allen, William Faversham and Henry Miller, nor yet the fact that its author was both famous and notorious, could make a success out of a comedy destined to be regarded as a classic of its kind. Oscar Wilde's *The Importance of Being Earnest* was as much a failure in New York as his *An Ideal Husband* in the same year.

During the month all the theatrical managers of New York were called to a meeting to consider action on several vital matters threatening their interests. One was the abuse of the free passes given for window display advertising which had developed into a huge cut-rate ticket racket. The others were two proposed bills in Albany—an amendment to the Gerry Law[1] further restricting the appearance of children upon the stage, and, most dangerous of all, the Mullins Bill to prohibit females appearing in tights on the stage.

Hammerstein, who had been the leading spirit in calling the meeting, arose and roundly took to task for their apathy those managers who failed to appear or sent substitutes. He then set the keynote by urging vigorous concerted opposition to any attempts by anti-vice activist Anthony Comstock or others to impose theatrical censorship through blue law legislation. "The public should understand," he told the meeting, "that we do not desire to stand in the way of a law prohibiting lewd or indecent exhibitions… but we don't want to get into the clutches of such fanatics as Gerry or Comstock."

A second meeting was marked by full personal attendance. At a third meeting Hammerstein, who had emerged as the dominant figure and driving force in the profession, was elected chairman, and there was talk of a permanent organization. Abe Hummel was engaged as counsel to oppose the threatened legislation, an assignment he carried out with brilliant success.

With New York the very heart and center of the theater world, a legal ban upon the display of shapely feminine legs might have had affects upon the future of show business in America too fearful to contemplate. Even serious drama and grand opera would have been affected. As for comic opera, musical comedy, burlesque and vaudeville, it would have struck at the very foundations upon which they stood.

Organizing his fellow managers for mutual defense was only a side activity for Hammerstein, busy supervising his two Harlem theaters and deep in detailed plans for Olympia He could already announce that he had contracted with producer E. E. Rice to present a new musical burlesque called *Excelsior, Jr.*, as the opening production in one of the projected theaters of the triple enterprise in Longacre Square.

And up north at the Harlem Opera House, his season was now reaching a climax of brilliance and variety. Beginning March 25 and all through April, Hammerstein was presenting in rapid succession a dazzling procession of outstanding male stars of the American stage. First came Richard Mansfield, bringing not only his familiar successes, as *A Parisian Romance* and *Dr. Jekyll and Mr. Hyde*, but his new *Arms and the Man* by Bernard Shaw.

Following this shining light among the new generation of actors came the grand old man of the American theater, the last of the titans of the older generation, now that Booth, Lawrence Barrett and the others were gone—the beloved Joseph Jefferson—in his famed portrayal of the immortal Rip Van Winkle. Hard upon his heels came the other rising star of the new acting generation, E. H. Sothern, in his repertory.

The next week saw a very different type of actor, the suave player of society drama and drawing room comedy—John Drew—to whose company society itself came as to a school to learn society dress and deportment and society manners and morals. In that company there were now three lovely and talented young girls beginning three remarkable careers.

One of the players, who had joined the company but a few months before, was Drew's own niece, Ethel Barrymore, destined to become a great star of the sage and one of its great ladies. The second of the trio was to scale the heights even sooner to become not only a great star but one of the theater's great legends. Her name was Maud Adams. The third was Elsie de Wolfe, debonair society girl in fact as well as fiction. She too was to become a star actress, but even more famed for her fabulous figure and clothes. After leaving the stage she would continue to hold the spotlight in two different careers, as the first woman interior decorator, who made chintz and period rooms fashionable in America, and then as a social celebrity, as Lady Mendl, leader of the international smart set, voted annually, almost to her dying day, one of the ten best dressed women in the world.

Ending the month of April and the procession of male stars came yet another type of acting personality, the singing comedian, Francis Wilson, one of the outstanding stars of the comic opera stage.

It was typical of Hammerstein that the greater his expenditure of effort in any one direction the more were his creative energies released in other directions. His energy seemed to grow by feeding upon itself. In the past invention had been the activity to which he devoted his surplus creative forces. In recent years musical composition had replaced mechanical invention as the expression of his genius. The new burst of energy released in the spring of 1895 now overflowed in all directions. To plan the construction and operation of Olympia down to the last detail was a superhuman task for a single individual to undertake. Hammerstein plunged into it with eager zest. There were no precedents for such an enterprise, and it bristled with difficulties and problems. When a particular problem seemed baffling and he found himself becoming irritable he would find relief by going to the piano and composing some music.

In planning a vast structure with three, and eventually four, auditoriums in which that many separate audiences would congregate, Hammerstein was much concerned with problems of fire safety. Numerous exits and fire escapes were provided in the blueprints but he was not satisfied. He wanted a virtually fireproof interior. The roof of the structure concerned him especially for it would eventually be the floor of the huge roof theater. With theater literally to be piled upon theater he felt a fireproof floor essential.

The architects said cement was the best fireproof material and Hammerstein was determined to have it. But, the experts told him, cement was impossible for a floor which was also a roof; the weight would be too great. Was there any method by which a thick cement floor could be made lighter, he inquired. There was not, he was told; it was quite impossible. Hammerstein shrugged his shoulders and smiled. Very well, he said, if no such method existed he would have to invent one.

Before long Hammerstein had devised an ingenious method that was simplicity itself. Hollow spheres were to be imbedded in the wet cement spaced out evenly in rows. When the cement hardened its interior, instead of being solid, would be studded with cells like so many air bubbles and the total weight drastically reduced. On May 8 Hammerstein celebrated his birthday by filing an application for a patent, which was duly granted, and the invention was incorporated into his building plans. Olympia never had a fire while he owned it, but a few years later the invention proved itself when a fire in the roof garden theater was effectively prevented from spreading by Hammerstein's patented fireproof floor.

Soon the reporters seeking interviews to learn more of Hammerstein's plans found their task arduous. The work of excavation and laying of foundations had begun and the east side of Longacre Square from Forty-Fourth to Forty-Fifth Street was one enormous hole filled with building materials, workmen, rubbish and mud. The reporters had to clamor down into this hole, for there, every day, rain or shine, was Hammerstein, spattered with mud up to his eyes, supervising every operation The brave and bedraggled newsmen who managed to reach him found him always smiling, full of ideas and plans. He had, he told them, some really novel surprises up his sleeve for New York theatergoers, no matter how blasé they might be. Surrounded by the dirt and chaos of excavations, he was obviously and radiantly happy.

The spring of 1895 saw nothing of artistic interest at Koster and Bial's. As testimony to Bial's stubbornness there was a fourth series of living pictures in April, and in May a return engagement for Harriett Vernon, the star who the previous season had aroused scant enthusiasm on the part of the audience and considerable disapproval on the part of Hammerstein. Perhaps it was Bial's way of expressing his defiance of Hammerstein.

The interesting developments in vaudeville entertainment were now taking place at Tony Pastor's Music Hall where the early May bill was featuring a famous singing star and two young unknowns who were not to remain unknown very long.

The famed star was the Englishwoman, Vesta Tilley, who always appeared fetchingly attired in a man's dress suit. The two unknowns were two talented young men, both comics. One was Sam Bernard, soon to become a leading "German" comedian. The other young man did burlesque imitations and would shortly become a noted Hebrew comic. It is quite possible that some who recognized his talent at Pastor's might have predicted for him a successful career in vaudeville and burlesque or even foresee his development into a great comedian. But it is quite unlikely anyone could have foreseen his subsequent career as a great actor in dramatic roles of heart-wrenching pathos. And surely no one could have suspected that young David Warfield would become the successor of Jefferson as the most successful and most beloved actor on the American stage and crown his career with a portrayal of Shylock in *The Merchant of Venice*.

Spring slipped into summer. With most of the legitimate theaters closed for the hot weather, the only real activity was at the music halls. At Koster and Bial's a remodeled roof garden opened with the addition of thirty-five private boxes—further evidence that Bial was girding his loins for the clash with Hammerstein. The summer shows he presented, however, contained little of novelty except for the first appearance there of Sam Bernard, fresh from his recent success at Pastor's, and for a new serio-comic singer, also a Pastor graduate, impish Cora Routt. The latter was shortly to attain a great deal of popularity and notoriety as the "Hooty-Tootie Girl," but only after a sensational engagement at Hammerstein's.

The theatrical world was buzzing with the coming war of the great music halls. Attention centered upon the Olympia project, with much speculation as to whether its scope would really be as grandiose as Hammerstein was intimating. All that was really known about it thus far was that its chief feature was to be a large music hall, with Yvette Guilbert, at a fantastic salary, its first big star. There was more involved than a new theatrical venture and a new rivalry. Both the music hall under construction and the impending war with the existing hall were symbolic of something new in American theatrical life. It was tangible recognition of the rise of a new form of theatrical entertainment called vaudeville.

More generally known as "variety," vaudeville had been existing upon the dark outer fringes of the theater, occupying a kind of disreputable nether world. Occasionally, it rose into the light of the respectable legitimate stage when vaudeville performers were used to provide interludes between the acts of melodramas or as specialty performers introduced into farces and musical shows. On its own it had flourished, for the most part, in low and vulgar dives. Ten years earlier no decent woman would be seen at a variety show. The music halls differed from the lowest dance hall shows only in being more expensive and attracting the wealthy "fast" set of men about town.

The one exception for years had been Tony Pastor's Music Hall, thoroughly respectable and not really a music hall since there was neither smoking or drinking and the place operated under a theater license. In recent years, Proctor and Keith had established large vaudeville theaters in several cities, introducing the new feature of "continuous" vaudeville (several shows a day in a continuous succession throughout the afternoon and evening). Keith's 14th Street Theatre and Proctor's 23rd Street Theatre permitted nothing objectionable and had successfully developed a family audience. In September, Proctor's new 58th Street Theatre was scheduled to open. On the music hall level, Koster and Bial's had achieved respectability and, undoubtedly, Hammerstein's new Olympia Music Hall would be a similar resort on a large scale, and presumably, on an even higher plane.

The sudden emergence of vaudeville into the Broadway spotlight was not viewed without misgivings and there were those who saw in this lusty upstart a growing threat to the legitimate theater. Some managers were especially aggrieved at the music halls because they were operated under a concert license, not a theater license, and therefore privileged to offer their patrons the refreshment and relaxation of liquor and tobacco—at a handsome profit. Their complaint was that although concert licenses were supposed to license only musical concerts, the music halls were giving acts in costume and even short burlesques, comic operas, ballets and dramatic sketches. This, they protested bitterly, was unfair competition. The only demarcation left was that the music halls did not present complete dramatic plays. And when eventually this last line was to be crossed by Oscar Hammerstein the storm would break in earnest.

Any lingering doubts of the colossal scale of Olympia were dispelled, as evidence of its financial dimensions became available. Official records established the land purchases as totaling up to a million and the recent negotiation of a $250,000 mortgage by the Title Guarantee and Trust Co. It was clear that the ultimate cost of the undertaking when completed in all its parts would reach to two million, unquestionably the financially biggest theatrical venture in the country. Skeptics could not bring themselves to believe that Hammerstein was undertaking this single handed solely upon his own risk and resources. All sorts of rumors circulated about his partners and backers, with self-styled possessors of inside information announcing various names, including that of James McCreery, the high-end dry goods merchant.

Hammerstein was not pleased by these persistent rumors and "authoritative" announcements and was to deny them repeatedly with considerable annoyance. One theatrical announcement at this time that must surely have pleased him came from Abbey and Grau, the successful managers of the Metropolitan Opera House, whose last opera season had netted a profit stated to be $200,000. As one of their new prima donnas they had engaged a soprano "direct from the Vienna Opera" where she was singing the past two seasons. Her name was Georgine von Januschowsky. There was more in this to please Hammerstein than his own one-time interest in the lady herself. He had starred her in his own opera company, to which critics and public alike had shown such indifferences, and now the great Metropolitan was vindicating his judgment.

Visible proof that Olympia would be the biggest thing New York had yet seen began to come fast after June 15, when the foundations were completed and the structure itself began to rise. Apparently the building was going to occupy every inch of the lot and extend the entire length of the block along the Broadway side of the square.

No longer did reporters seeking interviews with Hammerstein find it necessary to descend into a muddy hole. Now they were required to ascend rickety ladders and cross teetering planks of scaffolding to find their man. Smilingly, he took them on perilous journeys around the huge construction, blueprints in hand, pointing out where the different features of the building were beginning to take shape.

The general plan of the vast structure was becoming clear. In the middle of the block there was to be a main entrance and lobby, fronting directly upon the Concert Hall which occupied the center of the building. At the right of the lobby an entrance would lead into the theater on the 44th Street side of the building, seating 1,400 and containing 90 boxes. An entrance at the left of the lobby would open upon the Music Hall on the 45th Street side of the structure, with an auditorium seating 2,000 and equipped with the record-breaking number of 132 boxes. Two large elevators were to lead from the lobby to the Roof Garden, planned to extend over the entire area of the gigantic building and to be glass enclosed for year-round use.

The reporters were given the exact opening date—November 16—at which time Rice's show, Excelsior, Jr., would be presented in the theater, while a big vaudeville bill would be given in the Music Hall. Hammerstein was also able to announce the first of his major staff appointments, the engagement of Ted Marks as general manager.

There were still many who referred to Olympia as "Hammerstein's Folly," but those who had assured everyone the project would never materialize were silent. Even the skeptics were ready to admit that if Olympia was a folly it was certainly going to be the most daring and magnificent folly yet conceived and executed in the theater.

Each day, it seemed, Hammerstein was revealing some fact that set a new record for magnitude and scope. The rapidity with which the exterior was rising was itself record-breaking, and curious New Yorkers watched in fascination the army of masons and stone setters swarming over the huge edifice of white stone rising in Longacre Square. They got their climatic show in the first week of August. It was a great day for Hammerstein, as he watched a very well attended outdoor performance. Longacre Square was jammed with spectators as an enormous girder weighing thirty tons, said to be the largest ever made for any building in the country, was put into place in the Music Hall of Olympia. Hammerstein was able to announce that the roof would be on in a few days and the external structure complete.

The dream that had begun in a police station jail was standing there a visible reality in iron, brick and stone. From the West 30 Street Station House to Longacre Square was a distance of less than a mile. In Hammerstein's life and vision it was a long way and he had traversed it with giant steps in less than a year.

8

Olympian Splendor

September 1895 ushered in the season in which New York would witness the great war between the music halls. Koster and Bial's, as yet in undisputed possession of the field, opened early in the month. Bial's bill included another series of living pictures, the usual list of excellent variety acts, and one outstanding feature for which he was paying $1,000 a week—Lockhart's Comedy Elephants—a troupe of five performing pachyderms the like of which had not been seen. The huge beasts posed, teetered on see-saws, stood on their heads, played musical instruments, waltzed and put on a complete pantomime play. One of them even rode a bicycle and acted out a scene of getting drunk on champagne. The first night audience cheered the animals all through their act and Koster and Bial's season was off to a flying start.

Bial was also determined to meet Hammerstein's challenge to raise the artistic level of music hall presentation. He announced a new policy for the Sunday night concerts at Kosters and Bial's. Henceforth, no variety singers would appear in them, only the highest class of orchestral music and soloists. For these concerts he had engaged Gustave Kerker to conduct an orchestra of fifty pieces.

Among the other early fall openings were several smash hits and the launching of a number of notable careers. At the Lyceum, Daniel Frohman presented a dramatization of Anthony Hope's romantic novel, *The Prisoner of Zenda*, with E. H. Sothern in the dual role of Prince Rudolf and the gallant Englishman. An immediate success, the play was to remain so in repeated revivals on the stage and in repeated remakes on the screen, among which Ronald Colman's would be notable.

At the Empire, John Drew opened his season with several drawing room comedies, beginning with *That Imprudent Young Couple*. The three talented young girls in his company were all in evidence. Ethel Barrymore (it was her New York debut) and Elsie de Wolfe both won praise in small roles, but the third of the trio, Maud Adams, had now been elevated to the position of the star's leading lady and was already well on her meteoric way to fame.

And in a more curious fashion another future star was being introduced by a current star. When the great Shakespearian actress, Mme. Modjeska, opened her New York season with "Measure for Measure" the part of Angelo was played by a new leading man, a young actor with a soulful expression whom she had picked to develop and present as Macbeth, Benedict, Romeo and other Shakespearian roles. She considered him unusually promising and predicted a great career for him. This prediction was to prove entirely accurate but not in the way she imagined it. William S. Hart would indeed be a great star, but not on the stage—certainly not as a Shakespearian interpreter—but as one of the first great stars of the silent screen, as Bill Hart, tight-lipped two-gun hero of the early Westerns, who always played the strong, silent man, a good deal of the time with most of his face hidden behind a bandana.

On Longacre Square, Olympia, gleaming white on the outside, was a crawling beehive within, with carpenters, plumbers, plasterers, painters, sculptors, electricians, artisans of every description, swarming busily. To find Hammerstein it was necessary to plunge into this bewildering chaos within which, roaming about with an observant and critical eye, the overall designer and director watched every operation, checked specifications, straightened out snags, broke bottlenecks, exhorted foremen, cajoled contractors and negotiated jurisdictional disputes.

To those reporters who managed to catch up with him, he explicitly emphasized what his activities so clearly demonstrated. He told one: "I desire to emphasize that I, and I alone, am the manager of this place. I have no assistants and am in full control. Of course I shall employ some people to carry out my orders, but the direction of every detail will be in my hands."

To another, who asked if it was true that he had a partner or backer in this venture, he replied vehemently: "Not by the longest kind of a dynamite gun shot! No, no, no, and then again no, several times over. I have no partner, no backer, no manager, no anybody but myself. I am done with partners. I want to feel that I am the boss and that when I given an order there will be no one popping up to countermand it. You can say in the most emphatic way that I am alone in this business!"

It was the public impression that, since Olympia had not yet opened, the music hall war had not yet begun. Actually, the war had been going on for more than six months on the other side of the ocean on such far-flung battlefields as London, Paris, Berlin, Vienna and St. Petersburg, where Hammerstein and Bial agents scouted, maneuvered and contended for top talent across Europe. From their offices in New York the rival managers made the transatlantic cables hum as they directed their forces overseas.

Bial had the advantage of being able to present some of his novelties first. He had already shown New York those amazing elephants; in October he presented the first of the new ranking European artists he had engaged. His name was Segommer and he was nothing but a ventriloquist. But, as one reviewer put it, there are ventriloquists and ventriloquists; this one was an artist and a revelation.

No ordinary dummies sat on his knee. His figures were all life size, including a man, a woman, a clown, two little pigs, an ox, several dogs and a fierce-looking tiger. After the usual repartee, the woman sang in a shrill soprano, the man objecting to her vocal efforts, and finally all the animals join in a chorus of protest, the dogs barking, the pigs squealing, the ox mooing, the tiger roaring—all in such rapid succession that the audience almost suspected a hidden crew of assistants. There were also, some novel mechanical effects—the man's eyes lit up with colored electric lights, the pigs' tails gave off sparks, and when the woman reached a high note her neck stretched out a foot long.

At the end, Segommer played a final trick upon the audience. Picking up the clown, he carried the dummy off stage. A moment later, in response to the applause, the clown figure returned by itself, walking with a halting gait, and just as the audience was suspecting a mechanical figure, the clown removed his make-up, revealing Segommer himself. The *Dramatic Mirror* advised all ventriloquists to go to see him and learn to what artistic perfection their trade could be brought. New York had a taste of the kind of new artist performers the music hall rivalry would bring to the city. Whatever the outcome of the war, the public would have such entertainment as it had never had before.

To offset Koster and Bial's striking success in Segommer, Hammerstein released an announcement from E. E. Rice that made quite a stir. The cast of *Excelsior, Jr.*, the burlesque that was to open the Olympia Theatre, would include most of the brilliant players from Rice's previous success, *1492*, and, topping them as the star of the show would be Fay Templeton. This was welcome theater news. Delightful Fay Templeton had first skyrocketed into stardom when she won all hearts in Rice's memorable *Evangeline*. For some time now she had left the stage, where her talent and charm had been sorely missed. Now the opening of Olympia would bring back one of New York's great favorites.

As the month of November began Hammerstein was driving hard for the November 18 opening, the date he had set himself even before the foundations of Olympia were laid. His friends had pointed out the foolhardiness of setting a precise date so far in advance. In any building operation, especially one of such unprecedented magnitude, a target date should allow at least several months leeway. Hammerstein's response had been to smile and make a bet of $5,000 that he would open on schedule. He now had a force of a thousand men working day and night, and daily new revelations of the wonders in creation were trickling out.

The handsome exterior of Indiana limestone was to be matched by elaborate interior decoration. There was to be a profusion of stucco and plaster sculpture and ornamentation, following designs suggested and selected by Hammerstein himself. For the execution of much of this work he had imported skilled artisans and craftsmen from France and Germany. He had converted the offices and lofts in the Columbus Theatre into workshops where these artists were completing the sculptural figures and designs under the supervision of his son Arthur.

Heeding paternal advice about the uncertainties of the theater and the advantage of knowing a trade, young Arthur had become skilled in plaster and stucco decorative work and was well fitted to supervise this part of his father's vast project. But Hammerstein was not relying upon his family alone; almost every day he was announcing the appointment of experienced theatrical men to his executive staff.

The early part of November was marked by a variety of news of theatrical interest at home and abroad. From Paris came two items, one sad, one gay. Alexandre Dumas, the author of *Camille*, was dead. French dramatist Victorien Sardou and novelist Émile Zola were among the distinguished pallbearers and mourners for the man who had made countless audiences weep for a lost lady who loved camellias.

And Paris had a brand new scandal

Singer, actress and comedienne Fay Templeton (1865–1939), ca. 1895 (public domain).

and a new celebrity. In the ballet corps at the Opera was a young dancer noted for three things: the extraordinary angelic beautify of her face, the extraordinary way she wore her hair (down over her ears in an era of upswept coiffures), and the extraordinary infatuation she inspired in old King Leopold of Belgium. Upon these three foundations an extraordinary career was beginning. Already this $10 a week ballet girl was the toast of Paris and the possessor of fabulous jewels. Soon the name Cleo de Merode would blaze across two continents.

Currently re-visiting New York were several of England's greatest artists on two different levels of theatrical art. Stirred by the new music hall rivalry, Tony Pastor's was also presenting outstanding performers. The two leading women music hall singers of England were the two Vestas—Vesta Tilley and Vesta Victoria. Only recently Pastor had presented the former; now he was offering the other Vesta.

At each successive stage of her career, Vesta Victoria was identified with a particular song with which she captured the public fancy. Currently she was still being called "The Bow-Wow Girl" because of her phenomenal success with a song which she made the rage—a "little girl song" called "Daddy Wouldn't Buy Me a Bow-Wow."

At Abbey's Theatre, New York was seeing England's best of a quite different kind. This was the reappearance of the famed London Lyceum Company headed by Henry Irving in a repertory including *Macbeth* and *Much Ado About Nothing*. Until the passing of Booth, Irving had been considered one of the two greatest living tragedians; now he reigned as the foremost actor of the English-speaking stage. His leading lady, the lovely and gracious Ellen Terry, was the undisputed queen of the English theater. Even that irreverent young critic, Bernard Shaw, who stubbornly refused to acknowledge the greatness of Irving, was Ellen Terry's reverent admirer.

What made this visit of the distinguished actor especially significant was that he now appeared as Sir Henry Irving, but recently honored with a knighthood by Queen Victoria. This was an unprecedented honor, not merely for the recipient, but for the entire theatrical profession. For the first time an actor had been accorded royal honors; for the first time the actor as such was officially recognized as a dignified artist, no longer to be classed with vagabonds and mountebanks, but as a member of a reputable profession.

In Irving's present company there were also some young people who would bear watching. One of them was youthful May Whitty, herself destined for royal honors and revered status as Dame May Whitty.

At the same time New York was made sharply aware that there were other ways of acquiring British titles—ways open also to Americans. Fifteen hundred of the city's social elite packed St. Thomas' Church one early November morning to witness William K. Vanderbilt give his daughter Consuelo in marriage, and plebeian thousands milled about outside to catch a glimpse of the bride emerging from the church as Consuelo Spencer-Churchill, Duchess of Marlborough.

A week before the scheduled opening, Hammerstein invited the theatrical and music reporters and editors of all the newspapers and journals of the city to a dinner in the Olympia, to be followed by a tour of the almost completed building. An enormous table had been set in the huge cafe and dining room directly below the concert hall. When the doors were thrown open the assembled journalists gaped at the sumptuous repast prepared for them. Hammerstein was standing at the head of the table. Smilingly he motioned them to their seats. "Come in, boys," he called, "and enjoy yourselves. This dinner is costing me two million dollars."

At the table the host announced the engagement of various artists and staff members. Yvette Guilbert, it appeared, could not leave Europe in time for the grand opening; she would open the fourth week of Olympia. He had discovered a remarkable musician from Dresden whom he was appointing general musical director and who would conduct a full orchestra of seventy-five in Sunday concerts of classical and semi-classical orchestral music with distinguished vocal and instrumental soloists. He predicted a great musical career for his discovery, Herr Fritz Scheel.

The name meant nothing to the music journalists present. Five years later it would be a different story, for Hammerstein was launching a distinguished career that would make a striking contribution to music in America. Fritz Scheel was a superbly equipped musician from Dresden, but Hammerstein had discovered him in New York. He had come to make a career in America, but, after a single engagement leading a band at the Chicago World Fair, he was on the verge of starvation, ready to return to Europe, discouraged and defeated. Hammerstein was giving him a chance to prove his abilities with a full orchestra and bring himself to the attention of the New York musical world. Before long he was to be called to conduct an orchestra in San Francisco. Thereafter, returning east to Philadelphia, he would organize his own orchestra and develop it into a permanent musical institution. Before he was done, the Philadelphia Orchestra which he founded would take its place with the Boston Symphony and the New York Philharmonic as one of the ranking symphony orchestras of America.

After dinner, Hammerstein led the group on a personally conducted tour of the building. Into the marble lobby he took them, with its marble stairs, through a massive entrance on one side, and they were in the theater, looking up at the eighty-four boxes, the bas-reliefs and paintings on the walls, ceilings, and around the proscenium arch.

The general style of the auditorium was Louis XVI, the prevailing color scheme blue and gold, including the carpets and tapestries. All the surfaces were still wet with fresh paint. They went backstage, standing on the 31 by 60-foot stage equipped with the latest devices, peering up into the rigging loft 80 feet above their heads. The scenery for *Excelsior, Jr.* was already hanging there.

With special pride Hammerstein showed them the luxurious dressing rooms for the performers. It was one of the scandals of the theater world that even the most elegant houses relegated the actors to ugly, bare and drafty dressing rooms, devoid of elementary comforts. The profession had always blessed Hammerstein for the comfortable quarters provided in all his theaters. Those of the Olympia were the last word in elegance and luxury.

Up marble stairs he led them to the first tier, through a door into a lobby and then into the 85-foot Concert Hall. This hall was in the style of Louis XV, a frieze in high relief ran along the four mirror-paneled sides, cupids, flutes and lyres prominent among the motifs, and there was a small gallery around the hall. Here a special orchestra would play a nightly promenade concert from 7:30 to midnight. To lead this orchestra he had engaged Theodore John, well known musician and future head of the violin department at the New York College of Music. There would be tables around the sides of the hall for light refreshments and the center open for leisurely promenading.

Out again into the first-tier lobby, through another massive door, and they were in the first tier of the Music Hall, a solid tier of 32 boxes. In the spacious foyer behind the boxes heroic female nude statues standing on low pedestals served as giant caryatids reaching to the ceiling and seeming to support the tier above, the sculptured figures concealing the actual columns.

Down another marble stair, through other doors and passages, and Hammerstein led the group out onto the vast Music Hall stage, 43 by 70 feet, behind the huge curtain which cut off the auditorium. He showed them the automatic fire sprinklers strategically placed backstage. Other sprinklers were distributed throughout the structure, and he explained how these, plus the fireproof floors and numerous exits made the entire edifice the last word in safety. Gathering the group on the center of the stage he ordered the curtain rung up. For a moment they peered out into darkness. Then dramatically, the auditorium was flooded with light from every corner, the brilliance dominated by a central burst of scintillating radiance from the great crystal chandelier.

Dazzled and delighted, the group broke into exclamations. The Louis XVI Theatre had been ornately beautiful, the Louis XV Concert Hall more chastely beautiful, but here in the Louis XIV Music Hall, Hammerstein had given a Baroque fantasy free and extravagant rein. Every foot of the auditorium, with its five tiers of boxes—three of them solidly boxes—and its six tiers of proscenium boxes, was sumptuously decorated with sculptured bas reliefs of figures and designs, statues, mosaics, in a luxuriant profusion of motifs—floral designs, allegorical figures, flutes, lyres, cupids, gargoyles, shields, medallions wreaths. Red and gold, with old ivory for the relief work, were the prevailing color scheme, all glistening with paint and plaster not yet dry—the last of the scaffoldings and canvas had been removed that very afternoon.

Most flamboyantly decorated were the 132 boxes, almost twice the number in the Metropolitan Opera House and more than could be found in any theater in the world. The caryatid motif was carried throughout. On each side of the house a heroic female in full round sculpture supported the proscenium boxes, and on each tier above, the boxes were seemingly held up by smaller half-figures sprung from the wall partly in relief and partly in the full round. So profuse were the decorative patterns that, as Hammerstein pointed out, no two boxes in the house had identical ornamental designs. Even the shape of the boxes varied, some having straight fronts, others curved. Yet, almost miraculously, the total effect was harmonious and in good taste. Somehow the welter of intricate and varied detail fitted together into an overall pattern of coherent fantasy and orderly magnificence.

They went down on the orchestra floor. Hammerstein pointed out the roominess of the richly upholstered seats, the spacious widths of aisles and between rows, and such details as the slot machines on the back of each seat, which, upon insertion of a dime, would yield a pair of opera glasses. He gave them technical details of various original features of construction in the arrangement of seats and sightlines, in structural materials and design, and referred proudly to the more than 900 square feet of standing room and other innovations, many of his own devising.

They turned to look back at the stage and the rich designs and reliefs of the proscenium panels. Over the proscenium arch was the main sculpture group, 24 feet by 10, with figures representing Poetry and Prose being crowned by the goddess Fame. On the cornice above it they could detect the one visible sign of the builder's human vanity, a decorated shield in high relief bearing in its center the symbols "O.H." From its lofty eminence of cold command it appeared to be saying to all his theatrical compeers: "Look on my works, ye managers, and despair!"

Out into the main lobby again and into one of the two huge elevators, he conducted them, and now they were out on the roof gazing at the vast expanse extending a block long over the auditoriums. Here, he told them by next summer he would build a roof garden theater larger than any of the three theaters below.

8. Olympian Splendor

Hammerstein's Olympia on 44th Street was actually three separate venues—a music hall, theater and concert hall. The later addition of the roof garden made a fourth. Photograph ca. 1897 (public domain).

Back into the elevators. This time the group was led down into the bowels of Olympia. Below the street level were vast spaces stretching under the auditoriums. They were shown the great storage rooms, wine cellars and kitchens supplying the cafe, lounges and concert hall above. Armies of waiters were to carry refreshments to various parts of the building, smoking and drinking being permitted everywhere except in the theater. Every one of those boxes in the music call could serve as a small private dining room.

The host took them into the furnace rooms to show and explain the most modern rotary fans by which a forced draft heating and ventilating system would provide fresh air at the proper temperature throughout the structure, and into Olympia's own subterranean power plant and boiler rooms. Here four large dynamos provided electric power and Hammerstein discoursed on voltage, kilowatts and RPM's till the group was dazed with technical statistics.

He had many ideas for putting the vast underground spaces to use. Eventually there would be another small theater here for special purposes and he planned a number of recreational facilities in the nature of popular amusements and relaxations, as billiard halls and bowling alleys, perhaps even a Turkish bath. After all the installations were finally complete the cost of Olympia would reach to three million dollars.

When the journalists emerged from the building into Longacre Square, dazzled, exhausted and overwhelmed, each one had become a one-man publicity staff for Hammerstein's Olympia. They had endless material, not for routine news stories, but for feature articles.

During the next week, every paper in New York was talking about the wonders of Olympia in big columns and illustrations and in full page spreads. The *New York World* ran two separate feature articles, with headlines shouting: "Gorgeous Olympia—Hammerstein's Great Amusement Palace—Magnificent Decorations of This Wonderland of Pleasure—Nothing Like this in the World."

The columns fairly spouted superlatives in describing Olympia—"unique and unparalleled," "the most comprehensive, complete and beautiful amusement palace in the world," " a gem of a theatre," "a beautiful concert hall," "a superb music hall of vast proportions," "the most magnificent of its kind in the world," "lavish expenditure of money, good taste and artistic skill." One writer concluded: "There is no standard either in this country or in Europe by which Olympia can be measured. No theatrical manager ever before offered the public such a diversified scheme of amusement at such small prices and in such a building." All the news stories had accompanying drawings of the exterior of Olympia, various views of the interior and its different parts, with close-ups of details of the decorative designs and ornamental groups.

And every account repeatedly emphasized how distinctively there was stamped upon the enterprise the personality of the one man who conceived, planned and carried Olympia to a successful conclusion. The *World* paid a glowing tribute: "The successful completion of so great an undertaking in so limited a period, alone and unaided, and in the face of obstacles calculated to discourage any ordinary man, is an achievement of unusual magnitude, and Olympia will stand a monument to the indomitable pluck, energy, enterprise and genius of Oscar Hammerstein."

Nor were these outpourings merely the enthusiasm of the journalists moment; they were to be echoed and re-echoed in the technical books appearing in the succeeding years. Brown's *History of the New York Theatre* describes Olympia as combining under one roof "a great music hall, the like of which was not to be found in any other city of the world, a concert hall of noble design and ample proportions, a theatre built on unique lines."

Birkmire's *The Planning and Construction of American Theatres*, a book addressed largely to architects in discussing the technical details of this "large and magnificent palace," praises the stucco work in the interior decorations of the building as "one of the beautiful and artistic features of this immense amusement temple" whose "alternate strong and low reliefs and soft lines, with plain grounds well distributed, at once betray to the layman the quality of its execution." And Zeisloft's *The New Metropolis*, summing up at the turn of the century the memorable events of 300 years in the history of the city, does not fail to mention Hammerstein's Olympia as "the finest theatre building in New York."

The newspapers which told the public of the wonders of the Olympia structure also carried Hammerstein's own advertisements detailing the theatrical treasures the public would find offered within that structure when it opened on the night of the 18th. The large announcements were headed: "Hammerstein's Olympia—The Grandest Amusement Temple in the World—Three Auditoriums Under One Roof—Oscar Hammerstein, Sole Owner and Manager."

Each auditorium was listed separately: Olympia Music Hall, "presenting the first appearance in New York of 30 refined vaudeville artists selected from the principal stages of Europe"; Olympia Theatre, "presenting the first production in New York of Barnett, Tracy and Sloane's burlesque, 'Excelsior, Jr.,' by Rice's Olympia Burlesque Company of 80 artists"; Olympia Concert Hall, "presenting grand promenade concerts every evening from 7:30 to 12:30 p.m.—Fifty Cents Admission to All Three Performances." This was, of course, a general admission. Prices of seats for the music hall and theatre were listed as from 75 cents to $1.50, with boxes at $5.00 and $10.00. In the concert hall all seats were unreserved. The advertisements also announced the first Sunday evening concert featuring the first appearance in New York of Herr Fritz Scheel from Dresden, conducting the Olympia Orchestra of 75, assisted by eminent soloists.

During the week when all these announcements of good things to come fell upon an expectant public, and even as tributes were being showered upon their provider, Hammerstein himself felt as if suddenly the sky had cracked and fallen upon him.

For four days New York had been enveloped in damp fog and drizzle, four soggy days during which the wet paint and plaster of Olympia's interior should have been drying out, four days which created such havoc with Olympia's fresh decorations as to turn Hammerstein's pride and joy to horror. Not only was everything still wet; the dampness had caused the newly finished walls to sweat, colors streaked and sickened, gilding turned black, all the carefully worked out color schemes gone awry and surfaces ruined.

There was nothing for it but to recall the just discharged corps of carpenters. All the scaffolding which had just been taken down in the three auditoriums had to be hastily rebuilt. The army of painters, plasterers and decorators which had just been mustered out had to be re-mobilized with additional recruits and set to work on the double quick.

Under this unforeseen act of nature Hammerstein was forced to postpone the opening of Olympia one week to November 25, and his new advertisements carried the word "positively." To cap it all, the plasterers, aggrieved because carpenters were doing some work they regarded as rightfully their own exclusive prerogative, went on strike and walked out and Hammerstein was offering bonuses to attract replacements.

The loss of his $5,000 bet was a trifle among the additional unforeseen costs. Only one thing mattered. Olympia must open on the 25th—he could not disappoint a keyed-up public again. Unrelentingly, Hammerstein drove his workmen, day shift and night shift, around the clock, and drove himself hardest, even climbing up ladders and scaffolds to wield a brush with his men.

A *Mirror* reporter tried vainly for several days to get a personal interview with the manager. He finally found him, sitting on a wooden carpenter's horse in the lobby, so tired he could hardly move. Yet he consented amiably to be interviewed and, his mind fully alert despite his physical exhaustion, he was soon recounting the history of his career in the theater. He stressed the fact that in addition to building and managing theaters and producing shows, he had also written plays and composed music.

"I have composed any amount of music," he told his interviewer. "That's the way I calm myself when I am angry. I compose music to let out my wrath. I have been angry so often this summer that I have been able to compose a whole comic opera which I intend to produce here. I have named the piece 'The North Pole' and I think I will put it on in the summer. The name ought to make people feel cool, even if some of the music was not good enough, for though he copyrighted the name and plot of the show, he never did produce it."

The reporter had secured his interview and Hammerstein had secured a needed rest. Now he was off again, disappearing into the building to whip up once more his army of workers in the desperate race against time. Already many who knew what was taking place within the gleaming walls of Olympia were freely predicting further postponement, and his own men were warning him they could not guarantee that the paint would all be dry in time. But Hammerstein was grimly determined to keep his promise. Olympia would open as advertised—positively—wet or dry.

Meanwhile, Bial was taking steps to meet the challenge of Olympia's opening by strengthening his bill with new reinforcements. To the program headed by Segommer he added the remarkable mind-reading act of Lorenz and Kennedy, who completely mystified the audience, and the Baidis Sisters' trapeze act. This last was a deliberate counter to Hammerstein, whose opening program was featuring the Leamy Troupe, a group of European acrobats who had devised a sensational new act on a revolving trapeze which one member kept in motion by pedaling a bicycle set high over the trapeze. Bial had secured the Vaidis Sisters, whose act was a carbon copy in performance and mechanism.

For the week after Olympia's scheduled opening Bial announced that Koster and Bial's would present a startling novelty that would create a sensation. The living pictures had finally been abolished and it was intimated that the startling novelty was a new kind of living picture. It was called Kilanyi's Glymptorama, invented and presented by the original creator of living pictures, and Bial was sure it would be as sweepingly sensational as the original pictures of Kilanyi and Hammerstein. After its premiere, he was certain the opening of Olympia would be completely cast into the shade. He was soon made aware that anything which could accomplish that feat must cast a very large shadow indeed.

The labor was Herculean but Hammerstein kept his promise. On the night of November 25, Olympia threw open its doors to scenes of confusion and enthusiasm that made theatrical history in New York. Five thousand managed to gain admittance, overcoming the delays and confusions caused by their unfamiliarity with the building's plan and ticket-taking system, and the ushers' unfamiliarity with the seating plan. "Not only did every seat have somebody in it, but every bit of lawful standing room was occupied … in Hammerstein's big and gorgeous Olympia," observed the *Sun*.

That the pre-opening newspaper articles had not exhausted all superlatives was evident in next day's description of the scene at the opening. "Crowds, Confusion and Cheers" was the *World* headline. The *Herald* heading was "Olympia Fit for the Gods." The blasé reviewer of the *Mirror* wrote: "So great was the crowd and so eager were the people to get inside the building, that one literally had to fight one's way in. Such a struggle of modish people to get into a theatre has seldom, if ever, occurred before in New York… as beautiful as it is big…. Hammerstein's Olympia does honor to New York."

There was awareness, too, that more than theatrical history was being made; a new chapter was being opened in the history of the city. The *Herald* story began: "Longacre Square woke up last night! Its gloom and dullness is a thing of the past, for Hammerstein's Olympia has finally arrived." Times Square had been created, set on its path as the theatrical hub of the city and center of the nation's show business, soon to attract palatial hotels, and, within a few years, the great newspaper that would give the square its new name.

The brilliant first-night audience—the *World* described it as "composed of nearly all the well-known people in the city"—was less interested in the square outside and its future than in the interior of the great structure. The building itself stole the show before the curtain went up; indeed, it was the show as much as anything behind the footlights. The breathtaking brilliance of light, color and form and the lavishness of luxury and comfort brought forth exclamations of wonder and delight.

Even the critics and reporters who had already prevued the building and poured out their admiration in print were carried to new heights of enthusiasm at the spectacle of the auditoriums alive and vibrant with humanity. The 90 boxes of the theatre, the 132 richly ornated boxes of the music hall, rising tier upon tier, brilliant with gaily bedecked women and well-groomed men in evening dress, completed what the *Mirror* described as "a picture not soon to be forgotten." The Metropolitan Opera House itself had never presented so brave and colorful a sight. No bored dowagers sat in these boxes; there was pleasure and delight on every face.

So gay and happy was the occasion that the discomforts of the struggle to enter the jam-packed building were forgotten. The audience refused to permit even greater annoyances to mar its enjoyment. There were some walls and corridors where the paint was still damp, and some acquired unexpected souvenirs in the form of blue or red streaks on expensive evening coats and wraps. Yet most of them took it good humoredly. Those few who, with some show of indignation, sought out the manager to complain were quickly disarmed by Hammerstein's charming air of sans souci.

"That's all right, my boy," he told them cheerily, "Don't mind a little thing like that. It's only watercolor."

The dazzling wonders of the structure almost dwarfed the shows presented in the auditoriums, but the presentations proved themselves worthy of their environment, and as the evening progressed the enthusiasm quickened. The presentations also revealed what no pre-opening inspection could demonstrate; that both the sight lines and the acoustical properties of all three auditoriums were admirable, no matter where one was seated.

In the theater, E. E. Rice had outdone himself in the production of *Excelsior, Jr.*, a rollicking burlesque on Longfellow's hero, now transformed into a blasé fop always attended by four valets named, respectively, James I, James II, James III and James IV. As usual, the plot was merely a peg upon which to hang a lot of good lines, gags, and comedy scenes and a succession of tuneful songs, choruses and dance numbers, all set to catch music by Tracy and Sloane, with additional music provided by Rice himself. By final curtain time the audience was already humming some of the tunes.

In the title role, playing Aman's part—in tights, of course—Fay Templeton was warmly welcomed back to the stage. She was no longer the dainty ingénue of yore, for she had noticeably put on weight, but her singing and acting also carried added weight in artistry and effectiveness and her personality was as buoyant as ever. Her four valets were played by four beautiful girls whose tights revealed four pairs of magnificent legs. In this quartet, the stunning figure of May Hamilton was outstanding and there were those in the audience who recognized her as the gorgeous unclad Venus of Kilanyi's living pictures two years before. But the secret of her true identity was still being well guarded, and no one recognized her as Mamie Stevenson, niece of the Vice President of the United States.

All the female members of the cast were beauties. Among the specialty performers, attractive Therese Vaughn repeated her hit in *1492*, crooning street ballads to her own guitar accompaniment. The young and lovely Hengler sisters delighted with their graceful dancing and lively high kicking, revealing the beauty and talent that was to make them known for years to come as the most enchanting dance team on the stage. And Rice's chorus and ballet, always noted for the display of feminine pulchritude, provided that commodity in abundance.

The male side of the cast contained some of the cleverest and spriteliest comedians of the comic opera and burlesque field, among them Charles A. Bigelow, Walter Jones, Richard Carle, and little Arthur Dunn, whose burlesque of the idolized virtuoso pianist, Paderewski, which one review called "as clever as it was original," almost stopped the show. Rice had mounted the production with unusual care and taste. The *Mirror* called the last act "one of the most beautiful scenes ever placed on view before a New York audience." All in all, it was apparent that Hammerstein had a smash hit for the opening of his theater.

In the music hall, Hammerstein was offering a superbill of eighteen imported acts. After the playing of the national anthem and an operatic overture by the orchestra the monster program opened in the manner already traditional for all vaudeville shows—with an acrobatic act. What was not traditional was that the six acrobats of the Johnson Troupe were all star performers, each a headliner in his own right. Their remarkable acrobatics and balancing on revolving globes aroused enthusiasm at the very outset.

Other to-flight acrobats and athletic acts were scattered through the program. There was Lamore, who did "remarkably funny tricks on the bounding wire," the Kurschins,' "clever and novel performance on perpendicular poles," a French Hercules who held heavy weights while balancing on a slack wire, and the Avolos, who "performed thrilling feats on the triple bars." But it was the Leamy Troupe, which, despite the competition of their imitators at Koster and Bial's, "created a veritable sensation on the revolving trapeze," the effect heightened by the synchronized play of a rain of colored lights upon the trapeze during their "daring and graceful evolutions."

There were song and dance acts in abundance, French and English singers, skirt dancers, acrobatic dancers, clog dancers. There were clowns, a female impersonator, and there was young Giacinta Della Rocca, "whose beauty set the house a-buzzing," and who "played exquisitely on the violin." This was indeed a novelty. New York had seen beautiful girls who happened to play the violin. Here was a first-rate violinist who happened to be a beautiful girl. Hammerstein had launched more than an American vaudeville career, for this girl was a serious musician and was to have a long and successful career as a concert violinist. Hewlet's Theatre Mecanique, a highly amusing marionette performance, wound up the enormous program.

All the performers were new, making their American debuts. All, said the *World*, were "really superior vaudeville features and some notably so." "A first class show," said the *Sun*, and the *Mirror* called the bill "one of the best ever seen here."

This was also the obvious verdict of the audience, whose enthusiasm increased from act to act. Near the close it finally boiled over. A spontaneous cheer went up and there were loud cries of "Hammerstein!" mingled with more familiarly shouted calls for "Oscar!" The ruler of Olympia came out of the wings, his beaming face as shiny as his silk hat. During this period he wore, together with his mustache, not the small Van Dyke of later years, but a full beard, although closely cropped over his face. Yet nothing could hide his expression of extreme delight. It fairly radiated from him so that the *Herald* could assert, "the effulgence of his countenance actually made a halo about it." Hammerstein bowed and returned to the wings. The clamor intensified and he was forced to return. Now it was clear the audience wanted a speech. Still smiling, Hammerstein held up his hand. The house fell silent and, eyes twinkling, he said simply: "Ladies and gentlemen. I always liked this life, and I always liked this world. But never did this life and this world look so beautiful to me as it does tonight."

A little later a similar scene was enacted in the theater when the star brought Rice before the curtain and Rice brought Hammerstein, and again the audience would not let him go until the lord of Olympia had spoken.

The concert hall was a popular feature, its exquisite proportions and harmonious decor winning special admiration, and the promenade concert and tables attracted crowds both during and after the performances in the large auditoriums. Long after midnight the lights of Olympia still dispelled the murky gloom of Longacre Square, which was blocked by long lines of fashionable carriages, a wholly unfamiliar sight in that hitherto seedy area.

The crowds pouring out knew the disreputable old square would never be the same again. They did not know the new name it was destined to bear, but they seemed to sense that there a new era had begun. Thieves' Lair was dead. That night Times Square had been born.

9

The Great Guilbert

When Hammerstein read the newspaper reviews the next morning there was not a single dissenting voice in the chorus of admiration for the newly opened theatrical structure and the entertainment offered therein The only critical note of any kind was sounded by the *Herald*, which lamented the absence of a wide promenade linking all the auditoriums making it more easy to circulate from one to another to see an be seen. But the writer recognized that this omission was probably deliberate to discourage the musical hall practice of drifting in and out without purchasing a seat.

This surmise was eminently correct. Hammerstein did not care to encourage continual circulation at the expense of the box office. He wanted his patrons to purchase seats and see one of the shows. They could smoke and drink in the music hall, though not in the theater. For those who did not care to remain for the entire performance in the theater or merely wished to see a featured act or two in the music hall, there was the concert hall, the unique feature which Hammerstein had purposely placed in the center, accessible from both large auditoriums. Here the drifters could promenade to good light music, could see and be seen, or sit at tables and partake of light refreshment and conversation to their hearts' content. For those disposed to more serious eating and drinking, there were the cafe lounges, bar and restaurant on the ground floor below the concert hall.

The morning papers did not have room to sing all their praises of Hammerstein and his Olympia, and there were to be further follow-up articles during the week. The *Mirror* ran Hammerstein's photo with the caption, "Oscar Hammerstein—The Man of the Hour," and a feature article that began: "This is a likeness of the man who is being talked about and written about these days more than any politician or man of prominence now before the public. And why should he not be talked of and written of, when he has made more of a stir in the theatrical world since he has been in it than any combination of managers?"

Harrison Grey Fiske, the *Mirrors*' distinguished editor, paid an editorial tribute: "Many men talk about building theatres in New York … and while they are talking Oscar Hammerstein builds them… the only manager extant in this city who occupies a theatre or theatres the soil and the bricks and the mortar of which are his own individual property. Eccentric and bizarre as Mr. Hammerstein undoubtedly is, he nevertheless achieves wonders … and his promises, however extravagant they may seem to be, have always been carried to successful realization."

But Hammerstein had little time to relax and enjoy the handsome tributes in the press that Tuesday morning, for before the forenoon was much advanced Olympia was undergoing its first crisis.

The scene in Longacre Square was reminiscent of the night before, scarcely a dozen hours past. Again there was an excited crowd outside and again the square was blocked with vehicles. This time the vehicles were not carriages; they were fire engines, ambulances and police wagons, with additional ones still clanging into the square.

Olympia itself had almost disappeared, its entire facade enveloped in dense clouds of white smoke. Police and firemen were dashing into the shrouded structure and stretchers were being brought out. The wildest rumors circulated through the crowd outside—Olympia had blown up! The structure had collapsed!

At length the thick clouds lifted. Olympia was still standing. But the police were roping off the area and long after the fire engines and ambulances had departed a police cordon still barred that side of the square.

Down in the subterranean vaults of Olympia a defective feed pipe had burst in the boiler room, sending huge clouds of steam out of the vents in the sidewalk. Of the crew of engineers and electricians working below, two men had been killed and eight injured. Not until a careful investigation had established that the accident was purely localized and had caused no structural damage or hazard to the building, was the police cordon removed and the building made ready for the evening performance.

The accident was terrible enough, and Hammerstein foresaw serious consequences in future lawsuits, but he was thinking less of the remote future than of the immediate past. It must have caused him alternately to offer prayers of thanks and to break out into cold sweats merely to think of what might have ensued had the explosion occurred twelve hours earlier to panic the jam-packed audiences in the middle of the first night performance. But for that twelve-hour margin the opening of Olympia, one of the greatest triumphs in the theatrical history of New York, might have been one of its greatest tragedies.

Not far away that same morning an exciting event of a totally different kind was taking place. Another great family alliance was being cemented through a marriage. Only a few weeks earlier such an alliance had been consummated between the American aristocracy of wealth and the British aristocracy of birth. Now, this marriage was uniting two American potentates of industrial wealth by joining the dominion of Standard Oil with that of farm machinery. Oil magnate John D. Rockefeller, already one of the country's richest men, if not yet the richest man in the world, was giving his twenty-one-year old daughter Edith in marriage to young Harold F. McCormick, son of Cyrus H. McCormick, inventor of the famous reaper, and heir to the farm implement fortune.

It is doubtful if Hammerstein had the time or the interest to concern himself with such doings among the plutocracy. If he was at all cognizant of such matters he would scarcely have regarded the affairs of Vanderbilts or Rockefellers as anything that could ever have any connection with him. Yet, strangely, the time was not far distant when he would be on easy speaking terms with Vanderbilts, and Mrs. Edith Rockefeller McCormick was one day to be the financial backer of a superb grand opera company which he himself had created and developed.

And, indeed, the one theatrical event of the week that vied in importance and attention with the advent of Olympia was an event in grand opera which occurred two days after Olympia's opening. It was the greatest event of the season at the Metropolitan Opera House, one of the greatest occasions in the Metropolitan's history, and the artistic climax of Abbey and Grau's direction of that house. It was also the most curiously ironic climax of the great operatic revolution ushered in when those impresarios had returned to take over the management of the Metropolitan.

When the new millionaires had opened their big Metropolitan Opera House in 1883, Abbey had given them a lavish season of traditional Italian opera with great voices, high priced stars receiving $1,000 a night, and financially disastrous results. Ruined after losing $600,000, Abbey had forsworn grand opera. The Metropolitan stockholders themselves had been forced to pay out $60,000 on top of the costs of erecting the building. Worst of all, the stockholders, with their social aspirations, were in a predicament. They had their opera house and their boxes to sit in but no opera. Even if their interest was largely in opera as a social event alone, they could scarcely display themselves in an empty house. The performances were a social necessity.

In their desperation they had turned to the only available solution, and, under Leopold Damrosch and Stanton, had themselves supported an inexpensive German opera company to furnish performances without high priced stars and huge deficits. So for seven years the Metropolitan became the home of German opera, with amazing and ironic results. The Metropolitan Opera House went on, becoming the only fashionable house when the older rival, the Academy, soon closed, and in the theater built for fashionable Italian opera German became the only language of the performances, even the older works of Meyerbeer, Mozart and, on occasion, Verdi, being sung in German.

With the exception of a Lilli Lehmann and an occasional Amalie Materna or Albert Niemann, there were no great voices or magnetic and colorful artistic personalities in the company. The star system was out, but under the baton of the great Anton Seidl there was a highly integrated group of first-rate artists dedicated to the highest ideals of serious music. Above all, the company devoted itself to spreading the gospel of the "new music" of Richard Wagner. New York heard not only the popular early Wagner of *Tannhauser* and *Lohengrin*, but, for the first time, the advanced Wagner of the great music-dramas, *Rheingold*, *Siegfried*, *Gotterdammerung*, *Meistersinger* and *Tristan and Isolde*.

The large German element in New York was delighted, the lovers of serious music were ecstatic, and the music critics applauded the notable artistic achievements. Only two groups were unhappy: the genuine lovers of the old school of Italian operatic music, and the millionaire boxholders who found themselves the unwitting and unwilling novititates of New York's musical taste. For the latter, especially, it was seven long years of purgatory.

Where were the luscious voices, the displays of vocal acrobatics, the simple tuneful arias? Instead, in this "modern music" they were forced to listen to enormous men and women who appeared to shriek, belt and declaim in endless performances in which nothing happened on the stage—no duels, no murders, no passionate love scenes and no ballet dancers—with no tunes they could hum or even recognize, while an enormous orchestra made so much noise one could hardly carry on a conversation.

They signified their boredom by absenting themselves in droves, and on the fashionable nights when attendance was socially de rigeur they entertained their friends in their boxes and carried on animated conversations. Never had millionaires been so cruelly used. One would think the opera was for the audience instead of for the boxholders. Wasn't it their own house? Time and again they were on the verge of revolt which, only the remainder of that ghastly deficit could quell.

At last the long ordeal was ended, when in the overturn of 1891 the revolution erupted with the return of Abbey and Grau to the management of the Metropolitan. They were to provide Italian opera, (French for the few popular French works as *Faust*, *Romeo* and *Carmen*), with great voices and great popular stars. Not only was the German company ousted, the German language was out. The boxholders were going to have what they had built the house to get. Let the German element feel outraged, let the music lovers object, the critics thunder. The owners of the opera house would no longer be bored. With the overthrow of German opera they had come into their own. The seven lean years were over.

Abbey and Grau could not match the all-around artistic excellence of the German productions in perfection of ensemble, in dramatic fidelity, and in thoroughness of detail and finish. Their orchestra and chorus were frequently ragged, their stage management crude and their repertoire largely given over to the more obvious kinds of music. But they had more than made up for these deficiencies by presenting a galaxy of great voices and superb singers—Nordica, Eames, Lehmann (the only German holdover), Emma Albani, the great Adelina Patti (in special performances), Melba, Calve, and on the male side, Jean and Edouard de Reszke, Lasalle, Plançon, Tamagno, Maurel. Even the critics forgave other shortcomings in the sheer delight of hearing singers who were not only great voices and great stars but also great vocal artists. They were fully aware that a new era had been ushered in.

To posterity it became "The Golden Age of Song" or "The Era of Great Singers." And often it was termed "The de Reszke Period," for from the first it was these two male stars who captured the public and critical imagination and came to symbolize the new era. Handsome men of distinguished presence and bearing, the de Reszke brothers—Edouard, the bass, and Jean, the tenor—were no old-style Italian-type ranters and shouters, tearing every passion to tatters. They sang with taste and refinement, with purity and elegance of style. Naturally, it was the tenor, Jean, who became the great popular idol, the romantic Romeo and Faust beloved by the public and adored in the boxes, where he fluttered the hearts of dowagers and debutantes, while the stockholders beamed upon this symbolic knight in shining armor who had slain the dread dragon of German opera.

Yet, in this boxholders' paradise the serpent was already at work. To satisfy those who grumbled over the loss of Wagner, Abbey and Grau gave performances in Italian of early Wagner, as *Lohengrin*, and even of *Die Meistersinger* (disguised as "I Maestri Cantori"). While the critical scarcely regarded these as the real thing, the de Reszkes sang in them and their singing was a revelation to those who had thought no one not German or steeped in Germanic tradition could sing Wagner.

The brothers de Reszke were no mere self-adulating seekers of popularity and applause. They were serious musicians, ambitious to realize the highest possibilities of operatic art. Personally, they were Wagnerian devotees and they longed to attempt the challenging heights of the great heroic roles. Yet they feared they were lacking in the proper German traditions and training.

And now powerful influences began to encourage them. They were urged to undertake the heavy Wagnerian roles in German, by the two most influential music critics in New York, Henry Edward Krehbiel and William J. Henderson, and the London critic, George Bernard Shaw, added his eloquent pleas. Their hesitations overcome, the brothers threw themselves earnestly into the work of preparation. They studied German and, to perfect themselves, even spoke German to each other exclusively for two years. They persuaded Abbey and Grau, who also yielded to their insistence upon the reengagement of Seidl.

So it came to pass that on November 27, 1895, two days after New York had entered a new level of music hall entertainment, the city also entered a new level of grand opera performance when the Metropolitan presented *Tristan and Isolde* in German, with Seidl conducting, Nordica as Isolde, Edouard de Reszke as King Mark, and Jean de Reszke as Tristan—and what a Tristan! Six performances were to be given to enthusiastic audiences and critical acclaim, and the floodgates once open, ten more performances of German opera in German were to be presented, including *Lohengrin, Tannhauser, Fidelio* and *Die Walkure*. Henceforth, the Metropolitan was to offer Italian, French and German opera with the languages and singers of all three nationalities and traditions.

Once again the millionaire boxholders were discomfited, cruelly betrayed by their own champion. The bold Siegfried brought to slay the Wagnerian dragon now stood transformed before their very eyes and ears into a fearsome Wagnerian Siegfried himself. But if they were chagrined, their daughters were unconcerned, the debutantes fixing their opera glasses upon their beloved idol, Jean de Reszke, whether he played Faust or Tristan, Romeo or Siegfried.

For all of his preoccupation with the launching of Olympia, Hammerstein, a grand opera enthusiast, followed all the developments at the Metropolitan with close interest and one can be sure that this latest culmination did not escape his notice. What the critic, Henry T. Finck, called "the great de Reszke joke" (on the Metropolitan boxholders), was just the sort of ironic jest he would relish. His duties at Olympia would not allow much time for attendance at the opera, but he had a number of ideas about grand opera that were slowly ripening.

Hammerstein had always admired the fine ensemble and artistic ideals of the Metropolitan German company. Had he not himself presented them at his Harlem Opera House and did he not count Lilli Lehmann among his friends? At the same time he yielded to none in enthusiasm for great voices and great vocal artists. How hard he had tried to be the first to present Melba in America at his Manhattan Opera House.

What, he had often thought, if opera could be given with the high production standards and balanced integration of the German singers and with great voices and singing artists, and what if those artists were also great singing actors and stage personalities, as a Calve or Maurel? That would be an ideal worth trying for. Perhaps it was because it seemed an impossible ideal that he felt impelled to be the one to try it, and the time might not be far off when he would be ready to begin. For he had some great plans for Olympia that he had not yet disclosed to anyone.

Just now, however, Hammerstein's immediate concern was planning the build up for his first great star, Yvette Guilbert. In a few weeks, with her appearance, Olympia would meet its greatest crisis. He knew the risk he was taking. He knew she was a great artist. Yet the fact that she was the idol of Paris meant nothing. That with her French songs she had made a sensation with English speaking audiences in London gave no assurance. New York was not Paris or London. Many a European celebrity had proved a dismal dud in New York. Her art was new, original subtle, she called herself more a diseuse than a chanteuse, and much of the effect of many of her songs depended upon her realistic portrayal of purely Parisian types no one had ever used as subjects before—underworld denizens, Apaches, women of the streets, convicts, drunkards. Would her art and her subjects appeal to Americans?

Guilbert herself made no secret of her own doubts and misgivings. Like most continentals, she considered America a barbarous country. Although she was eager to succeed she wrote Hammerstein that the subtleties of her art might be lost upon Americans and she thought him foolish to pay her so much to come and find out. He knew he was taking a double gamble, on her ability to project her art and on the ability of the New York public to appreciate her greatness. He had said he was going to elevate the standards of music hall entertainment. What if he was aiming too high, over-estimating his public?

The very fact of the fabulous salary paid the Frenchwoman would key expectation to an extravagant pitch. The public and critics would expect something sensational. If she was

9. The Great Guilbert

only a moderate success, she would be a failure. Hammerstein was risking much more than the salary for her four-week engagement. It was an axiom of music hall entertainment that if the publicized star of a variety show made a failure the entire bill was a failure. The public would stay away no matter how good the other acts might be.

But this was not all. Guilbert was the first great star promised New York as the symbol of the kind of sensational new attractions Olympia would provide. If the first star fizzled, public confidence could be irrevocably lost. If Guilbert went down she might well drag the great new enterprise down with her. The risk was appalling—nothing less than the future of Olympia itself was at stake.

Despite his own anxieties, Hammerstein could not help being amused at some of his star's own evident fears. He had agreed to deposit in her name, as a financial guarantee, a substantial sum in a Paris bank. Just before sailing, she cabled, asking him to transfer the funds to her mother's name. Hammerstein remarked that either the lady feared drowning at sea—she had dreaded the voyage—or else she evidently expected to be scalped by Indians in this wild and barbarous land.

And now the build up began in earnest. Because Guilbert was the highest paid entertainer in Europe, it had been necessary to offer her a fabulous sum to entice her to America. But Hammerstein had also shrewdly realized that the amount he was paying would be itself the most potent single factor in creating sensational publicity. Already, in good press agent fashion, the figure had been increased to $4,000 in the newspapers. The amount was so fantastic anyhow, what did an added thousand matter.

French cabaret singer and actress Yvette Guilbert (1865–1944), pictured in 1913 (public domain).

Columns of material began to appear about this woman who had risen from poverty, after repeated failure, to make her first important success as the featured singer at the then new Moulin Rouge along with its colorful dancers, the saucy La Goulue and her high-hatted partner, Valentin le désossé, and the others; how she had risen in a few years to be the highest paid star of such music halls as Les Ambassadeurs and the Folies Bergeres, and had become the rage of Paris.

In none of these write-ups in the press was there the slightest understanding of what this woman did and why she was so great and so unusual. The papers played up her huge salary, the remarkable fact, for a music hall singer, that she was plain of face and angular of figure, her red hair, the long black gloves that were her trademark. They saw her as just another Parisian music hall chanteuse who sang indecent songs replete with double entendres and who had somehow captured the fancy of gay Paris. They dwelt upon the rumor that her songs were even more indecent than those of the ordinary French "cafe chantant" singers, as though this might explain her astonishing success and fame.

Only a few in New York, familiar with the artistic life of Paris, knew how absurd all this was. Guilbert was poles apart from the ordinary music hall chanteuse. She had created a new art form, part singing, part recitation, part mimicry, part pantomime of facial expression, gesture and pose. Her themes were contemporary Parisian types portrayed with vivid realism, moving pathos or merciless satire. Her songs were never indecent, except to the puritanical; her approach to sex was frank and straightforward, without insinuation and innuendo except where the subject called for it, as in "Les Ingenues," one of her familiar numbers in which she portrayed those young girls who are oh so innocent and demure and all the while know quite well what it is all about.

Those who knew the true position of Yvette Guilbert in Paris understood she was no passing fancy of lightheaded boulevardiers, no ephemeral beauty, for the moment the toast of the town. It was true that the gay public of the music halls adored her as a superb entertainer, but she was equally the darling of the sophisticated intelligentsia, the intellectuals and artists.

The poets, dramatists, musicians, painters were her devoted friends and admirers, eager to write verses for her, to compose songs for her and to capture her expressive features in charcoal, oil or clay. They treasured the intimate soirees at which she performed for them. After one such occasion Émile Zola wrote: "…she kept us all spellbound till two in the morning…. Quite another world was conjured up for us, a world half real, half fantastic…. I had never before realized so well that art, in the hands of a great artist, is only the reflection of nature in an exalted and slightly exaggerated form."

Shortly before she sailed for America, Yvette Guilbert had met for the first time a painter whose fame was rapidly growing. He was eager to do some sketches of her, and the playwright, Maurice Donnay, had brought him to her house for lunch. It was a meeting she never forgot and was later to describe vividly.

The butler who admitted the two men rushed to her in great agitation, blurting, "Monsier Donnay is there with such a funny little thing—like Punch!" She went in to greet them—"I was certainly taken aback by the sight of the 'funny little thing' standing beside Donnay…. Huge head… on the body of a tiny dwarf. A dark enormous head; oily, greasy skin; a nose large enough for two; …a mouth… like a cut from ear to ear… almost like a open wound!… lips thick… loose hanging like a hem round this gash…" Then she looked into the eyes of Toulouse-Lautrec—"How beautiful they are, large, wide, full of warmth, surprisingly bright and full of light."

Lautre was immortalizing the performers and habitués of the Moulin Rouge, including its current singer, Jane Avril. But he had missed its first and greatest singer and intended to repair that omission before his coming exhibition. He did a number of since famous drawings of Yvette Guilbert. Particularly well-known is the drawing of Guilbert singing the English song, "Linger Longer, Lucy," frequently referred to erroneously as a satirical drawing by Lautrec. The satire is there, but it is the subject's, not the painter's. It was her devastating caricature of the number as sung by a typical English soubrette. The hands joined coyly under the chin, the arch tilt of the head, the simpering expression—the genius of the painter has caught them all.

On her part, Guilbert found the artist the most unique subject among all the Parisian types she had studied. When he was evasive about bringing her one of his sketches for herself and she jocularly threatened to go to his home and get it he laughed, "I bet you don't," and astonished her with the information that he lived in a brothel. Yet she understood him and realized he was expressing his artistic credo when he told her, "Everywhere and always there is beauty, even in ugliness; it is thrilling to discover it where no one else has yet noticed it." She understood that very well for she, too, had discovered beauty where no one had suspected it, and, like him, she had discovered it in the sleaziest parts of Paris among its most sordid types.

There was another side to the genius of Yvette Guilbert—hers was the sharpest tongue in Paris. Having fought her way up from poverty she guarded her success belligerently against any criticism she regarded as posing the slightest threat to her pre-eminence. She would make a public reply in which the nimbleness of her wit and the caustic malice of her tongue were used so ruthlessly that the hapless critic found himself the laughing-stock of Paris. She would have occasion to apprise New York of her talents in this direction also.

As the build-up of its first great luminary began, Olympia completed its first week on a high artistic level with the first of the Sunday night concerts in the music hall. Leading an orchestra of seventy-five musicians assembled from the groups playing regularly in the three auditoriums, the new conductor, Fritz Scheel, on that December 1, made a successful New York debut. In the type of program, in the playing of the orchestra and the soloists, among them the lovely violinist, Della Rocca, a high standard was maintained.

For the second week of Olympia, Hammerstein continued the entire music hall bill unchanged, with only a slight structural alteration in the hall itself—the removal of the last four orchestra rows to permit freer circulation and more room for standees. The important program change that week was at the rival house of Koster and Bial's, for that Monday night was the premiere of Kilanyi's Glyptorama, Bial's much-touted grand riposte to the opening of Olympia.

Bial had never forgotten the furors over Kilanyi's original living pictures and how Hammerstein's pictures had run a solid year, the greatest single attraction Koster and Bial's had known. In Kilanyi's new creation he was convinced he had a novelty of sensational proportions sufficient to dim the glories of the launching of Olympia.

The Glyptorama pictures were immense, employing from five to twenty-five models each, shown in a frame fourteen feet high and twenty feet wide. The novelty was that they were moving pictures. There was no curtain, the pictures passing behind the frame as a moving panoramic view. Kilanyi had adopted Hammerstein's system of wheeled platforms moving on rails with the painted backgrounds moving in synchronization, but, lacking Hammerstein's mechanical ingenuity, his mechanism was cumbersome and difficult to operate.

Although a sick man, under doctor's orders to stay in bed, Kilanyi spent the days before the opening and far into the nights in the theater coping with the technical problems of production. There were all sorts of special effects, as in the picture, "The Deluge," in which sixteen maidens on a mountain top were realistically drenched by actual falling rain. Eighty-five persons were employed in the production and Bial had invested thousands of dollars in it.

The first night audience received the expensive production with considerable interest but no genuine enthusiasm. They had seen living pictures before; these were in no way more beautiful, in fact, they were less effective, artistically, than the stationary kind, and the factor of motion, while novel, was not in itself striking enough to create any excitement. As a promised sensation the Glyptorama had fallen flat. Bial kept it running several weeks but he knew from the first it had failed. He realized that to counter Hammerstein's Olympia he would have to provide much more vital attractions and being a stubborn man he resolved to do just that. Nor would he give up the idea of moving pictures. He was to try that again later in the season—and next time with real success.

Kilanyi, at least, was spared from witnessing the failure of his efforts. At the first night he was not there; he was home, lying on his death bed. Within forty-eight hours he was dead, another casualty of what the newspapers were pleased to call "the merry music hall war."

At the legitimate theaters there were a number of important changes of program that week, offering both familiar revivals and novelties. It was a rich bill of fare for the theatergoers of New York. At Daly's Theatre, the brilliant actress, Ada Rehan, was presenting her famous portrayal of Lady Teazle in Sheridan's "School for Scandal," regarded by many as her most delightful role. At the Empire, the fascinating new actress from England, Olga Nethersole, was appearing in several plays by the late Alexandre Dumas fils, including the remarkable *Camille*, in which she had won over critics and public.

At the Garrick, Richard Mansfield, the most distinguished and versatile of the younger American actors, was offering a repertory in which he alternated his popular successes—the Clyde Fitch comedy, *Beau Brummel* and the equally hardy *Dr. Jekyll and Mr. Hyde*—with a new play, *The Story of Rodion*, a dramatization of Dostoyevsky's *Crime and Punishment*. This last could only have been a labor of love, with the actor-producer knowing well that this unfamiliar Russian story of powerful and somber theme would never be a box office success.

Capping the week's offerings was Abbey's Theatre where the greatest living English actor's company was presenting *The Merchant of Venice*, Sir Henry Irving as Shylock, Ellen Terry as Portia. It was Irving who was the first to portray Shylock not as a half comic, half sinister villain, but as a proud and suffering being, a figure of tragic stature, turning what had been conceived as a comedy into a powerful tragedy.

Within the profession itself, the most interesting theatrical news of the week was the announcement that two of the most desirable and profitable theaters in New York were for sale—the Harlem Opera House and the Columbus Theatre. Hammerstein had decided to dispose of all his remaining major holdings in Harlem, including three large apartment houses, some lots on 135th Street, and the house adjoining his own—provided he got his price, a straight million.

He told the *New York Mirror*: "I find Olympia takes up all my time. That is as much as I can attend to. I could have sold my Harlem theatres several times last season, but I didn't want to let go of them before I knew if Olympia was a success. It is a howling success and so I shall sell. Several well-known managers are after the theatres, but nothing is settled yet."

The week's theatrical climax came on Sunday when the Etruria arrived in New York harbor that morning bringing the most talked of celebrity of Europe. The voyage Yvette Guilbert had dreaded had been a rough one and she had been deathly sick in her cabin all the way across, certain she was going to die and vowing that if she survived, never again would she go to America.

When the ship met the official tug, the passengers were gathered in the main salon, elegantly turned out and prepared to disembark. Yvette Guilbert was carried in half fainting, her face, by her own description, green, her lips blue, her hair lank and sticky, streaming from under a hat all awry, to find to her horror twenty reporters staring at her. What! Was this the famous Parisian star? Despite herself, she could not help laughing at their comical open-mouthed surprise. She refused any interviews; she would see the reporters that evening at her hotel, and she saw to it that no one sketched her in her present condition.

By the time the ship berthed she had recovered her ability to walk, if not her spirits. Hammerstein was there at the dock to meet her. The occasion of a great European star's first arrival and meeting with an American manager is always a momentous theatrical event. When the star is one of the most fabulous stage personalities in the history of the theater and the manager one of the theater's most fabulous managerial personalities the occasion assumes historic importance deserving to be recorded for posterity, as in this case, fortunately, it has been.

Having much to discuss with his star, Hammerstein sent her entourage on to the Savoy and took her into his private carriage. Although he was at his most charming, the great star was not in good humor and he was to have a taste of her acid tongue. Unused to the easy-going familiarity of Americans, she misconstrued his manner as an attempt to make an impression as a Don Juan who understood French women. She concluded he was attempting to seduce her.

As they drove along she was more certain than ever of her suspicions when he asked her to decide where she would have supper after her performances, mentioning various fashionable late supper dining establishments. Hammerstein was by no means averse to playing the Don Juan with a plump and pretty woman, which Guilbert was not. He was not a man who liked his women in any manner, shape or form, and in none of these three respects was she the type to attract him. His concern was with publicity. It was important in New York that a celebrity be seen in the right places after performances, and he wanted to be sure the reporters would know in what night spots to find her.

"I never go out to supper, monsieur," she said, coldly.

"New Yorkers always go out to supper," he told her.

"But I am not a New Yorker."

"Well, but what do you do after the show?"

"I go to bed, monsieur," was the sharp-voiced reply.

There was a chilly silence.

He began to talk about Paris. Now she thought he was trying to play the man of the world. What would a barbarian American manager know of Paris? He was interested to know if the fame of Olympia had reached Paris, whose greatest celebrity it had enticed away.

"Do they know my name in Paris?"

"Yes, monsieur."

"What do they say?"

"That you're a fool." She buried her hands in her muff with finality, satisfied at having offended him.

She did not know that Hammerstein's tongue could be as sharp as hers. She was wide open for a devastating reply. Undoubtedly he had it on the tip of his tongue but thought better of it. It would hardly do to begin quarreling with a star whom he was paying a fortune and upon whose success or failure might hinge the fate of a vast enterprise.

Perhaps never has a frostier and more hostile first meeting taken place between a great manager and a great star. It is a pity we do not have his account of it, only hers.

Later they were to get on fairly well, despite her prejudice against Americans, especially American managers, whom she regarded as motivated solely by unlimited greed. She appreciated his intelligence and, recognizing his unique position, was even to describe him as "a legendary and popular figure." Once, in a burst of enthusiasm, she even called him a great man. But she refused to take seriously his pride in his design and decoration of Olympia and in his abilities as a musician, scoffing at him as a conceited man who thought himself a great artist in decorative design and a Beethoven in music. She could not admit that an American manager could have any artistic taste and talent, let alone versatility.

For the rest of her life, although she was to make repeated American visits, find a husband here, and once spend seven consecutive years as a resident, she never conceded that America was anything but an unbroken cultural desert. With her, as with so many Europeans, it was an article of faith.

When Hammerstein left his caustic star at the Savoy it was agreed she was to have several days rest before beginning rehearsals. She refused all "those dreadful reporters" until the evening with one exception, a journalist who had known her in Paris, whom she could regard as a spiritual Parisian and therefore a kindred soul in this wilderness. To him she unburdened herself at luncheon, talking at length, seriously and illuminatingly about herself and her art her hopes, fears and anxieties.

"I am so frightened," she admitted, "that I don't know how I shall be able to summon enough courage to face my audience at Olympia next Monday night." She told him it would be her first and last trip over. "We see so many Americans in Paris that it is interesting to see them at home. I wonder how the untraveled American will like me. The lower classes in England didn't understand me a bit.... I would like, were it possible, to explain to my American audience, before I sing, the meaning of each of my songs, give by verbal description the types they portray.... For, in my opinion, that is the secret of my success from the old fashioned and hackneyed music hall song, and it was because my listeners recognized the characters I assumed that they accepted my work.

"It is an error to think, as many do, that my reputation has been made by singing equivale [sic] songs, for I hope my art is better and higher than that. Each of my songs presents a distinct type of humanity, the humanity we elbow each day in the street, and they sing of life as it is, not as we would have it. But ... the actual words of the songs are only secondary in artistic importance to the pantomime and facial play with which I accompany them. I even object to be called a songstress. I am a diseuse."

She met the "boys" from the press that evening. Her English, despite a strong accent, was quite adequate. Knowing well the importance of publicity she answered politely all their questions, even though she thought them tiresome, stupid and irrelevant—how much money did she make, would she marry and what sort of man, what was her opinion of New York, of American men and American women (after ten hours in the country).

While this séance was in session, the second Scheel Sunday concert was making a first-rate success at the Olympia. Scheel held a nice balance between serious and lighter classical music, and the soloists included, besides Della Rocca and several vocalists, a virtuoso performer on the mandolin who made such a tremendous hit that Hammerstein promptly signed him up for the Music Hall bill. The rival concerts at Koster and Bial's were not doing well—Koster and Bial's clientele proving impervious to anything but popular music, and they were creating an increasing financial drain for Bial.

For Olympia's third week Hammerstein's bill, like that of the rival house, was held over almost intact. The Olympia advertising which announced the American debut of Yvette Guilbert for December 16 also carried a statement nicely calculated for its publicity value: "Notwithstanding the extraordinary expense attending this engagement, there will be no advance in the prices for seats and admissions." To this stroke the Koster and Bial advertisements could only counter by carrying the legend: "The handsomest Music Hall in America," unintentionally paying a handsome compliment to Hammerstein.

The Olympia publicity was rolling in high gear. What with the daily papers full of Guilbert write ups and with various items of theatrical news coming from Hammerstein's office, Koster and Bial's was just not in it that week when it came to news. Among other things it became known that during the period of Olympia's launching Hammerstein had sought relaxation from his cares by, as usual, composing music, and was working on an operetta which he intended to produce. It was also announced that, being too busy to leave for European trips, he would shortly send Ted Marks, his chief executive, to open a permanent London office as Hammerstein's European agent.

In the middle of the week there occurred an artistic event which almost took the play away from Hammerstein and Olympia. On December 11 the Metropolitan Opera House presented Calve in the American premiere of *La Navarraise*, the melodramatic one-act operatic thriller that Massenet had composed expressly as a vehicle for the great French opera singer, and she gave an electrifying demonstration of her dramatic powers.

It was also a demonstration of some of the grievous lapses of artistic good taste characteristic of the Metropolitan management. As a curtain-raiser to the little blood and thunder opera, an effective dramatic vehicle of negligible musical value, the Metropolitan offered, of all things, Gluck's *Orfee and Eurydice*, one of the most sublimely serene and noble classics in all grand opera, and a shoddy performance of it to boot. For such an egregious gaffe even Calve's sensational portrayal could hardly atone.

But within 48 hours the spotlight was back upon Olympia and the French music hall singer who was its star. This was the climax of the build up Hammerstein had prepared for the Friday of the week preceding Guilbert's opening.

For that afternoon, at the Savoy Hotel, Hammerstein had arranged a private reception and performance by Yvette Guilbert. To this he had invited representatives of the leading newspapers and periodicals, not their reporters, but their experts, music hall critics, drama reviewers, music critics, literary men. Most of them came, the variety critics in the line of duty to witness a prevue, the others out of curiosity to see what all the shouting was about and with great skepticism about this music hall singer over whom Europeans made a fuss appropriate only for a great artist. Those who did not deign to come were to regret it.

With Hammerstein acting as a genial master of ceremonies, his star entertained the distinguished group with a number of songs from her repertory, to which she supplied some explanatory remarks. Those present who were on the staffs of the dailies lost no time reporting their impressions in print the next day.

One wrote: "The revelation of the new art that this famous singer possesses made no uncertain impression. No report of her powers that has come to this country over-rates them." Another said: "Mlle. Guilbert's methods differ widely from those of any French artists who have visited this country… changes tones of her voice in a manner at once startling and effective… wonderfully convincing… indicated profound study of the character of the people depicted in her songs."

The accounts gave detailed reports of the songs she had sung, terming many of them "wicked ballads." The *Herald* writer descried how in Beranger's "La Grandmere," "she put on a lace cap, sat in an armchair, and with a few deft touches to the lace round her neck transformed herself into an old woman who volubly tells of her early loves and conquests to her granddaughter."

The *Sun*'s account said: "She can make an effect with the brief words of a song that is more moving and impressive than many an actress can do in a 5-act tragedy. She is a genius in miniature. The hearers who listened to her yesterday had no idea of what her real powers were and whether she was a fad… made by puffery or the artist she was said to be…. The same question will be in the minds of the audience Monday night. If her art bears transfer to the wider field of a theatre, there will not be much doubt of the answer… the people will not only listen to a new singer, but learn a new form of art. Our stage has never seen performances of the kind and some element of her success will depend on what her audiences expect. The singer herself understands what she has to encounter."

"I wrote to my mother," she had confided to the group, "that the newspapers have all described me as so ugly that the people may be disappointed in that respect when they see me. But if they expect me to dance and skip, why then—"

After this unanimous accolade of the connoisseurs, Hammerstein's star was already a *succes d'estime*, but the question of her popular success at the box office was as moot as ever. To sing in a hotel reception room was one thing, to project her subtle art in the vast spaces of Olympia quite another. And what would a public used to frivolous music hall entertainment make of this new and subtle art?

Just at this moment there was a short-lived international crisis agitating the newspapers. Because of the strong line President Cleveland was taking in the Venezuelan dispute, timid folk feared imminent war with England. The financial market, always a sensitive barometer of vain hopes and vainer fears, reacted sharply, and there was a panic in Wall Street. But no trace of political crisis or financial panic showed itself at Olympia Monday night.

It was the opening night all over again, the house packed to the doors, long lines of carriages filling the square and fashionably dressed people struggling to enter through the crowded sidewalks and lobby, made more choked by swarms of ticket speculators plying a thriving trade. At one point it was necessary for young Arthur Hammerstein, assisted by a corps of attendants, to forcibly eject all speculators from the lobby and have one of the more recalcitrant ones placed under arrest.

Inside there was an even more brilliant audience than on the opening night. The five tiers of balconies and boxes were a glittering sight. In addition to the usual gay music hall habitués, a good part of the Diamond Horseshoe of the Metropolitan Opera House seemed to have transferred from Thirty-Ninth to Forty-Fifth Street. Society notables were easily spotted—Mr. and Mrs. James Hyde Beekman, Mr. and Mrs. Charles F. Havemeyer, the Theodore Havemeyers, Mrs. Herman Oelrichs, various titled foreigners, notables of the French colony, ex-Mayor Thomas Gilroy, even the Metropolitan Opera management was represented by both Mrs. Abbey and Mrs. Grau. An air of expectancy hung over the house as an audience curious to hear a singer of French songs, although only a small fraction could understand any French, hardly concentrated on the eight numbers on the bill preceding the main attraction.

The two most nervous persons in the house were Guilbert herself, waiting tensely in her dressing room, and Hammerstein, wandering through the lobbies with a serious and abstracted look, not at all his usual smiling self. At last, at 9:30, number 9 on the program was reached, and Yvette Guilbert stepped out, wearing a long, simple dress of light color and long black gloves. The audience greeted her with hearty but not prolonged applause. In the wings, Hammerstein stood nervously beside Ted Marks. He knew his star's reputation and publicity would insure applause at her entrance and after each number. That meant little. What counted was sustained attention and the summatory applause at the end. Would they recall her, demand more? That would be the real test.

In a voice seemingly at conversation pitch but which reached clearly to every corner of the house, the French chanteuse sang her first number, "Les Ingenues," the song about the presumably innocent girls who are not. Although the French words were incomprehensible to the great majority, the audience followed with hushed attention and a salve of applause at the conclusion.

In the second number, "La Soularde," a vignette of a drunken woman of the gutter who had once known a happier life, the mood changed completely. No winks, no smiles, sorrowfully, earnest—a song in which one reviewer said, "she all but touched the height of tragedy." Another account observed, "one could have heard a pin drop in the vast auditorium usually so noisy with revelry," and noted that "when here and there noise from the boxes broke the almost oppressive silence it was speedily rebuked by impatient hisses."

Another change of mood as the singer reappeared, her face encircled by a quaint white cap, for "La Grandmere," the old lady who tells of her youthful amours so proudly and with such wistful recollection. Even the jaded Mirror critic who admitted his French was limited to "bon jour" and "garcon" and that he expected to be bored, found himself fascinated as he sat, opera-glass in hand, and was to write, "Yvette Guilbert can express as much with a toss of her head or a wink of one eye as a dozen of our best serio-comics can by using all their features and their arms and legs into the bargain."

Then the frank "Ca fait toujours plaisir," of which the *World* reviewer said, "what pleased I dare not say in English, ... for instance, 'Les baisers sur son sein.'" This was succeeded by the gay "A La Villette." And now came Jules Jouy's tragic tale of the gutter, "La Pierreuse," the story of the pathetic streetwalker who loves a criminal and loses her lover to the guillotine.

The whole audience was now completely under the singer's spell. Another reviewer described it: "Her personality permeates the audience room.... Even though you do not understand a word you are convinced that an artist of prodigious talent stands before you. It makes no difference what she sings... witty or pathetic... the effect is the same. Not a music hall singer at all, but an artist so great that you wonder that she was not born within the very walls of the house of Moliere.... Such diction you cannot hear even at the Theatre Francais... the greatest mistress of the art of diction upon the French stage. You may not know the exact significance of every word... for much in these songs is in the Parisian argot of today. Nevertheless, you will catch every word she utters. Some Parisian friend will tell you the meaning afterward. Bear in mind, however, not to ask a female friend."

The seventh and last song was one the singer would term "for the gallery," a song in English, the hackneyed, sentimental. "Linger Longer, Lucy," But sung with what a difference, not merely in the quaint accent, but, as in the *New York World*'s description, "the drollest, cleverest, cruelest burlesque of one of those English music hall 'gals' we have been paying our good dollars all these years to hear—before we knew Yvette." This brought thunders of applause, not only from those who appreciated the point, but equally from those unsophisticated who clearly "took it straight."

As the conductor handed floral tributes across the footlights, the applause swelled in a mighty crescendo. In the wings, Hammerstein stopped his pacing up and down, listened almost incredulously to the deafening roar and turned to Marks:

"Is it genuine, Ted?" he asked.

"Did you hire any people to do it?" Marks rejoined.

"No."

"Well, then you can depend on it that it's genuine."

And now, a reporter watching Hammerstein closely was able to report that, for the first time, the manager smiled, a slowly spreading smile of such radiant satisfaction as to be one of the newsworthy events of the evening. "It started under the black mustache, usurped all the neighboring features and was finally lost among the outskirts of the close-cropped beard bordering on the Hammerstein ears." Nor did it stop there. As the great chanteuse was forced to respond to recall after recall, to add encores, the Hammerstein smile spread from face to body until "satisfaction fairly radiated from every point of his plump figure."

He was the first to congratulate his star when she came to her dressing room carrying great bunches of roses. She sat down happily at the dressing table to remove her stage make-up. To supplement her own hair she wore a switch of red curls, and no sooner had she removed it than Hammerstein snatched it gleefully as his personal souvenir of a memorable occasion. Guilbert protested strenuously that she had paid $3 for those curls in London. He said, laughingly, he would not relinquish his trophy for less than a fortune as great as—well—Mademoiselle's salary for a week. She stopped protesting and he complimented her again upon her triumph. Yet though she was happy she had reservations.

"The audience was so kind," she replied, "but was it because they thought me good? … Is it not strange that your audience understood my risqué songs better than my more artistic ones? I think they liked best 'Les Ingenues,' 'Ca fait toujours plaisir' and 'A la Villette.' When I sang 'la Soularde' and 'La Pierreuse' I could see that they did not understand … that they did not quickly follow the changes in the serious songs…. Now, in London they did not understand the delicate points of my shocking songs. They were lost on them, but the serious artistic efforts they appreciated…

"They did like that foolish song, 'Linger Longer, Lucy,' n'est ce pas? If I should sing such a silly song in Paris people would say: 'This Yvette, has she gone crazy?' Non, Monsieur Hammerstein, I tell you all the while you lose money on me, but if they want shocking songs I will sing them all the shocking songs I know. Wait till next week and I will sing 'Les Vierges' and many chansons like that.

"And you sincerely think they liked me? I do hope so. I am so pleased that they receive me so well, but I hope they will like my serious songs more. We shall see!"

The rest of the evening's all-star program was all anti-climax. Even when a performer on the slack wire lost his footing on the bounding line and fell to the stage, sustaining a severe concussion, there was little stir. The audience had already expended their emotions on one sensation. And backstage swarmed with reporters seeking interviews with both the great star and the great manager. Hammerstein gave them a statement for publication.

"Yvette Guilbert is a great success," he told them, "there can be no doubt of that. Tonight has shown that an American audience will appreciate true artistic worth when presented in a music hall. Yvette Guilbert is a great artist, and her success tonight has justified my faith that she would be a drawing card, and has also justified the great outlay that was necessary to induce her to come here. I think the public will appreciate her serious songs quite as much as those in lighter vein. I am proud to have Yvette Guilbert at Olympia."

As a showman, no one understood better than Hammerstein what an astounding triumph it was and how well it illustrated the dictum that great art is the bringing out of the universal in the particular. Here was an artist who practiced a highly specialized art dealing with particular types of a particular city in a particular country. And by a miracle of communication she had succeeded in breaking through the barriers of space, nationality and language by the sheer projective force of her art and personality.

If Hammerstein's pride and faith were amply justified, some of the French-woman's reservations may also have been justified in part by the reactions and emphases in some of the news accounts. The *New York World* devoted a full page and numerous illustrations to the debut of the French chanteuse. The headlines read: "All Hail! Guilbert!"—"Yvette, the Divette Scatters Prudishness to the Wind"—"Art Triumphs Over Indecency"—"Matchless Art Displayed in Songs Typical of Modern Degeneracy." Charles Henry Meltzer, dramatist, translator, music critic and future executive secretary at the Metropolitan Opera House, who wrote the review, wet off on the tack that Longacre Square had become a bit of Paris:

> Yvette Guilbert made Gallic humor acceptable to prudish ears by the force of art.... Hammerstein has established a great truth, exposed the national sin of hypocrisy and given all his brother managers a great lesson. The fiction of American prudishness has been killed, the word "shocking" eliminated from the dictionary.... No more need managers use the pruning-knife. No more need French plays be adapted. The self-appointed censors may resign, for Yvette has sung her songs verbatim... with their Rabelaisian wit and their Zolasque naturalism and they have been applauded and encored. Hammerstein is himself wiser. He hissed Di Dio for a milk-and-water skit... he heard thousands acclaim Yvette for her naked expositions of vice and crime.

The *New York Sun*'s headlines carried a similar slant: "An Event in Vaudeville"—"Bold Yvette Sings Her Indecently Wicked Songs at Hammerstein's Olympia with Unquestionable Success." The reviewer went further, conceding, "She is fully the genius which Paris took her to be," but insisting that the nature of her songs, "the indecencies of which are not to be particularized in respectable print," constituted a "degradation of theatrical business."

The headlines in the *Herald* were more to the point: "Captured by Mlle. Guilbert"—"She Carries vast Audience in Hammerstein's Olympia Completely by Storm." And the critic undertook to describe the impact of her personality and her art: "A frail young woman of distinguished bearing, dressed charmingly and simply.... Not a beautiful woman, you say. Listen! After two minutes you will swear that nothing so bewitching, so seductive, has ever been painted or chiseled. Her magnetism is tremendous. The moment she parts her lips the audience is spellbound...

> "Mlle. Guilbert sings, you say; so tell us about her voice. Mlle. Guilbert does not sing, she chants... she is not a music hall singer in the common term. She is the most gigantic histrionic satirist of the day, and she is quite familiar with the fact that hers is not a fine voice. Accordingly, she chants her music... half speech, half song.... But the vocal means that are at her command she controls with a virtuosity that is amazing. No instrumentalist, no prima donna phrases with more exquisite taste.
>
> "Incomparably, the most astounding feature of her artistic equipment, however, is her face. It expresses every thought, every shade of thought. A more mobile countenance I have encountered but once upon the stage... the face of Duse.
>
> "...during the last ten years two artists have over-thrown all the schools, the traditions and the methods that had gone before. Duse created a new tragic style, and Yvette Guilbert—well, will it be possible to listen to the smirking, prancing, painted, short skirted dolls after hearing her?...
>
> "It was a memorable evening. No one will forget it."

If any final seal of critical approval was needed it came eventually from the *Evening Sun*, which was to admit that art is art whether found in the Metropolitan Opera House or in a music hall, agreeing that "It is no longer possible to argue the question of Yvette Guilbert's supremacy in her line, any more than that of Calve and Duse in theirs. What these geniuses are to the operatic and dramatic stage, Guilbert is to the music hall."

What Hammerstein found so satisfying was not the mere fact that the S.R.O. sign was out at each performance of Yvette Guilbert. It was that all sorts of distinguished people from the realms of society, the arts and professions, many of whom had probably never set foot in a music hall, were present nightly to hear the great new artist.

There was a standing rule at the box office that no money for tickets was to be accepted from theatrical celebrities; they were to be given the courtesy of guest status in Hammerstein's own box. Apparently, this rule applied impartially to all such celebrities who were beautiful women. On Wednesday, the third night of the Guilbert engagement, sitting beside a beaming Hammerstein was a woman of a peculiarly serene and radiant loveliness, and there was much turning of heads and craning of necks as word spread that Ellen Terry was in the house.

A few nights later a world-renowned celebrity caused an even greater stir. Although this personage, being a mere male, had to procure his own box, no one could fail to recognize the leonine face and might mane of Ignacy Jan Paderewski, the most idolized of living virtuoso pianists, a great artist and a great personality who would one day crown his fame by becoming the first prime minister of his country. Paderewski caused a flutter in two audiences, for after hearing the star of the Music Hall he went over to the theater in time to witness the hilarious burlesque of himself by Arthur Dunn in *Excelsior, Jr.*

Everybody who was somebody of distinction, it seemed, came to visit the star in her dressing room after her night's performance. The chanteuse was always pleased to meet those who were European; the Americans she tolerated, for she considered them, with few exceptions, uncomprehending bores.

One of the exceptions was a young man, slim, well-groomed, who had sent her some magnificent American Beauties and asked her if she was not disappointed in her American audiences. "On the contrary," she replied, "I see that although they don't understand my art, they applaud enthusiastically."

"How can you expect them to understand Montmartre?" he said to her. "It is your personality that they applaud." She thought him charming and perceptive. She did not know until later that, young as he was, he was the millionaire owner of a newspaper and already becoming a great power in New York journalism. At the time, the name on his card—William Randolph Hearst—meant nothing to her.

And it was a perceptive remark. One of the most discerning and sensitive of critics, Carl Van Vechten, thought that Guilbert's songs were really only of secondary importance because she re-created them entirely with her own personality, and once said: "Sometimes, indeed, it seemed that the genius of this remarkable Frenchwoman could express itself directly, without depending upon songs."

The first week of the Guilbert engagement (the fourth of Olympia itself) came to a triumphant conclusion Sunday evening at the fourth Scheel concert with the sensational chanteuse as the star soloist before a packed house. For Guilbert's second week Hammerstein continued substantially the same bill with a few changes affecting the star. Her appearance on the program was set back from 9:30 to 10:30 p.m. In part this was an act of mercy to spare a few more of the acts from the impossible position of going on after the star. And since many of the audience only came to hear Guilbert, it was also a shrewd move to increase the sale of liquid refreshments by way of easing their impatient anticipation.

Guilbert's own program was changed by the introduction of several new songs, "Les Vierges," one of her "shockers," "La Morphinee," a tragic tale of a drug-addict, and a love song, "Par Un Clair de Lune." As a special concession she also added a song in English, the well-known, "Her Golden Hair Was Hanging Down Her Back," with the familiar line about that "naughty little twinkle in her eye." What she did with that line was a revelation.

It brought down the house. The triumphal progress of Hammerstein's star continued unabated. All through the week every performance was sold out—seven performances plus the Sunday concert.

At Koster and Bial's, Bial had prepared an unusually strong bill that week in an attempt to counter the great attraction at Olympia. In addition to a program of high-quality acts that still included the remarkable Segommer, he had added a star feature that cost him $1,000 a week—the reappearance after five years of the Paul Martinetti Pantomime Troupe.

This was an event of artistic distinction, for Martinetti was the greatest living pantomimist, he and his company masters of a great and subtle art ranging from farce to tragedy. When he played at the Folies Bergeres in Paris, the actors of the Comédie Française, including the great Benoît-Constant Coquelin[1] himself, came eagerly to admire and to learn. For their opening program on Thirty-Fourth Street the company gave their hilarious farce, "A Terrible Night." But although the return of these important artists should have been a major event, it drew poorly against the over-shadowing attraction at the rival house. Bial realized again he would have to do much better to match Hammerstein's sensations. He made no secret of his stubborn determination to keep trying until he succeeded even if it ruined him or killed him. And eventually he was to succeed and in the end it would do both to him.

Despite the new and spectacular prominence of music hall and vaudeville in the public attention, this was still but a small segment of the New York theater world. In that larger segment known as the "legitimate theatre" it was a week of rich activity—renowned artists in new productions, debuts of distinguished performers, and appearances of young performers of future renown.

Most important of the week's events was the debut of the celebrated English comedian, John Hare, in the first American performance of Pinero's "The Notorious Mrs. Ebbsmith," in which a minor part was played by young C. Aubrey Smith, now at the beginning of his long stage and screen career.

At Abbey's Theatre, Sir Henry Irving had just given one of his young actresses, the future Dame May Whitty, the opportunity to play his feminine lead in *Don Quixote*. Now, he and Ellen Terry were presenting *Charles I*, in which the tiny part of a page was taken by another of his talented fledglings, young Martin Harvey, who would one day appear in New York at the head of his own company as the distinguished Sir Martin Harvey.

At the Garden, talented Marie Dressler was appearing in a musical travesty called "A Stag Party" and giving further evidence of developing into one of the most entertaining young comediennes before the public.

But if anyone had thought the Guilbert furor would exhaust the public's capacity for sensations he would have been quite mistaken. For, at the Empire, another sensation was provided by the young woman who had so recently burst like a skyrocket over the legitimate stage and who, that week, provided New York with another display of pyrotechnics. This was Olga Nethersole's performance in a new adaptation of Merimee's *Carmen*, and at her first night she demonstrated that the jingle about "Little Olga" whose "plays are so warm" did not begin to do her justice. This one was not warm; it was sizzling.

New York was not unfamiliar with sultry Carmens—there was Calve's voluptuous portrayal in the operatic version—but it had never seen anything so torrid as this. One critic wrote that in depicting the depravity of Merimee's heroine and her passion for her various lovers, she "gave an exposition of female sensualism which on a stage less respectable than the Empire's might have exposed it to the wrath of Dr. Parkhurst." Such passionate lovemaking, such fiery kissing; not in the history of the city had an audience seen osculation of such depth, intensity, temperature and duration. Another reviewer calculated that had each kiss been shortened to ordinary length the performance would have finished a half hour earlier. In his editorials, Harrison Grey Fiske warned that the frankness of Guilbert's songs had opened the footages to scandalous animal eroticism on the stage, in the newsprints Olga Nethersole's name closely crowded that of Yvette Guilbert, and at the Empire as at the Olympia the nightly legend appeared—"Standing Room Only."

At the end of the week Hammerstein himself made two public appearances, though not on the stage—one as a defendant in police court, one as an author in print. On Saturday he was summoned to court on a charge of violation of the law prohibiting the sale of liquor in any place giving a theatrical performance other than a purely vocal or instrumental concert. Police detectives, probably at the instigation of some legitimate managers fearful of the growing popularity of the music halls, had suddenly decided to enforce a law long a dead letter.

Hammerstein was not without company, for Bial, George Kraus of the Imperial and other managers of halls operating under a concert license had also received summonses. The lord of Olympia, acting as his own counsel, pleaded not guilty and demanded a hearing, as did lawyers for the other managers in several courts. Luckily, none of the cases came before Magistrate Mott, the irascible old curmudgeon who ran his court like the Queen's in "Alice in Wonderland," finding every defendant guilty and venting his spleen impartially on police, lawyers and court attaches. The other magistrates, finding the District Attorney not pressing for conviction, and reluctant to enforce a moribund statute, finally dismissed all the cases. It was only a temporary flurry, but it revealed a potentially recurrent threat and it was a portent of trouble ahead.

On Sunday, the *New York World* had a special feature in its section devoted to the arts. It published a group of signed articles surveying various fields of artistic activity, each written by a leading authority in the field. There was an article on American Painting by the distinguished artist, William Chase, "The English Stage," by John Hare, "The American Play of the Future," by producer Charles Frohman, "Dramatic Authorship," by playwright Bronson Howard, "Public Taste in Plays," by Olga Nethersole, "Modern Stage Ideals," by Henry Miller, and "Music Halls in America," by Oscar Hammerstein, now unquestionably the greatest recognized authority on the subject of vaudeville.

It was Hammerstein's first appearance in print since the days of his editorials in his own journal and his first signed article in any journal of general public circulation. During the next twenty years there would be many others, not counting innumerable lengthy verbatim interviews which were actually articles given by dictation.

Clearly and concisely he traced the history of the amazing rise of vaudeville from its disreputable and degraded past. "In those days," he wrote, "vaudeville or variety had no permanent home, and the only opportunity it had to present itself was during the act-pauses of a tragedy or melodrama at the old Bowery theatres, when the specialty performer was introduced to fill in the long waits and quiet the impatient demonstrations of the gallery gods. What a contrast to the palatial amusement temples now devoted exclusively to vaudeville and its accompaniments.

"The music hall of today has eliminated all the vulgarism formerly associated with the old time variety theatre. (It) has brought a dignity to its performer equal to that enjoyed by those who follow the legitimate, and to many it has added great fame and fortune. Yvette Guilbert, the most interesting and talented music hall artist now before the public, whose recent debut in America was a great a stage sensation as that of Jenny Lind, derives a revenue from the music hall equal to the combined salaries of the President of the United States and his entire Cabinet."

He then went on to analyze the two chief functions of the vaudeville stage:

"The mission of the music hall is to provide a panorama of varied stage features which will fascinate the eye, ear and mind, and not strain the emotions too severely. Its mission is to amuse and entertain rather than to educate or instruct. It appeals most strongly to the busy and hard-worked brain in need of relaxation and diversion from the cares of business.... In addition, the music hall affords a social comfort to its patrons such as is not found in any other place of amusement" (referring to the facilities for lounging and refreshment).

"The mission of the music hall and vaudeville stage is not only to entertain the public, but it is the primary school for many performers who aim for higher roles in comedy, opera or drama. Some of the greatest stars of the stage of today owe their positions to their early training in vaudeville..."

It is doubtful if Hammerstein's statement of 1895 has ever been improved upon. Sixty years later it would still hold true, with due allowance for changes of outward form, whereby the entertainment features would persist through the media of the continuous vaudeville theater and eventually in radio and television, while the entertainment plus "social comfort" features would be continued successively in the cabaret and night club.

At the Olympia the third triumphal week of Guilbert opened with no sign of diminishing interest. But on its second night all records were broken. For Tuesday night was New Year's Eve, and, as though all of gay New York had decided that Olympia was the logical place to celebrate the old year's passing, fashionably dressed people packed themselves into every one of the three auditoriums until the walls fairly bulged. Revelry was the order of the evening in every box of the music hall and there was a special air of exuberance in the enthusiastic applause that greeted the performers. As the night wore on more and more people from both theaters wormed their way into the concert hall for convivial refreshment.

Just before midnight Hammerstein slipped into the gallery of the concert hall and seated himself quietly at a table to watch the gayety of the throng. Their happiness seemed to match his own expansive mood. He had good reason to be joyful at the end of this year, the most climactic year of his life so far, his greatest dream, Olympia, successfully launched, already established as one of the city's unique institutions, its first great star an unprecedented artistic and box office success.

He could pride himself in the acknowledged fact that no one had ever spread before New York such a bounteous feast of entertainment, when now, for an admission of fifty cents, it was possible to watch a hit musical show with the inimitable Fay Templeton and a brilliant cast and then look in on some superb vaudeville acts topped off by the songs of the great Yvette Guilbert. Already he had raised the level of American music hall entertainment to an undreamed of height by presenting the founder of a new art form—the art of the chanteuse-diseuse—who was to remain its greatest exponent, towering in artistic stature over the whole long line of her successors from the most talented to the lesser lights, from the Raquel Mellers and Maria Tubaus to the Edith Piaffs.

Hammerstein had also another cause for private satisfaction. He had just completed complicated negotiations for a large-scale refinancing of Olympia. In a few weeks the documents would be signed whereby the New York Life Insurance Company would give him a three-year mortgage of $900,000 at four and a half per cent. Part of this would be used to retire the existing mortgage of $225,000 and to repay other building loans, and the rest to complete the structure, especially the large theater on the roof. Olympia would be clear of all indebtedness save the single mortgage.

At the stroke of midnight, all the lights in the Concert Hall were darkened for one minute. When they were turned on again and the revelry was at its height, the creator of Olympia was spied sitting in the gallery. There was a spontaneous outburst of applause, then someone proposed three cheers for Hammerstein. The crowd took it up with a will and the hall resounded with enthusiastic cheers to which Hammerstein responded with a smile and bow.

But the crowd would not let him return to his seat. Now the hall rang with cries of "Speech! Speech!" Still smiling happily, Hammerstein advanced to the gallery rail and made a speech, certainly the shortest speech he ever made, and probably the most popular. He did not even address it to the crowd. He looked around until his eye caught the head waiter. To him he addressed his speech. "Head waiter," he said. "Give every gentleman in the place a quart bottle of champagne, with my compliments."

No piece of oratory every evoked greater acclaim than that eloquent sentence. Someone called out, asking if the host's generosity included any brand of champagne. "Any brand you like," answered Hammerstein, "except one—we don't serve Moet and Chandon here." There was general laughter. Everyone knew that was George Kessler's brand and it was already a Broadway legend that Hammerstein's celebrated fight, arrest, and rupture with Koster and Bial that night fifteen months ago had set in motion the train of events that culminated in Olympia.

But they did not know the full dream of Olympia that what they applauded Hammerstein for was but a partial realization, and as he received their tribute he must have smiled to himself with the thought of the much greater vision he would some day unfold to them.

To only a very few had he ever intimated the full extent of his dream of Olympia. The critic, Hillary Bell, was one of those who knew that Hammerstein had set his sights upon a higher aim than the establishment of the greatest music hall in the world. Raising the artistic standards of vaudeville was not his ultimate goal—indeed, vaudeville was for him not an end in itself but a means to a greater end.

Often his friends heard Hammerstein say that once Olympia was completed he would never build another theater; he would not need to, he would have the facilities for every type of theatrical production. They did not always grasp his meaning—that his goal was nothing less than a temple of all the theater arts, devoted to the highest form a every type of stage presentation.

For the theater part of Olympia he planned greater things than *Excelsior, Jr.*, fine as that was of its type. He would continue to have burlesques and comic opera in the spring and fall, but for the winter seasons he would have the finest achievements of the dramatic stage from comedy to tragedy, classic and modern. There would be Shakespeare and Sheridan and Ibsen, not only the Fay Templetons or Francis Wilsons but the Mansfields, Irvings, Terrys, and he would have Bernhardt and Duse too.

The concert hall would remain a concert hall but on a higher level, reserved exclusively for vocal and instrumental recitals and concerts of chamber music. The tables and refreshments would be banished to the cafe and lounge below.

The great music hall, however, would cease to be a music hall. Here in spring and fall there would be spectacular musical extravaganzas, operettas and ballets, but the winter season would be devoted to grand opera. Hammerstein had not forgotten the failure of his venture at the Manhattan Opera House, and this defeat, too, he was determined to turn into final victory. Eventually, however, he might even challenge the great Metropolitan Opera House itself with grand opera on a truly grand and lavish scale. He would have de Reszkes, Melbas and Calves to grace his stage. He had had that in mind when he built those 132 boxes. One day the society aristocrats of the Metropolitan might be sitting in them.

And what of the music hall and variety entertainment? That would be transferred to the huge theater on the roof. Here he would continue to present the best in vaudeville, the greatest variety artists obtainable, and in the basement of Olympia there would be even more popular forms of amusement.

The beauty of the vision was not merely in that it encompassed all the arts of the stage but that the different theater arts would balance each other financially as well as artistically. The serious drama, music and opera would occasionally show a profit, sometimes they would merely break even, and at times they would lose money. He knew well how heavy the losses could be. He had learned, also, from his experience with Koster and Bial how enormously profitable a music hall and vaudeville could be. Whatever the box office fluctuations of the drama and opera, they would be supported by the more popular arts and entertainments going on above and below. To Hammerstein's mind, the fascination of vaudeville was that not only was it a splendid and popular entertainment in its own right and on its own level but that he saw it could be used to serve and support art forms on a higher level.

This was the dream in all its completeness, the great dream of Olympia that Hammerstein did not reveal to the public. For he knew that first things must come first. Before Olympia could become a temple dedicated to the theatrical arts, the huge costs of the structure must first be paid off and one theatrical art alone was capable of doing this rapidly—vaudeville. For that reason the music hall and lighter entertainment would have to be the principal feature of Olympia for a time.

He had now consolidated all the indebtedness on the structure in one large mortgage. In a few years, perhaps in three years, if all went well, that $900,000 debt would be cut down to manageable size. Then, with a long-term refinancing, Olympia would be ready to march to its greater and nobler destiny. Hammerstein was only at the beginning of the realization of his vision. To make a dream of such scope and magnitude come true, this was for him a worthy life goal to strive for. And here, at the year's end, with his Olympia but five weeks old, he was already on his way.

10

The War of the Music Halls

The first Sunday of the new year of 1896 enabled Hammerstein to mark up another victory in the war of the great music halls. That evening the sixth School Concert, with Yvette Guilbert as soloist, played to a house packed to the doors. At Koster and Bial's, however, there was no rival concert that evening. After piling up uninterrupted deficits, Bial had conceded failure and abandoned the Sunday series conducted by Kerker, who promptly brought suit against Bial for the balance of his contract. Scheel had carried off the musical honors and Hammerstein had won the battle of the Sunday orchestral concerts.

Monday night at the Olympia Music Hall, Guilbert began her fourth triumphant week before a capacity audience which included a box party headed by Chauncey M. Depew, New York's most celebrated railroad magnate and after-dinner speaker. And the same night at the Olympia Theatre saw the fiftieth performance of *Excelsior, Jr.*, duly celebrated by the management with pretty souvenir clocks distributed to all the ladies in the audience.

The phenomenal success of Hammerstein's enterprise was fully reflected in the advertisements of Olympia which carried such boastful statements as "The most successful and popular amusement temple on the face of the earth," "Embodies the most original and attractive amusement scheme ever conceived," and, "To be in New York and not to visit Olympia is like a journey to France without seeing Paris."

If Hammerstein did not believe in hiding his light under a bushel, neither did he have any reason to doubt the accuracy of these phrases. Compared to the extravagant praises of Olympia and its creator in the news columns they were almost understatements. Olympia had become the city's greatest attraction for out-of-town visitors and Hammerstein was combining civic pride with self interest when, in this election year, he contributed $500 to the fund raised to bring the Democratic Convention to New York—in vain, as it turned out, the prize going to Chicago.

It was not enough for Hammerstein to have conceived and built Olympia and to manage its colossal operations down to the supervision of the last detail, all the while still supervising his Harlem theaters. It was not creative enough merely to secure and present varied attractions; he could be satisfied only if he himself personally created at least some of Olympia's productions. When Olympia would present a show written and composed by Oscar Hammerstein, only then could he feel that Olympia was fully his own. Although the strenuous period of Olympia's completion he had found relaxation in composing music, much of which he had discarded as not good enough to be heard. Now he was seriously at work on *Marguerite*, a ballet-opera which he intended to produce under his own direction in the near future.

Every moment that could be spared from the myriad financial and executive details of running his vast enterprise found Hammerstein in his second-floor office immersed in composition. At times he alternated so rapidly between managerial and musical labors that he seemed to be doing both at the same time. Once, one of his sons—at least three of them were on the Olympia staff—came into his office to find him writing at his desk. Before him were two piles of paper, one a heap of bills and financial statements, the other a pile of music paper.

"Go away and don't bother me now," said Hammerstein, pointing to the two piles. "I'm busy writing notes—some to be paid and some to replayed, and I hope none of them will be protested."

Against Hammerstein's resounding successes, Bial had been feverishly preparing some weight counterblows. The rival house on Thirty-Fourth Street already could boast of the reappearance of Cinquevalli, King of Jugglers, still unquestionably the world's greatest in his line, but Bial had an announcement of greater interest to follow. Since Hammerstein had secured the greatest music hall singer of France and the greatest living artist of this kind, Bial was countering by engaging the artist who was England's greatest music hall singer and undoubtedly the world's second greatest of the kind.

This singer was the celebrated Albert Chevalier. Little was known of him here except that, like Guilbert, his star had risen in the last few years and he was the idol of the London music hall stage. Like the Frenchwoman, he combined the talents of actor, singer and pantomimist, and, like her, his songs had a special subject, portraying the life of a distinctive type of London Cockney—the costermonger—a type with its own customs, philosophy, slang, and even costume, including an addiction to innumerable pearl buttons.

Like Hammerstein, Bial was taking the gamble that such an unfamiliar and specialized subject matter would find acceptance in New York, although, in a way, Guilbert had blazed a trail for the appreciation of exotic character type portrayals in song. Chevalier's salary was announced as $3,000 a week for a four-week engagement, although the actual figure was closer to $1,200. He would arrive in March, giving two months to prepare an extensive build-up. Bial had not failed to profit from observing Hammerstein's methods of promoting Yvette Guilbert.

Meanwhile, the engagement of the great chanteuse, which had been extended into part of another week, reached its final triumphant climax on the night of January 15. The audience, crowding the huge hall from pit to dome, was loath to let her depart. Each time the orchestra attempted to proceed with the next act the singer was called out for yet another curtain call and more floral tributes. Finally, she scattered flowers over the front rows and said simply: "I weesh I knew enough English to tell you how grateful I am."

The most sensationally successful and talked-about engagement of any singer in New York since P.T. Barnum's presentation of Jenny Lind had come to a close. In her dressing room the star was in expansive mood.

"I have liked this engagement very much," she told the newsmen. "Good theatre, good journalists, good public. The manager a great man—Oscar Hammerstein, but why is he not here? He make his Marguerite; eh? His music, is it good?"

But the reporters, by this time, were quite familiar with her less genial moods and had already acquainted the public with the great artist's equally great talent in the art of malicious repartee. That very week New York had been enlivened by two demonstrations of how sharp the singer's tongue could be in demolishing an adversary.

The two women who were the hapless victims of her malice—not unprovoked, to be sure—were no ordinary women but adversaries worthy of her mettle. One was no less a person than one of the two greatest living actresses, the other, one of the two greatest of living prima donnas.

To the question, who was the greatest living actress, only two answers were possible. Those who were converts to be the new dramatic style of inner emotional expression awarded the palm to Duse. But to those, and they were still the majority, who remained faithful to the older persuasion of dramatic acting in the grand manner, there was only one answer—the one and only Sarah Bernhardt, the incomparable, the divine Sarah.

When Henry E. Abbey introduced Bernhardt to the United States in 1880, she had taken the country by storm, put a clear profit of $100,000 into his pocket and catapulted him to the heights of managerial greatness. Since then each American tour of the great French actress had been highly profitable to her, to her manager, and to the public. And now, this week, she had arrived, bringing her own company for another tour to begin with a repertory season in New York.

One reporter managed to get an interview and fired questions at her while she was still in the midst of all the details of unpacking. Among other things, he wanted her comment on the phenomenal New York success of her compatriot, the great French singer, Guilbert.

"Don't know the name," was the curt reply.

"But," the not too bright newsman persisted, "we've been told she's a great celebrity in Paris and are paying her $4,000 a week."

"$4,000 a week for a singer!" exclaimed the divine Sarah. Then, shrugging off this preposterous nonsense:

"Never heard of her," she snapped.

"Good heavens!" said the reporter. "Then we have been taken in by an imposter and she's really a nobody." And he was off with a sensational scoop for his paper.

When the story broke Guilbert was in a fury. By the time the "boys" from every paper in the city were storming her door for a statement she had composed herself. She had also armed herself with some precious mementos she carried with her in her trunk. Only a few weeks before leaving Paris, she told them, she had been a guest in Sarah Bernhardt's home. She showed them the actress's gift to her, her own fan with an inscription and a signed note in Bernhardt's own hand expressing her admiration for the art of her distinguished guest.

But how then, the reporters asked, did she account for the great lady's amazing statement. It was then that Guilbert gave them her saddest, sweetest smile and unleashed her sharpest claws.

"It is very sad, about Mme. Bernhardt," she signed. "This poor lady, who at 55 has already lost her youth, is now beginning to lose her memory as well."

In a second a roomful of newsmen were out the door with a whoop and a scoop, and next morning New York was gayer at the expense of the great Bernhardt.

As for that lady's strange behavior, it might have been due to lapse of memory, or, possibly, harried by an inconvenient interviewer and confused by his pronunciation of "Guilbert," she might not have recognized the name. But no one ever convinced Yvette Guilbert it was not a simple case of mean and petty jealousy.

This diverting incident as but a piece of by-play in a much more regaling imbroglio that in the same week added even more substantially to the gaiety of the metropolis.

One of the established and popular traditions at the Metropolitan Opera House was the institution of the Sunday evening concert. It was kind of weekly gala performance, both an artistic and social occasion. Various stars appeared on the stage and those not performing were usually present in the boxes. Occasionally, a guest star performed, usually a distinguished instrumental virtuoso.

Maurice Grau conceived the notion that it would be a novel and effective attraction to have the great French chanteuse appear as guest artist. He offered Yvette Guilbert an engagement for the concert of January 19 which the music hall singer accepted with pleasure. What more fitting climax to her New York success than to crown it with a guest appearance at the Metropolitan Opera House. Grau had prepared a program including some of the Metropolitan's brightest luminaries—Melba, Nordica, Plançon and the two de Reszkes.

Led by Mmme. Melba, they drew themselves up in aristocratic hauteur. They refused to lower their artistic and social dignity by appearing on the same program with a mere music hall singer. They told Grau that if Guilbert appeared they would withdraw. Guilbert, however, made it clear that, having been engaged, she had no intention of withdrawing. With the great prima donna and the great chanteuse thus locking horns, Grau was neatly impaled and it looked as though there would be no Metropolitan concert on the 19th.

It was Guilbert who extricated the impresario from the horns of his dilemma. She offered to take over the entire program with the help of a company of assisting artists, which Ted Marks, as her manager, would engage for her. Grau accepted the offer, and so, for the first time in its history, the Metropolitan presented a non-operatic guest artist and supporting company in what was the farewell appearance in New York of a music hall chanteuse.

The Metropolitan artists, from their point of view, had every reason for maintaining a position of dignified hauteur and cold disdain. Not only did they belong to the top aristocracy of singing artists out they moved in the most exclusive social circles.

Melba herself had an especially exalted position. She was the ranking prima donna at the Metropolitan, and, except for Calve, its highest paid star. At Covent Garden in London she now reigned supreme. For more than a generation "the divine Patti" had been universally regarded as the world's greatest singer. But Patti was now past her prime and already beginning those "farewell" tours that would continue for years and increasingly Melba was being hailed as the greatest of living prima donnas.

She was at home in the exclusive drawing rooms of the English aristocracy and basked in the favor of British royalty. Nor was her position less exalted on the continent. A member of the French royal family was her devoted admirer and so

Australian soprano Nellie Melba (1861–1931), autographed publicity image, ca. mid–1880s.

marked were his attentions that there had been much speculation recently that his interest was more personal than artistic—a tidbit of international gossip much relished in the newsprints on both sides of the Atlantic.

All through the week the concert controversy was aired in interviews and commentaries. Pronouncements were coming from both sides, with the Metropolitan striving to maintain a dignified neutrality. One statement on behalf of Melba and her colleagues read: "Mlle. Guilbert is a charming woman—an artist if you will—but the boards of the Opera House are not her proper place. She is a music hall singer and no matter how artistic her work her place is not among our great singers."

Guilbert's statements were less restrained. Her hackles were up. During her final evenings at the Olympia the reporters practically camped in her dressing room. To one she said vehemently: "I put on no airs but I have my place as high up as theirs.... I meet these people in the hotel and they pinch my arm and say, 'Bon jour, ma petite Yvette,' but in the salon... they pull down the face and say, 'Ah, here comes that music hall singer, we must not know her.' Bah! It is disgusting!... They are all so jealous.... But I do not care for them.... I will sing on the stage with any of them and let them choose their own place. Yvette fears none of them."

To another she said: "If Melba wanted to sing here for Hammerstein I would say yes. I would not object to sing on the same stage with her; we are both artists. But I will sing at the Metropolitan... with my own company and we will make a success and I will give all the money to charity."

Sunday night the Metropolitan Opera House was well filled, though not sold out. In addition to assisting vocalists, Marks had engaged Gilmore's famous 22nd Regiment Band, now conducted by that brilliant musician, Victor Herbert. The vocalists, according to the *Herald*, were fearfully and wonderfully bad but Herbert and his band made a great hit, even if a military band seemed incongruous in the opera house. Guilbert herself was enthusiastically applauded even though she was not at her best. The vast spaces and good but difficult acoustics of the Metropolitan made it necessary for her to force her voice and exaggerate her facial expressions so that much of the subtlety of her art was lost.

But the occasion was a personal victory. She had appeared as the star soloist of a Sunday concert on the stage of the Metropolitan Opera House. The reporters were there, backstage, to witness her triumph and she was sharpening her tongue for a final thrust She got her chance when they asked if she was now still resentful of Melba.

"Of course not," she said. "I quite understand her position. I am only a Frenchwoman of humble birth, a mere commoner, while everyone knows that Mmme. Melba *belongs* to the Royal Family of France!"

Melba and the other Metropolitan stars had maintained their position of aristocratic hauteur to the end, pointedly absenting themselves from attendance at the concert. Only one Metropolitan star had as pointedly dissociated herself from her colleagues. Not only was she present but she went backstage. There, before the admiring assemblage of newsmen, the great Calve embraced the music hall singer.

The reporters described it as an affectionate kiss for a sister in art. It may have been that. Perhaps it was merely that the chanteuse was a fellow Frenchwoman and blood is thicker than hauteur. And, then again, it may have been not so much that Calve loved Guilbert the more but only that she loved Melba the less.

11

"Stop Hammerstein!"

Olympia's first great star having come and gone, Hammerstein proceeded to maintain the high level of variety entertainment by preparing for the week of January 20 a huge bill of fifteen acts, all top-flight performers in their line. Except for a few holdovers the acts were new and most of the artists making their first appearance in New York.

The superb bill was a veritable cross-section of the finest vaudeville talent obtainable in the world. There was Watt, the change artist, who, one critic said, "did the most remarkable quick change act ever seen here," and there was Urdohl, the international female impersonator, and Hertz, the magician and illusionist.

Particularly successful was the debut of the London music hall favorite, Fanny Wentworth, who did a sophisticated musical monologue at the piano. Her act included clever imitations of French and German singers, interspersed with amusing remarks, and her arrangements of "Her Golden Hair Was Hanging Down Her Back" in the styles of Mendelssohn, Mozart, Gounod, Chopin and Liszt. It was a type of clever entertainment combining wit and humor with musical versatility, and those performers who could master this combination have always been in the front rank of entertainers for sophisticated audiences, from Fanny Wentworth down to Alec Templeton or Victor Borge.

But the sensation of the program was the Spanish beauty, Virginia Aragon, with her dark, lustrous eyes and stunning figure, who, perched upon the high wire, "performed astonishing feats with the greatest ease and apparent absence of effort." Upon the almost invisible thread of wire she poised on one foot, jumped, waltzed, and did tricks with a hoop, sometimes with a tiny Japanese parasol for balances, at other times with only her shapely arms to steady herself Finally, with infinite ease and grace she executed the maneuver which many acrobatic dancers find difficult upon the solid boards—she nonchalantly did a "split" and brought down the house. There was no question that this newcomer was the queen of the high wire and many critics thought her the world's finest single wire performer bar none.

To a reporter who interviewed the lady after her phenomenally successful American debut she displayed her proudest possession, a large autographed photograph of Oscar Hammerstein inscribed, "To Virginia Aragon, the finest and most charming artiste who has so far appeared at Olympia." She could not know how many other artistes already were or would be proud possessors of an identical inscription. And yet, Hammerstein was probably entirely sincere whenever he penned such sentiments, especially when the recipient was a beautiful woman.

The printed programs of the Olympia Music Hall with their gay colored lithographs on the cover have become rare theatrical playbill items. One of the few, perhaps the only copy surviving, happens to be for the week of January 20. Besides listing the bill and the arrangement of the hall with its five tiers, the program had become a profitable source of advertising revenue and the various advertisements afford a glimpse of some of the pleasures and amusements appealing to sophisticates of the Gay Nineties.

The theatrical advertisers included McBride's Theatre Ticket Office and, of course, Hammerstein himself, who used his playbill to advertise all his own theaters, calling attention to his Olympia Theatre next door, with *Excelsior, Jr.* in its third month, to his Harlem Opera House, where this week he was presenting Olga Nethersole in *Carmen*, direct from its sensational Broadway run, and to the appearance at his Columbus Theatre of "primrose and West's Minstrel Show," the most famous of the remaining great companies carrying on the tradition of black-face minstrelsy. The reader was also informed that a new opera and ballet, "Marguerite," words and music by Oscar Hammerstein, was in preparation, to be produced at an early date under the personal direction of the composer.

Fine food, drink and clothing were, as ever, prominent interests of Hammerstein's patrons. The advertising included Brill Brothers' men's clothing, Huyler's candies, Maillard's chocolates, and, interestingly, Moet and Chandon White Seal Champagne. Evidently, although Hammerstein refused to serve Kessler's brand of champagne, he saw no reason to refuse his money to advertise it.

The advertisements left no doubt as to the favorite outdoor sport currently the rage among New York's sophisticates. No less than five bicycle manufacturers, including Spalding Bros., extolled the virtues of their makes. B. Altman and Co. advertised the latest Cycle Suit, "an ideal ladies' dress for wheeling, combining style and utility, with a graceful and genteel appearance," and announced a new patented bicycle muff, which would simultaneously keep milady's hands warm, in fashion, and in control of the wheel.

Yet the most interesting advertisement of all was for a new deice and service that in two decades would become more fashionable, more useful and more ubiquitous than even the bicycle. "An appearance through a trap," it read, "is always a startling effect on the stage. Telephone service gives you a trap door into 13,500 establishments in New York. Rates from $75 a year. Metropolitan Telephone and Telegraph Co."

The night that Hammerstein presented his new music hall bill was also the night on which the New York legitimate stage unfolded one of its supreme glories. Sarah Bernhardt opened her repertory season at Abbey's Theatre with a French verse drama, *Izeyl*, to be followed by such dramatic warhorses as *Adrienne Lecouvreur*, Ssardou's *Gismonds*, *Fedora*, and Dumas' perennial *La Dame Aux Camelias*.

But vaudeville was also scoring some triumphs at the expense of the legitimate theater with the announcement that two well-known actors, Mr. and Mrs. Sydney Drew, would go into vaudeville and appear at Keith's in a comedy sketch. And, as further evidence of growing trends, Tony Pastor's cozy house on 14th Street, the little theater in which Neuendorff and Hammerstein had once presented German performances, converted to continuous vaudeville, after the Proctor and Keith pattern.

At Koster and Bial's, there was no new bill on the stage to match Hammerstein's but there was feverish activity in the front offices. Bial had become a dedicated man, his own life and the resources of his organization bent to one single-minded aim—"Stop Hammerstein! At all costs!" His agents abroad had instructions to sign up every performer Hammerstein might possibly want and to secure every celebrity by topping any offer Hammerstein might possibly make.

Already Bial had secured Albert Chevalier, a London celebrity, but this was only a beginning. Hammerstein had scored a sensational triumph with a female celebrity from Paris. Therefore, Bial was determined to have stars who were celebrated Parisiennes.

Apart from the stars of the legitimate stage, Paris now had four sensational female celebrities. Greatest in fame and artistic stature was Guilbert. The other three were dancers. Second in artistic stature was Loie Fuller. She was, of course, an American and it must have made Bial wince to recall that it was in Hammerstein's theater that she was first introduced to New York, where her serpentine dance became enormously popular. But it was Paris that hailed her as a great artist, made her a reigning star of the music halls and took her to its bosom as La Loie. And in Paris she had developed her peculiar art further into sensational elaborations of drapery movements and lighting effects that were practically a new art form. If she could be brought back it would be as a Parisian celebrity practicing a new technique New York had never seen.

The third celebrity stood lower on the artistic scale. She was the Spanish dancer and beauty, La Belle Otero. Unfortunately, she too had already appeared in New York some years back, indeed at the very time of Carmencita's sensational engagement at the old Koster and Bial's on Twenty-Third Street. Consequently, no one had paid any attention to the voluptuous Spanish woman whose dancing, while it had less grace and abandon than Carmencita's, was probably more authentic. Since then Otero had come a celebrity, not solely through her dancing, although she was recognized as a first-rate Spanish dancer. She had become one of the most famous and most notorious of the grand courtesans of Paris. One of that city's sights was Otero, riding daily in the Bois in an open carriage, bedecked with fabulous jewels exhibited like trophies, even as the military men flaunted their exploits in displaying their medals and decorations.

The fourth and latest celebrity was Cleo de Merode, in artistry the last, in publicity the first. She was not even a featured dancer, only a member of the corps de ballet at the Opera. But her demure and angelic beauty, the infatuation of a king, and a collection of jewels that already bid fair to soon outstrip Otero's made her the talk and the toast of the town.

These were the four female celebrities of Paris. Hammerstein had presented the first of them. Bial was determined to secure the remaining three. During the week of January 20 he made the proud announcement that he had engaged Loie Fuller for four weeks. She would appear next month, her engagement to precede that of the English star, Chevalier. With further lavish offers Bial was hopeful of eventually snaring Otero and Merode to make up the tally of three.

And Bial's hope went even further—if possible to present all four of the Parisiennes, including the great Guilbert. If Hammerstein had presented her first American appearance Bial could present her second. When the chanteuse had made her unprecedented success, Koster and Bial's had immediately begun to make her offers for next season and Hammerstein had promptly made that fact public. The result was considerable editorial denunciation of the low level of managerial ethic whereby a manager, after taking great risks, no sooner makes a success with a performer before another manager tries to entice the artist away. And there was satisfaction at Hammerstein's statement that his contract fully protected him against such low tactics.

The atmosphere had been frosty at the first meeting of Hammerstein with Guilbert. Later it had thawed. But when the chanteuse left for Paris it was positively glacial. The star was no longer on speaking terms with her manager, and all because of their contract.

By this document, Hammerstein had first call on Guilbert's services for the following season, provided he met any bona fide offer she received. Bial had continued to ply the singer with offers to a final bid later reported at the unprecedented figure of $4,800 a week (which actually must have been in the neighborhood of $4,000). Guilbert, whose distaste for this barbarous America was more than matched by a taste for the American dollars, claimed she notified Hammerstein of the offer but he made her no offer of his own, thus setting her free. Hammerstein, for his part, claimed she had failed to inform him according to the specifications of the contract. He threatened a lawsuit if she contracted elsewhere and she denounced him with vehemence.

It is scarcely possible to determine whose allegations were true, but even if Hammerstein's claim was correct it is apparent that this was a minor issue, nor is it difficult to see why. Hammerstein had obviously been doing some hard thinking. Guilbert had been a great financial as well as artistic success. Yet he was fully aware that more than her artistry was involved. She was also a celebrity and a complete novelty and upon this foundation he had been able to build the greatest publicity promotion since Barnum's puffing of Jenny Lind. Next season she would still be a supreme artist, but a novelty no longer. Art alone would not attract sold-out houses, only fair-sized audiences, and at Guilbert's further inflated salary fair-sized houses would mean large-sized deficits. Clearly then, the smart thing to do was to let Bial have the singer he had once thought not worth $100 a week. Let him have her for $4,000 a week and let him lose his shirt.

But there was the public relations aspect to be considered. Hammerstein did not wish to appear to have lost confidence in the artist he had introduced, nor would it do to appear as having supinely permitted his rival to carry off his star. Hence the legal issues of the contract must be raised. When Bial would announce his acquisition of the great chanteuse, Hammerstein would be ready to announce a lawsuit and be in the position of an aggrieved manager whose star has been underhandedly lured away from him. Guilbert herself could not be expected to understand these complex maneuverings. To her it was only the crude rapacity of American managers. She could never understand that though she might be one of the greatest of living artists, here she was only a pawn in a war between two music halls.

Meanwhile, Hammerstein was not idle in the search for celebrities. He had his sights upon a star of such exalted magnitude that she transcended the music hall and would require separate presentation. For next season, he was trying to entice Emma Calve away from Abbey and Grau at the Metropolitan Opera House, where she was now the top-paid singer at a reputed $1,500 a performance.

Hammerstein's proposal was a special engagement for fifty performances of *Carmen* with a specially organized company. Beginning with a limited number of performances at one of the theaters in the Olympia structure, the remainder of the engagement would take the form of a tour of the principal cities of the land where the fabulous Calve and her famous Carmen were only a legend. For these performances the manager had made Calve an offer never yet made to any singer save Patti—$2,400 a performance, or $120,000 for the engagement. It was a novel and daring plan and the French prima donna gave the break-taking offer serious consideration. But in the end she decided against it, evidently fearing to place her American operatic career in the hands of one she knew of only as the manager of a music hall.

Once before Hammerstein had failed to secure a great prima donna and had vowed that someday he would have her. Now, his second failure only doubled his resolve. The time would come, he promised himself, when both Melba and Calve would sing upon his stage.

But Hammerstein as not worrying over his failure to secure a great star for the next season; he was faced with greater worries over the current season, here and now. In the

Olympia Theatre, *Excelsior, Jr.* was still a smash hit, bringing in some $2,500 a week as Hammerstein's share, but there had been an alarming fall in receipts at the music all.

It was not that the new vaudeville bill inaugurated on January 20 was playing to empty seats; it was merely that capacity audiences had been reduced to good or moderate size. Yet so huge were the running expenses of Olympia that a good house meant no profit, a moderate house a loss. With its luxurious appointments and enormous staff, Olympia had to operate at or near capacity to stay on the profit side. The bills for heat, light and ventilation alone dwarfed the total costs of an ordinary theater.

At first Hammerstein could not understand what had happened. The vaudeville bill was first-rate, even stronger than the one which had opened the hall, yet the packed houses were no more. Then he began to comprehend. In making Olympia a place of unprecedented entertainment values, in seeking to raise music hall standards to new heights and to provide sensational artistic novelties he had succeeded too well. Now the public expected always to be dazzled and surprised. Anything that was first rate in a more conventional manner was a disappointment. He had created a demand he could not continuously supply.

At the beginning, the wonders of the great structure itself had been the sensation, then it had been the appearances of a sensationally new kind of performer, a great artist and personality who was the talk of New York. Now, for fifty cents general admission, New York evidently expected to find every week a Fay Templeton in the theater and a Yvette Guilbert in the music hall. A variety performance of merely top-notch international vaudeville artists no longer sufficed to fill the music hall. Hammerstein had spoiled his public!

One did not find new Yvette Guilberts every week. All over Europe Hammerstein had his agents looking for another sensation, for a performer who was absolutely without a peer in his or her line and whose line was itself a complete novelty, at least to New York. He would provide his public with another sensational novelty as soon as he could find one. In the meantime, he would have to solve the problem in the way he had always solved seemingly insuperable difficulties before. If no novel and sensational attraction existed for him to engage, he would have to create such an attraction himself. He was preparing an opera-ballet, *Marguerite*. Very well, he would have to make *Marguerite* so original, so novel and effective a show as to provide a sensational attraction. It was the kind of challenge to his own resourcefulness that he liked to meet.

Marguerite had been announced vaguely for production "at an early date." Now Hammerstein moved up the opening to February 10. Time was of the essence. He could not afford to run Olympia at a loss, what with Bial preparing to counterattack with celebrities like Loie Fuller and Albert Chevalier and with his own great plans for the future requiring money, a good deal of money. He gave himself three weeks to complete the book and score, engage his cast and whip the production into shape.

The first step was to engage his chorus. To Hammerstein, the chorus was the musical backbone of any show and he personally auditioned each applicant. Later, he laughingly told a reporter that he had not only spoiled the public, he had even spoiled New York's chorus girls Several applicants had assured him privately that although their voices were ten times better than Yvette Guilbert's, they would be willing to work for half her salary.

When his newly picked chorus of fifty voices arrived for the first rehearsal, Hammerstein suddenly remembered that although he had written much of the music for the soloists and for the ballets, he had not as yet written a single note for the chorus. Nothing daunted, he told them to wait and dashed up to his office. Ten minutes later a messenger came down with a sheet of music manuscript and instructions for the chorus master to rehearse it with the chorus. By the time they had run through it a second sheet arrived. It was the Gilsey House with a new twist—Hammerstein upstairs, composing the music, and the chorus rehearsing it downstairs as it came down page by page.

Marguerite would have to be something strikingly original and Hammerstein had decided just how he would achieve this. He was under no illusion that he could accomplish it by the originality of his music. There were those of his admirers who regarded him as a great composer of serious music and did him the disservice of spreading the legend of his great, creative, musical gift, a legend the musically critical delighted to demolish. He himself constantly and deprecatingly poked fun at his own music, thus creating a contrary legend, believed by many, that his music was the most atrocious ever foisted upon the public. When *Marguerite* was being cast and someone asked Hammerstein who was to be the comedian in his new opera, he replied, "I haven't any. There's nothing comical in the piece—except my musical efforts."

Actually, Hammerstein's own estimate of his ability was extremely well-gauged. All he claimed was that his music was just as good as that of the average Broadway production of operetta or musical comedy—no better and no worse—and his pride was in the fact that he, wholly self-taught in musical composition, was able to match the professional composers in effectiveness.

Neither did Hammerstein expect to create anything striking in the book and lyrics of *Marguerite*. He knew that his dramatic ability was not on a level with his remarkable musical facility. He could manage on occasional witty line or effective scene, but on the whole his dramatic structures were nothing but adequate framework for getting performers and production numbers on and off the stage. If there was in Hammerstein any innately original talent as a librettist and lyricist it remained largely latent and was to reveal itself only in his grandson.

The originality he was trying to achieve would lie in the way he was combining all the elements: an adequate dramatic framework, tuneful and effective music, novel and striking costumes and scenery (he was assuring their novelty by designing them himself), and novel and spectacular ideas of production and staging (he was making certain of originality here by being his own producer, director and stage manager). This would be an Oscar Hammerstein production from first to last and having himself provided all the ingredients, he alone would best be able to combine them in ways wholly unique.

Next to music, Hammerstein's greatest love was for the dance, and it was upon the ballets in *Marguerite* that he was lavishing his powers of invention, in costumes, scenery, subject matter and even the general outline of the choreography. In Signor Francioli he had an expert ballet master to carry out his ideas and train the enormous corps of seventy-five dancers. For the four singing parts he had engaged two fine artists, Alice Rose and Marie Brandeis, to sing the parts of Marguerite and Martha, and two very competent men for the roles of Faust and Mephisto. And in the pit with the full Olympia Orchestra, presiding over the musical direction of the entire performance, he would have his sterling conductor, the future founder of the Philadelphia Orchestra, Fritz Scheel.

For the first half of the program Hammerstein was going to present the cream of his current vaudeville bill, including Fanny Wentworth and Virginia Aragon. *Marguerite*, running time an hour and a half, would take up the second part of the program. It was the most ambitious theatrical creation of his own that he had yet ventured. With the music hall war rising in fury and Olympia falling in box office receipts, much was at stake. As the date of the premiere approached, Hammerstein was becoming increasingly nervous.

Faced with the unpredictability of public taste, everyone concerned with a new show is normally highly nervous before opening night—the author, the composer, the director, the producer, and, as a rule most nervous of all, the investing "angel" financially backing the production. Being author, composer, director, producer and "angel" all in one, Hammerstein had cause for more than the normal degree of anxiety.

At one point he began to doubt if he could face the opening night and confessed to one newsman that he was thinking of enlisting the help of Magistrate Mott in order to avoid it. Everyone knew Mott was the most irascible old curmudgeon on the judicial bench and the reporter was dubious as to how this cantankerous judge could possibly help the situation. "I think," explained Hammerstein, "I'll get Magistrate Mott to commit me until the agony is over. How? Easy. All I'll have to say will be, 'Your Honor, I have composed an opera,' and the Judge will say 'Ten days,' and there you are."

Monday night, February 10, Olympia was packed as it had not been since the departure of Guilbert with an audience curious to see and hear Hammerstein's first stage creation of his own since that gem of glorious memory, *The Kohinoor*.

The author-composer had termed *Marguerite* a spectacular opera and ballet, and the simple plot, designed to provide a vehicle for exploiting the ballet and spectacular aspects of the production, was a modernized re-working of the Faust legend. In Hammerstein's version Marguerite is the pure and noble wife of Faust, a struggling and ambitious artist-painter who yearns for the fame that has eluded him.

The curtain rose upon Faust's studio, its walls covered with pictures. Marguerite is worried by her husband's despondency, but Faust, embittered and morose, is unmoved by her loving solicitude. Alone, he sings of his frustration. He dreams of painting a picture—a single female nude—of such supreme beauty that this one painting would make him famous and he is obsessed with the idea that if he could only discover a model of ideal bodily perfection her beauty would inspire him to create his masterpiece. Mephisto appears and offers to supply a subject of perfect and supreme female beauty—upon the usual terms.

To impress a hesitant Faust, Mephisto waves his wand at the pictures on the wall and they begin to glow with color and light and come to life. They become three-dimensional, all the figures turning into live human beings—living pictures. The delighted artist readily consents to sell his soul, and, the bargain sealed, Mephisto gives him the magic wand. Faust is cautioned, however, not to let Marguerite possess it. In her pure hands it will create only sacred pictures.

Faust is invited to accompany Mephisto to his palatial residence and the scene changes to an elegant artist's studio of huge proportions. In the center of the wall stands an enormous, curtained picture frame. Faust is told he can waive his wand and create any picture he conceives. The artist imagines a courtly scene—the court of Louis XV with courtiers dancing a gavotte—and before his delighted eyes the curtains part revealing the scene in the form of a brilliant living picture.

Now Mephisto makes a conjuring gesture and the courtiers begin to move, troop gracefully out of the frame, to come down and go through the evolutions of a gavotte. As the dancers finish and group themselves on either side of the stage the curtains part again and a new picture is conjured forth, *The Fishers*, revealing a group taking in nets on a shore. These figures in turn come to life, moving out of the frame to do an appropriate dance based on characteristic motions of casting and hauling nets. Picture after picture is disclosed and comes alive, the graphic form within the frame transmuted into the choreographic upon the stage.

By this time, the entire audience was sharing Faust's delight at the spectacle the *New York World* called "a combination of living pictures and ballet in the most novel and picturesque manner." Nothing of this sort had been seen before. The entire conception, soon to be imitated to the point of becoming a commonplace, was to the Olympia audience something delightfully fresh and new.

There were eleven pictures in all, including such varied subjects as *The Peasants, The French Dancers' Can Can, The Wedding Party, The Dressing Room Girls, Cooks and Chimney Sweeps*, each one, the *Herald* was to say, "presenting new and delightful scenes and surprises."

In the audience there was mounting enthusiasm as each successive tableau was unfolded and animated. Two picture-ballets in particular made overwhelming hits. One, *The Hussars*, was a new and original version of a standard musical comedy and burlesque number—"The Amazon March." Instead of the usual statuesque females in tights heavily tramping the boards, these were graceful dancers, their dainty and diminutive figures making all the stronger the contrast between the military nature of the subject and the femininity of its protagonists. Nor was it merely a march. The tableaus revealed the charming Hussars at bivouac. At the sound of the trumpet the animation began, an intricate march with all sorts of precision formations, the whole led by a brass band of young women in rousing style. "The stage in this scene," one reviewer write, "presents a kaleidoscopic picture of animated action and brilliant color." The entire number had to be encored.

But it was *The Circus Dancers* that really stopped the show. A sawdust circus ring was revealed with a striking tableau. In the background a magnificent live horse posed rearing up on its hind legs before a feminine ringmaster in the style of an equestrian "haute ecole" act. In the foreground, a "team" of four pretty dancers in scanty costume with mane-like headdresses and held in rein by another ringmaster, struck a similar rearing pose.

At the crack of the whip the group moved out of the frame. The horse was put through its paces, trotting galloping, leaping, rearing, posing, while the feminine "steeds," in perfect precision, duplicated each maneuver with subtle terpsichorean variations of their own. The whole ballet was so delightfully novel in conception that there were shouts of approval and there had to be two repetitions before the show could go on.

When all eleven pictures had spilled their human contents out of their frame the scene worked up to a climax. The *World* critic described the scene, when now the stage "gorgeously set and illuminated was peopled with more than a hundred beautiful and shapely women in the handsomest costumes that have yet been seen in a spectacular production." And now all the groups from the various pictures were dancing together in intricate patterns, intermingling in a riot of color and movement for a spectacularly climatic ballet ensemble.

At this moment of heightened fantasy the revelry is suddenly interrupted by the appearance of Marguerite, who pleads with Faust to give up his obsession before it is too late. Mephisto, fearing to lose his victim, prepares to summon the ideal nude beauty of Faust's desire when Marguerite snatches the wand and waves it. The entire scene changes miraculously into the interior of a great cathedral. An invisible choir sings, Mephisto is foiled, and Faust, saved from perdition and brought to his senses, is reunited with his loving Marguerite as the curtain falls.

There was thunderous applause with numerous curtain calls for the principals, especially Alice Rose, the Marguerite, for the ballerinas, the conductor, the ballet master, and repeated shouts for the deviser and creator of this delightful entertainment. When Hammerstein finally appeared there was an ovation, but despite the usual calls for a speech, the ruler of Olympia, whether overcome with happiness or with modesty, did not respond. He merely bowed his acknowledgments again and again.

The enthusiasm of the first night audience was fully reflected in the praises of the critics. The *Mirror* found the music tuneful and the lyrics well written and stated flatly: "The ballets have created a sensation."

The *World* review carried the heading: "Hammerstein in All His Glory," and began by saying, "It was Oscar Hammerstein's night at Olympia…. Marguerite… a remarkable effort," It observed that while frequently conventional, the music "was sometimes original and distinctive and always tuneful… of the vocal numbers the audience particularly liked a quartet in the first scene, the waltz love song, and a spirited ensemble. Hammerstein's dance music was continuously appropriate and pretty."

The critic went on to emphasize *Marguerite*'s amazing success as a ballet spectacle—"The dances are all conspicuously beautiful"—and like the first-night audience, signaled out the Hussar's march and the circus ballet, "which will be the talk of the town for its charming originality and the skill of its dancers."

"Last night's performance," the review concluded, "reflected glory upon Oscar Hammerstein, author, composer, and stage manager; upon Fritz Scheel, musical director, and Signor Francioli, ballet master … 'Marguerite' should restore the ballet to the local stage."

The *Herald*'s review equally emphasized the wonderful ballets—"The greatest praise is due Hammerstein for the fertility of invention displayed in the arrangement and subject matter of these tableaux," and summed it up neatly with: "The versatile Hammerstein last night accomplished the apotheosis of the living picture in his… 'Marguerite.' He took it out of its frame and made it dance and sing."

One or two reviewers were inclined to be more severely critical of the music of *Marguerite*. Hammerstein did want to have his music taken seriously—just as seriously as that of the professional composers of Broadway musicals. However, these critics were among those who had the notion that Hammerstein took himself seriously as a talented and original composer of great music, that he meant his *Marguerite* as a rival to Gounod's *Faust*. They felt it necessary to suggest that Hammerstein had neither the talent nor the technical equipment for serious composition, that his musical efforts, while occasionally original, were usually reminiscent of the beaten track of popular musical shows and that any of the Broadway composers could have furnished similar music. The severest of the critics ended by saying: "There is no fault to find with the music of 'Marguerite,' but why did Hammerstein waste so much of his valuable time on it?"

The composer of *Marguerite* would certainly have agreed that the current professional composers of Broadway could write music like his, for this was to admit that his music was as good as theirs. But he would have rejected the suggestion that he should have employed any of them to do it for him. The music was the backbone of a musical show and if he did not write it himself he could not consider the production his own.

Since the ballet was the high point of *Marguerite*, several reviews advised cutting down the purely vocal parts. One critic suggested: "Hammerstein is a man of expedients. Let him cut off the first and the last scene of 'Marguerite.' Let him send one to heaven and the other to Harlem and there will remain a delightful act of picturesque dances—a feast for the eye." Hammerstein did not resent the advice, in fact he concurred. He did prune the vocal music considerably and expand the ballet music.

Capacity houses of enthusiastic spectators continued throughout the week. Each night the Hussars were rapturously encored, and the circus dancers given a double encore. The one, a huge production number, the other, a miniature involving only six performers and a horse, the two were direct opposites in more than one sense. If the Hussars were a new and original variation on the standardized old marching Amazons, the circus ballet set a new standard form. It was to be copied and imitated until finally no musical show was complete without the inclusion of what came to be called a "pony ballet."

Hammerstein himself was taken by surprise at the resounding success of *Marguerite*. He had hoped to provide a substitute for a sensational star's engagement, one that would run successfully the usual four weeks of such an engagement. He had hardly expected a sensational success that would run thirteen capacity weeks to be taken off only to make room for another attraction. Not only had he solved the problem of Olympia's post–Guilbert slump; he had created a box-office hit whose duration was three times the run of Guilbert.

After the second phenomenal week of *Marguerite*, Hammerstein was still a little dazed at his success. "I've done it!" he told an interviewer. "How, I don't know, but I've done it! Why, just look at the crowds that are coming to see it and lots of people have been here two or three times." He was even talking of permanently devoting only part of the bill to vaudeville, with ballet the main attraction of Olympia.

Sometime later, in reviewing his first Olympia season, Hammerstein summed up the whole episode in pithy and characteristic fashion. "After Yvette Guilbert left," he wrote, "I fell back upon the old vaudeville. From playing to $60,000 in four weeks I dropped to receipts which didn't pay the ushers. I had spoiled the public. For a while I stood aghast. Then, getting tired of standing, I sat down and wrote 'Marguerite.' That pulled things right up again."

12

Counterattack—Thrust and Parry

For two weeks all was serene at Olympia. Seeing that *Marguerite* was in for a run, a second cast of principals was engaged, headed by Francis Wilson's former leading lady, Laura Moore, who alternated with Alice Rose in the role of Marguerite. Hammerstein, for his part, was basking in the role of successful author and composer. Each night he was the recipient of praise and congratulations from a varied assortment of admirers. The ballet girls even gave him a surprise party backstage with the presentation of a laurel wreath—quite a ceremony, with Hammerstein making a pretty speech and kissing all the prettiest ballerinas. It was a congenial role and the lord of Olympia played it with modesty and good humor.

But the Saturday night on which *Marguerite* concluded its second triumphant week saw Hammerstein in a different role, equally congenial, perhaps, if not at all good humored, and quite familiar. That night he appeared in the Forty-Seventh Street Police Station. Hammerstein had been arrested! And his adversary was also a familiar foe from his old Harlem days—the New York Fire Department and its minions.

For some time, Hammerstein had been much annoyed by a particularly officious inspector from the Fire Department. This official was in the habit of issuing all kinds of arbitrary orders, not only to the fireman on duty, but to Hammerstein's engineer, electrician and other employees. Hammerstein did not take kindly to anyone but himself giving orders to his staff. The inspector also made a practice of testing exit doors during performances by opening them wide to the discomfort of patrons. This, too, did not endear him to the lord of Olympia, Probably, the inspector was seeking a little discreet bribery, but had he been familiar with Hammerstein's history he would have known better.

On this Saturday night the crowd in the music hall was enormous and there was some difficulty in getting people seated. The inspector, arriving at the peak of the rush, decided there were too many people blocking the aisles and told the fireman on duty to order the head user to clear them. The harassed usher was protesting that he was keeping the aisles as clear as possible when Hammerstein came up, telling him to go about his work and to ignore the fireman. That brought the inspector up to insist upon his orders being obeyed and by now the commotion was attracting a dense crowd around it.

Angrily, Hammerstein said that if the aisles were being blocked the Fire Department men were chiefly responsible. He ordered the inspector to leave the theater immediately or he would personally throw him out. The inspector promptly left but returned in a few minutes with a policeman and had both Hammerstein and his head usher placed under arrest, the usher on the charge of violating the safety law, Hammerstein on a charge of technical assault for interfering with an officer in discharge of his duty.

Off to the Forty-Seventh Street Police Station they went. Young Harry Hammerstein came with them, plentifully supplied with cash with which he posted bail for his father and the usher and the two prisoners were promptly discharged for appearance in Police Court next morning.

When the group of men left the station house the captain at the desk heaved a sigh of relief. He did not like being caught up in a dispute between representatives of a city department and the famous—and redoubtable—Mr. Hammerstein. But he had signed too soon. Within twenty minutes the whole party was back with a different policeman and a new prisoner.

The inspector and fireman had hurried back to Olympia, but Hammerstein had gotten there ahead of them. At the door the fireman was permitted to return to his station, but the inspector was informed that he was barred by strict orders of Mr. Hammerstein. While the inspector was arguing with the doorkeeper, Hammerstein had come up, observing sarcastically, that the inspector was blocking the entrance and again had offered the representative of the Fire Department the choice between leaving the lobby or being thrown out into the street. Once again, the inspector had left to return with a policeman. This time he had the doorkeeper arrested, charged with technical assault, Hammerstein being already out on bail on the same charge.

Again, Harry was brought along and when the formalities of booking and posting bail were concluded Hammerstein stepped up to the desk and pointed his finger at the inspector. "And now," he said to the Captain, "I want this man told to keep away from my theatre until this matter is settled. He has other theatres to visit. Let him go to them and not stand around my house all night."

"But," protested the Captain, "I have no right to give him orders."

"Well," said the manager sternly, "I shant let him in. Every time he tries to get in I'm going to throw him out and I suppose he'll keep on having me and my employees arrested all night."

The prospect of having this go on the rest of the night looked grim to the Captain. It impelled him to put forth his greatest powers of persuasion. After a long parley a compromise was reached. Hammerstein promised to admit the inspector who, for his part, promised no further interference of any kind.

Word of the dispute had gotten around, and when the ruler of Olympia returned to his office a few inquiring reporters were already on the scent. Hammerstein unburdened himself in a vigorous statement:

"I want to make a test case of this. This man has annoyed me for a long time. He gives arbitrary orders without consulting me, just as if he owned the place. I shall not submit to it any longer…" (some specific illustrations of annoying acts and orders were supplied).

"And tonight he insisted upon an impossibility. He wanted the aisles kept clear when the crowd was coming in. The ushers were seating the people as rapidly as they could, but of course some had to stand a little while. We couldn't tell them to wait out in the street…

"No, sir! I don't propose that any man shall tell me how to run my house. I know the law and I obey it. It's preposterous. Here the Building Department says I must give up so much room in my house to aisles and passages between the seats that I can hardly accommodate an audience large enough to pay for keeping it open, and now the Fire Department comes along and makes me more trouble. I won't stand it. Why, it's just like telling me I mustn't have big audiences. Goodness knows, they're hard enough to get, and I'm not going to keep them out."

Just what orders Fire Department inspectors had the right to give in theaters was a moot point, and it was a sore point with all the managers. Aware of this, the reporters asked a number of other managers for their reaction to the current imbroglio. All were delighted that the Olympia management had taken a stand. If a test case was to be made Hammerstein was the man to make it. Some were even ready to take bets upon the outcome, and the odds they were offering were two to one on Hammerstein.

When Magistrate Kudlich arrived at his Sunday morning Police Court for the usual quota of Saturday night "drunk and disorderly" arrests he found, to his surprise, a celebrity on the docket and his courtroom filled with reporters and theatrical folk. All of them knew that when Hammerstein created and produced his own show on the stage he did everything but act in it himself, but that when he created and put on a show in court, there he was also the star performer.

And put on a show for them he did. Not that Hammerstein was not genuinely angry. No one could interfere with him in his own theater without arousing his ire, and, if the interference came from official authorities, that only added zest to the battle. Yet in the role of a wrathful Jupiter hurling Olympian thunder, he was fully aware of the effect he made and intended to make. He came not to defend himself and his employees against charges but to denounce the fire department officials who had brought them and to make his complaints heard in a public forum. His lawyer, Fred House, was present but it was the client who did all the talking.

"This sort of thing is an outrage," he exploded before the magistrate. "Of course there was a great crowd in the Music Hall Saturday, for didn't they come to see my 'Marguerite?' But there was no law violated…. Hundreds of persons bought admission tickets and then squatted in the reserved seats. Then lots of other persons came with reserved seats and of course there was a tangle. And while this was being straightened out, these men (pointing accusingly at the Fire Department men) forced their way into my property … arrested me … and lugged me off to a police station. It was an outrage."

"But," mildly interposed the magistrate, "these officers did have the right to see whether the law is enforced."

"They didn't come to find that out," the manager exploded again. "They came to plague me…. I didn't like it and I put them out, quick! … they are the men who got in the way and caused all the disturbance. They would accept no explanation. They came to make trouble for me, and they succeeded. They have been trying to own my theatre and they can't do that. I'm going to see, Your Honor, what I can do to secure private rights to citizens in this city. If these men are allowed to do as they choose wherever they choose this city will be worse than Harlem was in the '80s. I never have allowed and never will allow any crowding in the aisles of my theatres, but I am better able to regulate matters of that kind than these men are. I want protection from the Fire Department, and I'm going to have it before I'm through."

The magistrate, impressed but calm under the blast, then read the charges to Hammerstein, and seeing the great manager was about to explode again, quickly arranged an adjournment to a later date, with the prisoners paroled in custody of their lawyer.

At the next hearing the charge of violation of the fire regulations was dismissed for lack of jurisdiction. The Fire Department would have to bring its own suit if it wished to impose a fine. The Department never tried it. Hammerstein's blasts in the courtroom had been heard, as he had intended, all the way to Department Headquarters, where, with memories of Harlem still rankling, there was no disposition to tangle with this fiery millionaire manager. Even the fire chiefs had found him too hot to handle. At a final hearing, the charge of assault was also dismissed, and Hammerstein had won a clear-cut victory. Olympia was to have difficulties with other representatives of the law, but the Fire Department, having burnt its fingers, left it alone.

During the first two weeks of *Marguerite*'s run, Bial was busily preparing his great counterattack, the "stop Hammerstein" movement spearheaded by his first great European celebrity, Loie Fuller. The publicity promotion for the dancer had been made easier by the fact that this American girl had already become something of a celebrity in New York, when, a few years earlier, she had introduced her serpentine dance. Now Bial was bringing her back as a famous foreign star to present the sensational dance creations which had captivated Paris, where she reigned as the admired La Loie.

For days, at Koster and Bial's a corp of technicians had been busy backstage, installing the electrical equipment the dancer had brought with her. Although her freedom of movement and plastic expression made Loie Fuller one of the forerunners of the modern interpretive dance, she obtained her novel effects not so much through bodily movement as through the imaginative use of drapery and stage lighting. She had created a new technique and unique form in which the dancer dissolved into a phantom of disembodied moving forms and colors.

When, in later years, experimenters attempted to develop a color organ to "play" light and form in motion they were carrying further a trend that Loie Fuller had initiated. For she was one of the first to realize the potentialities of the electric light for stage lighting effects and became one of the foremost authorities on the subject. When Boston was to build its grand opera house, not only was Loie Fuller engaged to direct the ballet but she was called in as the consultant to plan and direct the installation of the lighting system for the stage.

For the American reappearance of Loie Fuller on February 24, Bial demonstrated his readiness to go to any cost in his "stop Hammerstein" offensive. The bill was probably the costliest the house had yet known. The starred celebrity was receiving $2,000 a week. Yet, the program also included the great juggler, Cinquevalli, and the celebrated Martinetti pantomime troupe. Most amazing of all, this famous troupe, for which Bial was paying $1,000 a week, actually opened the program in the place usually reserved for an acrobatic act, the number one spot, in which acts played to an almost empty house, no fashionable music-hall goer ever arriving that early. It was a humiliation the Martinetti had never experienced before.

By 10:30 the house was crowded to capacity for the appearance of the star. She presented five dances. In the first, "La Nuit," she danced on a darkened stage, moving through shadows in shimmering black drapery agleam with silver, setting a mood of darkness and mystery. During her second number, "Le Feu," she never moved from one place. Standing immobile over a glass plate set in the stage, only her draperies in motion, she was able skillfully to move her drapery without seeming to move herself. From the sides, overhead and from underneath came fiery light in saffron, orange, blue and ruby, and flames seemed to lick at her feet. Then, as she waved enormous scarves about her and over her head, she seemed to be enveloped in fire, illuminating the interior of her swirling drapery as well as the exterior. At the climax her scarves became great tongues of flame, her body a living pillar of fire, and the house rose and cheered.

"La Dame Blanche" followed, a complete contrast—a study of movement in white. Then came the exquisite "Le Firament," where, in the *Herald*'s description, "the lights were gradually withdrawn from her until only the great scarves waving in the air could be seen... illuminated like a Turner[1] sunset dying out until only a fleecy bit of veiling was seen, studded with stars." And now, the concluding "Le Lya du Nil." Here, critic Charles Meltzer wrote in the *World*, "by what appears a miracle of skill she twisted her voluminous and dazzling draperies into the forms of flowers of most varied hues," and another reviewer noted that "her draperies seemed to fill the space about her in great waves to a distance of ten to twelve feet, showing all the colors of the rainbow while the audience fairly howled its delight."

There was bedlam when the curtain fell, cheers, shouts, flowers galore. La Loie kissed her hands to the audience, was called out again and again, finally dragging out a reluctant but happy Bial. The owner and manager of Koster and Bial's had good reason for happiness. At last he had a sensational celebrity and a smash hit. His great counteroffensive was under way. Yet the full measure of satisfaction was denied him and he knew it was a triumph without victory.

When Hammerstein had presented a sensational celebrity while Bial had none, Olympia had played to sold-out houses and Koster and Bial's had played to deficits. Now he had a sensational celebrity and Hammerstein had none, yet the fortunes were not reversed. There again was that unpredictable something men called Hammerstein's genius that had enabled Olympia to have a sensational hit nevertheless, a sensation of Hammerstein's own creation out of his own versatility and resourcefulness. Now both rival houses were playing at capacity.

The night that Loie Fuller revealed her sensational new dances at Koster and Bial's was also a gala night elsewhere on Broadway. At the Broadway Theatre, the Bostonians, the most perfect operetta ensemble in the country, was again reviving its famed production of the most successful operetta yet written by an American composer. This night the company celebrated the two thousandth performance of the beloved *Robin Hood*, with Reginald De Koven, its distinguished composer, himself conducting the orchestra.

But the most distinguished event of the night was taking place at the Fifth Avenue Theatre. Only two days before, Sarah Bernhardt had closed her season. Now, before a brilliant audience headed by the mayor of New York, Eleanora Duse began her repertory season with a magnificent performance of *Camille*. A happy public, within the space of a few days, could see the two foremost tragic actresses interpret the same role in two different languages and in two different styles of dramatic art.

Before Duse's season ended, she had also presented her unforgettable performance of Sudermann's *Magda*. So now, already in this season, New York had been privileged to see, in close succession, the great dramatic artists of England, France and Italy—Irving and Terry, Bernhardt, Duse.

Following these renowned geniuses of the European stage, the first three weeks of March presented a rich and varied array of personalities of the American stage. There was beauty and talent in profusion, performers of established reputation and young artists of future renown.

Beauty was ideally personified in the appearance of the two reigning stage beauties of America. The incomparable Lillian Russell starred in *The Goddess of Truth*, a musical on the Pygmalion theme, and in *A House of Cards* there appeared the stunning Maxine Elliott, universally acknowledged the most beautiful woman of the speaking stage, together with Henrietta Crosman, herself on the threshold of stardom.

Established reputations were represented by the distinguished actress, Rose Coghlan, appearing in *Madame*, a play written by her equally distinguished brother, the actor-playwright, Charles Coghlan, and by such well-known performers as Cora Potter and Kyrle Bellew in a production of *Romeo and Juliet*.

At the Empire Theatre, a whole galaxy of young actors and actresses of increasing popularity, each one a future star, presented *Bohemia*, a play adapted from Murger's book, *La Vie de Boheme* (In Italy a young composer named Puccini was completing his operatic setting of the same book under the title *La Boheme*.) The group included Henry Miller, William Faversham, Viola Allen, May Robson and Elsie de Wolfe.

Attracting special critical attention were two rising actresses destined to be particularly bright ornaments of the American stage who now first showed New York their true stature. Both had appeared here some years earlier and had been noted for their promise. Both had since married and now both returned with maturing talents and heightened artistry.

Lovers of the serious drama remembered the skillful portrayals of Minnie Maddern. Now, appearing as Minnie Maddern Fiske in Daudet's *Murie Deloche* and Ibsen's *A Doll's House*, she was received with critical enthusiasm clearly foreshadowing the position of esteem Mrs. Fiske would soon attain and retain for a quarter of a century as queen of the serious drama in America.

Perhaps the most distinguished and interesting first night assemblage was the large audience gathered at Palmer's Theatre for an opening of *Romeo and Juliet*. They had been drawn there to see if the young woman who played Juliet had fulfilled her great promise. All the arts and professions were represented in that brilliant opening night. Representatives of the theater world ranged from young Ethel Barrymore to lawyer Abe Hummel. Officialdom was represented by Police Commissioner Theodore Roosevelt. A veritable "Who's Who" of the world of art included such notables as author William Dean Howells, sculptor Augustus St. Gaudens, and Stanford White, brilliant architect and man about town, whose talents would continue to give the city so many elegant buildings, and whose proclivities as a *bon vivant* were to cost him his life.[2]

It was eight years ago that a young girl had first appeared in New York in a performance as Juliet that was unconventional, imaginative, and gave promise of a future Shakespearian actress of genuine distinction. Since then Broadway had seen little of her, although Hammerstein had presented her Juliet at his Harlem theater. She had married the actor, Robert Taber, and now, as Julia Marlowe-Taber, she and her husband were presenting a repertory season at Palmer's. And so confident of her maturing powers that, although the Potter-Bellew *Romeo and Juliet* was still running at Daly's, she opened with the same play.

Taber was a competent Romeo but it was Julia Marlowe who had drawn that distinguished gathering. Everyone found her Juliet delightful and enchanting, as would a whole generation of Americans, in whose memories Julia Marlowe would remain forever Juliet. It was freely predicted that this gracious girl with the lovely voice would become the successor of Modjeska. As further evidence of her powers, she also appeared in *She Stoops to Conquer* and in *King Henry IV*, taking the role of Prince Henry to Taber's Hotspur.

The rich theatrical repast of new and familiar offerings and interpreters during these weeks did not exclude the field of serious music. At the Academy of Music, Walter Damrosch was presenting a season of German (largely Wagnerian) grand opera by the Damrosch Opera Company, including as a novelty his own opera, *The Scarlet Letter* with Johanna Gadski singing the leading role.

Up at Hammerstein's legitimate theaters in Harlem the offerings were continuously rich and varied, presenting, as always, the best of the past and current Broadway seasons. Following the established Hammerstein policy that the most interesting Broadway productions were immediately booked for the Harlem Opera House, he was presenting Julia Marlowe's *Romeo and Juliet* as soon as her downtown engagement ended.

Only the week before, Hammerstein had delighted Harlem by presenting the comedian, De Wolf Hopper and his wife, spritely Edna Wallace Hopper, in a revival of *Wang*, Hopper's great musical comedy hit of 1891. It was Hammerstein's grandson and namesake who was one day to write the book of a hit musical show about a king of Siam. But, half a century earlier, *Wang* had a Siamese king as its central figure, except that the potentate portrayed by Hopper was far more benevolent and gentle, given to merry quips and puns. Asked how he managed his rule with such mildness, Hopper's King of Siam replied, "I don't reign. I merely sprinkle."

During these weeks, Bial was developing the publicity build-up of Albert Chevalier, the next Koster and Bial star and the foreign celebrity who would spearhead the second attack in the great counter-offensive against Hammerstein. He was getting the English music hall character singer cheaply, for a paltry $1,200 a week, and planning to support him with an extremely costly all-star bill.

Loie Fuller's engagement being limited, Bial had arranged an extension in which her sister Ida would take over and perform the same dances, and though Ida Fuller was far from the equal of La Loie, her salary was not much lower. In addition, both the $1,000 a week Martinettis and the highly paid Cinquevalli were retained and there would be a reappearance of Harriett Vernon, who had never received under $600, plus some new acts.

To Carver Cline, Koster and Bial's business manager, this extravagant policy of "stop Hammerstein at any cost" could only lead to ruin. Even packed houses would show only very small profits. When Bial proved deaf to his protests, Cline found it necessary to resign and Will McConnell became the new manager of Koster and Bial's.

At the same time, Hammerstein was taking a leaf from past Koster and Bial policy by adding a Wednesday matinee and announcing that henceforth both Wednesday and Saturday afternoons would be "family matinees"—smokeless and drinkless. He had announcements on other matters, too, for at this time the stage, especially the vaudeville stage, was facing another recurrent threat from Albany, where a bill had been introduced to ban Sunday concerts of any kind, and, as usual, Hammerstein took the lead in heading the opposition.

When the reporters, who had come to look to him as the natural leader among the New York managers, approached him for a policy statement, he told them: "Of course we shall oppose the bill. It would deprive New York of any form of public amusement on Sunday. The highest class of music at the Metropolitan or Carnegie Hall will be illegal. The thing is preposterous, transcending all bounds of toleration. If we should submit the public will not. Why, New York would become worse than New Lebanon."

This particular threat was averted but the issue was to plague the managers again and again with increasing pressure.

It was during this period, also, that Hammerstein offered a special matinee performance of *Marguerite* that afforded him peculiarly keen satisfaction despite the fact that the box-office receipts were exactly zero. One of the most distinctive institutions of the theater, unfortunately now vanished, was the professional matinee, in which actors performed before an audience of their fellow actors, admittance by invitation only and without charge. A manager had to be very sure of his show before he risked exposing it to an audience so knowledgeable, so hyper-critical of inferior quality, yet so keenly appreciative of genuine artistry—an audience that might not even show up for the free performance it if doubted its worth.

Hammerstein had good cause to be gratified. A capacity house contained representatives from every theatrical company playing in New York, Brooklyn and Jersey City, as well as performers currently "at liberty" in the city. They were all there, artists of reputation, and rank and file professionals, stars, and future stars, glamorous celebrities, ambitious newcomers, row on row of beauty and talent filling the huge auditorium—Lillian Russell, Fay Templeton, Sadie Martinot, Marie Dressler, James T. Powers, Aubrey Boucicault and all the others—a visible directory of the theater world.

For a curtain-raiser Hammerstein presented the remarkable act of Virginia Aragon, his beautiful "Queen of the High Wire," whose marvelous feats evoked applause and cheers. But it was Hammerstein's own *Marguerite* that aroused the greatest enthusiasm. This professional audience immediately recognized the originality of the ballets, the theatrical effectiveness of the music, dancing, scenery, costumes and staging in their total impact upon the eye and ear. No lay audience had yet proved so demonstrative as this house of sophisticated professionals. Every number, dance and scene was warmly applauded. Many of the vocal numbers were encored and three of the ballets had to be repeated in their entirety.

At the end there were vociferous shouts for the owner-manager-composer-librettist-producer, and when Hammerstein appeared before the curtain the house rang with cheers. There were loud calls for a speech but the creator of Olympia and of *Marguerite* only bowed and smiled. It was, the *Herald* observed, "the one great disappointment at the professional matinee."

Within the profession, Hammerstein's wit was widely known, his reputation as a delightful conversationalist already a legend. The general public was less familiar with this side of his personality, for it knew him only through press interviews, and at this period of his life Hammerstein was usually quite earnest with reporters. The audience of professionals had hoped for some of his characteristic pithy and humorous comments, but nothing could elicit a word from him. Perhaps he was too deeply moved by this ovation from within the profession itself.

And now the time had come for the unleashing of Bial's second great counterattack against Olympia. The Koster and Bial publicity campaign for the American debut of Albert Chevalier was well organized. Although it fell far short of the unprecedented amount of newspaper space Guilbert had received, it was extensive. New York was made aware that, like the Frenchwoman, the Englishman combined singing, acting and pantomime in his character songs, that he portrayed a particular type of London Cockney, the colorful costermongers, a type quite unfamiliar to New York, in their own peculiar dialect, and that the humor and pathos of his coster songs had made him for five years the idol of the London music halls.

Like Guilbert, Chevalier himself was not too confident of success. To a reporter who asked why he had not come to America before he answered: "To tell the honest truth, I was afraid the people here would not understand my songs." Bial, like his rival, was taking a gamble, and perhaps for this reason, had bolstered the star with a star-studded bill of such variety and costliness.

Yet, on the night of March 23, Bial might well have spared himself the outlay. Not that the crowded house did not appreciate the rich array of top-flight entertainers—the Martinetti Troupe, Ida Fuller (in Loie's dances), Cinquevalli, Vernon, Sabel. Even the new acts were unusual. There was, for example, Olschansky, a Russian who did an animal act with, of all creatures, trained cats and rats, at one point fifty rodents following him about the stage as he played a fife, a Pied Piper in the flesh. It is unlikely that this particular act was relished by the feminine patrons.

The audience applauded them all but it was clear that they had come to see the much-heralded English star. When Chevalier appeared in a gray coster suit, cap in hand, a broad comical grin on his face, he was given a hearty welcome. The novelty of his characterization, the effectiveness of his pantomime and facial expressions, his perfect diction and his cleverly delivered patter between verses made his very first song, "The Future Mrs. 'Awkins" an immediate hit.

Chevalier's repertory ranged from the broadly humorous to characterizations that were sentimental or pathetic. For "My Old Dutch" he appeared effectively made up as an old workingman in a love song expressing the love of an old man for his "dutch" (coster dialect for wife) with whom he has lived for forty years. In "The Little Nipper's Lullaby," Chevalier sat in shirt sleeves by a little cradle singing a plaintive melody to the sleeping little "nipper." There were effective little touches of stage business, as when he lit his pipe and unthinkingly blew a big puff into the cradle, hastily fanned it away, then, with a glance at the infant and another at the pipe, after a moment's hesitation, quietly giving up the comfort of a smoke.

And in triumphant "Wot Cher, or Knocked 'em in the Old Kent Road," he came strutting out, resplendent in a coster's sartorial best, his coat bedecked with enough pearl buttons to decorate the dresses of forty-fine ladies.

His range was narrower than Guilbert's, his humor never reached the heights of subtle satire nor did his pathos plumb the depths of stark tragedy. His costumes were realistic, his movements more literal, where the Frenchwoman's gestures were evocative, and costume merely suggested by a single imaginative touch or detail. But his characterizations were direct and effectively recognizable, projected with deft skill, and within his more restricted range he was a polished artist. His appeal was immediate and warmly human, and the audience responded with tumultuous enthusiasm, recalling him again and again until he finally made a short speech of thanks.

"Truly an artist," said the *World*, "a master of diction and expression … colors his singing voice … variety of facial expression…. The success of Chevalier was instantaneous." The *Herald* summed it up: "His success was immediate, unqualified, unexampled." The most critically severe and authoritative of all critics of music hall character singing called him an artist and said that though his style was conventional, some of his interpretations were really first-rate and that he was a delightful, cultured man who knew how to choose his music and contrive an excellent make-up. This was high praise indeed, coming from no less an authority than Yvette Guilbert.

Only the distinguished editor of the *Mirror* grumbled: "Chevalier is an artist in his way…. Nevertheless, there may be doubt… whether his specialty represents a type of art sufficiently high to warrant all the attention being paid to it by most of our newspapers. This performer, like Guilbert, is… visiting New York during a season when the papers have turned the stage upside down, placing the singers of London and Paris gutter songs on a pedestal of importance above such interpreters of dramatic art as Duse or Bernhardt."

Every night now Koster and Bial's played to sold-out houses, drawn by the new English celebrity. Every night the great coster singer sang his scheduled four songs and the audience refused to let him go until he had sung three or four more. Bial had a second smash hit, another hit at Hammerstein, coming right on the heels of the success of Loie Fuller, and an even more satisfactory victory because, in Chevalier, Bial was presenting a wholly new performer.

But the object of victory is the defeat of the enemy. Bial's great counterattack to stop Hammerstein was well under way, yet Hammerstein was not being stopped. Bial's victory was not Hammerstein's defeat. Even as Chevalier was making his sensational debut at Koster and Bial's, at Olympia, *Marguerite* was going into its seventh big week. Sold out houses were the rule at both of the rival music halls.

All this time Hammerstein had not been idle. He had opened a booking office in London with Willie in charge. His agents were scouring Europe to find either another great celebrity who would be a sensational novelty in New York or to discover some sensational unknown performer of striking originality who could be publicized into a celebrity in New York.

Reports had come to Olympia of a young Italian named Leopoldo Fregoli. For four months he had been appearing before packed houses in a Madrid theater where he was the sole attraction and that city had gone wild over him. Hammerstein lost no time in dispatching Alfred E. Aarons, as his special agent, post-haste to Madrid. Aarons came, saw, and was completely captivated. Fregoli, he cabled Hammerstein, was not a performer, he was a phenomenon and would create a greater sensation than Yvette Guilbert. Just what did this young man do? What did he not do!

To begin with, he was a "quick change" artist, but his changes were incredible, lightning fast. He was an impersonator, capable of impersonating anyone living or dead, a character actor and pantomimist. He could walk off stage through one door as a doddering old man and immediately enter through another as a beautiful young woman, and could enact entire plays, playing all the roles himself. He was also a singer, in all vocal ranges, male and female, could perform whole operettas, and in addition was a dancer, ventriloquist, juggler, pianist and more besides—a complete theater in himself. All these things he did with artistic brilliance, withal writing and adapting his own sketches, plays and operettas.

If the man did only half what Aarons said he could do, he was a world-beater. Yet Hammerstein hesitated before signing a contract and the negotiations were protracted. He had taken a great risk with Guilbert despite her great fame in Europe. This man had as yet no reputation, was a virtual unknown. At the beginning of his career now, he had appeared only in some minor Italian music halls and in South America. Even his great Madrid success meant nothing. Spain was a theatrical backwater, and Madrid no international entertainment capital such as London, Paris, Berlin, Vienna and St. Petersburg.

Not that Hammerstein was unwilling to build an unknown into a celebrity if he was a sensational performer, despite the greater risk. The hitch was the expense. He knew Fregoli's act was not cheap. It employed a crew of ten assistants backstage and a vast amount of scenery, properties and costumes and he was prepared to pay $600, $700, even $800. The trouble was that this young man had a very high opinion of his worth; he demanded $2,000 a week, a salary appropriate for a top-level international reputation. A famous celebrity was worth a great price, the reputation lessened the risk of failure and helped to create publicity. But it was poor business and against all reason to pay a great star's salary to an unknown quantity.

The cables were kept busy between New York, London and Madrid, but Fregoli's manager would not budge. Finally, it was Fregoli himself who cut the Gordian Knot. In a cable to Hammerstein he said, simply: "My price is $2,000 a week. I make no contract. I come. If I do not earn my money at the end of one week you send me back."

Hammerstein liked that. This was a fellow after his own heart, a man with unlimited confidence in himself, willing to risk everything upon his own ability. He accepted the offer, but not without a contract. Fregoli's suggestion was incorporated in a special clause permitting Hammerstein to cancel the contract at the end of the first week—a wholly unilateral contract that bound the performer but not the manager.

Fregoli's debut was set for May 11 and Hammerstein promptly set his publicity staff to work. As a newsworthy item he gave them the unique clause in Fregoli's contract to set the tone of expectation and confidence and start off the build-up of a man no one in New York had ever heard of.

Pending the development of the Music hall's sensational coming attraction, Hammerstein was presenting some minor sensations to provide novelties, maintain public interest and attention and to counter Koster and Bial's. Although *Marguerite* maintained itself as a hit attraction, he insured its continued popularity by adopting the methods of E. E. Rice. He was constantly introducing new numbers and new performers into it and those who came to the show more than once could always find new features to enjoy. The picture-ballets easily lent themselves to such interpolations.

On the evening of March 30, a capacity audience waited expectantly for the much-advertised appearance of two new dancers in *Marguerite*. Each constituted an event with some sensational overtones. One of these was the first appearance in America of the Countess Kielmansegg. From time to time various vaudeville artistes arrived who styled themselves as countess this or that, their claims to aristocracy usually as dubious as their claims to artistry. Hammerstein had discovered a genuine countess who was a real artist and with a romantic personal history for his publicity department to exploit.

The Countess was a personage in her own right in her native Vienna, where she had been Nina Conti, prima ballerina at the Royal Opera House. When the young lieutenant, Count von Kielmansegg fell in love with her this was entirely fitting and proper. Normal young aristocrats were expected to have discreet love affairs with beautiful dancers and the fact that this young woman was a distinguished artiste only displayed exceptionally good taste.

Unfortunately, this young man flagrantly committed the most unpardonable of all indiscretions—he insisted on marrying the lady! Since the Count's father was no less a personage than a field-marshal of the Imperial Army and privy counselor to the Emperor, and his uncle was Imperial Governor of Upper Austria, the entire royal court was scandalized. The outraged family interposed a firm veto which the young lovers as firmly defied and in the best romantic tradition they eloped to America.

In America, however, opportunities for unemployed titled lieutenants were meager; prospects for beautiful ballerinas far brighter. Hammerstein had lost no time in snaring the Countess to grace his *Marguerite*. She performed three numbers and her beauty, grace and artistry captivated everyone. To provide an extra romantic thrill the audience could see the handsome young Count himself every evening, watching his wife's performance from a stage box, drawn there by the inexorable dictates of love, pride, admiration—and Hammerstein's publicity staff.

With the prestige of her American debut at Olympia, the Countess was soon touring the leading vaudeville theaters of the country. The Count's prospects also took a decided turn for the better when, upon the death of his father six months later, the Austrian Consulate in New York was advertising for him to come home and take over the vast estates of his great family. Evidently, they had forgotten to disinherit him.

In presenting the Viennese ballerina Hammerstein was introducing a new personality. In the other dancer he was featuring in *Marguerite* he was presenting a name familiar from coast to coast. The Chicago World's Fair of 1893 was a monument to progress, but to millions it was best known for its Midway, both celebrated and deplored. And what had made the Midway famous had been two women who introduced to America a new dance, an oriental dance that respectable folk considered of such lascivious depravity as to make the Midway synonymous with the abominations of Sodom and Gomorrah. It was known variously as the "muscle dance," the "danse du ventre" or "belly dance," the "coucheo," or more vulgarly, the "cootchie-cootchie."

Hammerstein was presenting, for the first time in a New York theater one of these dancers, the celebrated Fatima, whose fame (or infamy) was exceeded only by the even greater notoriety of her Midway rival, "Little Egypt." The very names, Fatima and Little Egypt, had become household words, heard by the respectable with feelings of dismay or horror while the less straitlaced rolled them on the tongue with winks, smirks and leers.

The mere announcement that Fatima would appear at Olympia was enough to create a minor sensation and major expectations. Something wicked and shocking was anticipated despite Hammerstein's assurance that he had so expurgated her performance that even the most fastidious need not be offended. "She has reformed, terpsichoreally," he announced. "She will dance a Spanish dance in my 'Marguerite' and it will be pure and graceful."

She appeared in a fairly decorous Turkish costume. Hammerstein had indeed protected the morals of the community. Not a muscle quivered, there was only "a general hip movement" of a "snaky" type and she followed this with a fiery Spanish dance which brought an encore. Hardly in the artistic category of the Viennese ballerina, yet she turned out to be a competent performer and made a hit. And despite her failure to be shocking the audience was satisfied. They had seen the wicked Fatima herself—in the flesh.

Next door in the theater, *Excelsior, Jr.* reached its hundred and fiftieth performance, and with signs of reduced attendance beginning to appear, it was decided to have Rice transfer it to a less expensive house. It had already enjoyed a highly profitable run by 1896 standards, when even an expensive musical show could recover its investment in eight weeks. A three-month New York run to good houses meant a real hit—*Excelsior, Jr.* had been going four moths—and after that, normally, came the road tour, which, whatever the rigors of travel and one-night stands for the performers, could bring even vaster profits and might continue for several years.

In the Olympia Theatre, *Excelsior, Jr.* was followed by a one-week engagement of *The Strange Adventures of Miss Brown*, a farce already familiar from a previous successful run in New York. The company was headed by that remarkable acting couple, Louis Mann and Clara Lipman, and both the inimitable comedian and the charming comedienne made a hit in this reappearance.

Not having another suitable show in sight to put into the theater and not wanting to keep it untenanted, Hammerstein saw a chance to kill two birds at once. The unforeseen long run of *Marguerite* had created a serious logjam of acts already booked for the music hall. Because his own opera-ballet took up half the program, Hammerstein found himself with variety performers holding contracts to appear at Olympia and no room for them upon his stage. Although he managed to cut back some contracts by postponement, advance bookings made this unfeasible for most. He decided upon the expedient of putting his surplus acts into the theater and running two complete variety shows simultaneously for several weeks.

So for the week of April 13, Hammerstein was competing against Bial with two music halls at Olympia. In the music hall auditorium, the sensational Virginia Aragon still headed the vaudeville bill, followed by *Marguerite* with its new twin sensations—the beauteous Countess and the iniquitous Fatima. In the theater, Hammerstein was presenting a number of American debuts of outstanding performers, such as Pablo Diaz, who did remarkable contortions on the flying rings, and the London dancers called the Tiller Troupe who headed the bill.

The Tillers were eight very pretty dancers who executed high kicks with technical virtuosity and perfect precision. In his own "Circus Ballet," Hammerstein had already anticipated this kind of precision dancing, but this troupe carried it out on a wider scale. They made an immediate hit and were to establish a tradition that became an institution. For the next thirty years, Broadway musicals were to feature troupes of Tiller Girls as a standard specialty and the Radio City Music Hall Rockettes would be their lineal descendants.

But the greatest hit of all was the New York debut of an American dancer, the first important native performer Hammerstein had presented—the attractive Papinta, the Myriad Dancer. A first-rate artist, her specialty was gorgeous lighting effects. Like Loie Fuller, she also did a fire dance over a glass plate with vivid light thrown from below. The uniquely original feature of her performance lay in the mirrors strategically placed behind her so that when she danced, not one but a myriad Papintas danced—a solo ballet, in effect. Combined with artistic lighting of great beauty, the effect was stunning. When, the following week, the Aragon engagement terminated, Hammerstein transferred the myriad dancer to the Music Hall in the place of honor on the bill preceding "Marguerite." She was to be one of the most popular performers ever to appear at Olympia and would be re-engaged again and again. And very soon there appeared on her dressing table, too, an autographed photograph of Oscar Hammerstein, suitably inscribed with a flattering sentiment.

The wonder was that with Hammerstein, for the time being. Operating two music halls in opposition to Koster and Bial's, yet all three were playing to packed houses. The war of the great music halls had lifted vaudeville into the most vital form of current theatrical entertainment, and it seemed New York could not have enough of it. The rivalry between Hammerstein and Bial had resulted in an unprecedented profusion of constant surprises and sensations for the public to enjoy. Even the continuous vaudeville houses felt the effect. Before long, almost all of the foreign performers introduced by the expensive music halls found their inevitable way to the Keith and Proctor vaudeville theaters as the starring headline acts, raising cheap continuous vaudeville to a new level.

The bill at Proctor's that week of April 13 was especially noteworthy for both current interest and future portent. Heading the program was the great Sandow. Although his appeal as a remarkable attraction had been well exploited and ably managed, yet the phenomenal strongman and his young manager were now parting company. Young Florenz Ziegfeld, Jr., was free to set out upon his career of exploitation and glorification of feminine beauty.

In next-to-top billing on the program was an American comedy team, Weber and Fields. Lew Fields, the tall, thin member, and Joe Weber, his short and stout partner, were still young, but they had been acting together many years. Beginning as black-face comics, they had changed to Hebrew and finally to Dutch (i.e., German) comedy, and rung by rung they had climbed the ladder, from playing the lowest dives to the $500 a week class. Their hilarious act, in which they committed equally murderous assaults upon each other's person and upon the English language, was known throughout the vaudeville houses of the country and they also owned a controlling interest in two other popular vaudeville acts. They were talented, had come a long way and were ambitious to go further.

A few people thought they were more than low comedy, knockabout, funny men, that they were really comic geniuses. One of the few who thought so was Oscar Hammerstein. He had written them a special invitation to play at the Columbus Theatre, where they had concluded a successful engagement earlier in the season. This had been a milestone in their career, the first time they had ever played a legitimate theater. Now, they were featured performers at a leading continuous vaudeville house, but they had never played a first-class Broadway Theatre.

Yet the goal was within their grasp, for they had in their pocket the most coveted prize in vaudeville—an engagement to play the Olympia early in May. If they could make a hit with the sophisticated audience of the greatest of music halls, they would have reached the summit. Weber and Fields would become great vaudeville stars. They were full of confidence, yet even they could not have foreseen how that engagement would not only raise them to stardom but would lead to the emergence of Weber and Fields as a national institution.

Far down the listing on the same Proctor bill was an obscure young girl billed as doing "dashing character changes." She, too, was fiercely ambitious, but her attempt to achieve a New York success was premature, doomed to failure. It would be a number of years before she would try to storm the metropolis again to become one of the most fabulously successful of all song and dance stars and one of the legendary personalities of vaudeville, and her New York successes would be intimately bound up with Hammerstein's stage. But for the present neither critics nor public took the slightest notice of Eva Tanguay.

13

Mechanization of the Living Picture

It was in this week, also, that there came some important announcements from Koster and Bial's, news that included new developments whose future significance neither Bial nor anyone else was aware of at the time.

Bial was leaving for Europe on his annual trip to round up new performers for next season, and for that season he was announcing a change in policy. Impressed by the astonishing success of *Marguerite* at Olympia, he was paying Hammerstein the sincerest compliment of imitation. Next season, he said, he would present comic operas, ballets and pantomimes, interspersed with only a small number of vaudeville acts to complete the bill of fare.

For this season, he announced, Koster and Bial's would shortly present a novelty developed by Thomas A. Edison called the Vitascope, a kind of enlarged and improved form of the inventor's familiar Kinetoscope, suitable for showing in a theater. Once more Bial was trying living pictures that moved, the experiment that had been such a costly failure with Kilanyi's Glyptorama. He did not regard it as a genuine substitute for that lamented attempt, for these were not live pictures but a mechanical device to simulate them. Yet it was something new, and similar devices were already being shown in London and Paris with great success and he expected that at least for a time, while it was a novelty, it should prove a hit attraction. Even as Bial sailed, his press agents were playing up the Vitascope, exploiting to the fullest the publicity value of the name, Edison. In the frantic search for new attraction to counter Hammerstein's, Bial had at least a minor novelty to throw into the fray as the war of the music halls mounted in tension and in tempo.

A constant flow of announcements was coming, also, from Hammerstein's publicity staff, but it was concentrated upon a single aim, the build up of Fregoli. Although the Vitascope was due at Koster and Bial's in little more than a week, so well-known a name as Edison required no extensive advertising campaign. Fregoli's debut at Olympia was still nearly a month off, but Hammerstein had the more difficult problem of puffing an unknown into a celebrity.

Pictures of Fregoli in various character roles were appearing in the newspapers with descriptions of his protean diversity, including data enumerating the total number of characterizations he assumed, the number of changes he made during his performance, the number of costumes and wigs in his wardrobe, and detailed accounts of his versatile feats of vocalism and ventriloquism as a multi-voiced phenomenon.

One story that received wide circulation recounted an incident during Aaron's negotiations in Madrid. In one of his discussions with the remarkable Italian, Fregoli, being tired, had gone to bed early and Aarons continued discussions with Fregoli's manager. In the course of the conversation the manager mentioned, casually, the presence in Madrid of a young French soubrette who had just made a great success in Paris. Aarons, always on the lookout for a "find" for Olympia, immediately expressed interest in meeting her and the manager agreed to take him to her hotel. There, Aarons was introduced to a charming young woman, very blonde, chic and Parisian. When he began to question her she unaccountably began to laugh at him in a high, silvery soprano which suddenly changed into a resonant baritone and then into a sturdy bass. Off came the blonde wig, and Aarons, delighted at Fregoli's hoax, was more than ever convinced he had discovered a phenomenon.

Good publicity as such a story was, it is quite likely it was also true. Fregoli was famous throughout his career for the tricks he played upon people as exercises of his amazing powers of make-up and impersonation. Once in London, it is said, he even deceived his own wife, answering her advertisement for a domestic servant and passing himself off for three days as a housemaid, during which he drove the good woman to distraction by deliberately planting the suspicion that her "maid" was secretly carrying on an affair with her husband.

The latter part of April saw two well-publicized openings. At the Broadway Theatre there was the opening of *El Capitan*, a musical show. The composer was John Philip Sousa, the successful writer of stirring marches whose band was already the most popular in America and even more famous than Gilmore's Band had been. Sousa's efforts as a composer of operettas were never more than competent, and the most effective parts of *El Capitan* were its marches. That it had a successful run was due largely to its stars, DeWolf Hopper, droll comediation of the long, lugubrious face, and his vivacious wife, petite Edna Wallace Hopper.

The important novelty, its real importance unrecognized at the time, came on Thursday evening, April 23, when Koster and Bial's offered the first showing of Edison's "latest marvel," the Vitascope. It was added to an already star-studded bill as number seven on the program that included Chevalier, Ida Fuller, Harriet Vernon and the rest. There was much curiosity about this latest Edison device, further whetted by the sight of the strangely shaped machine perched in the center of the balcony. According to some authorities, the wizard himself was present in one of the boxes, but if so, the reviewers do not appear to have noticed it.

When number seven was reached, the packed house saw, first, a large screen lowered, then the house lights darkened, then the machine on the balcony began to sputter and whirr and throw a beam of light upon the screen, and suddenly, there was a picture of the Leigh Sisters doing their familiar umbrella dance.

The novelty was one of degree rather than of kind. The audience was long familiar with lantern slide images projected upon a screen. It was also acquainted with Edison's Kinetoscope, a machine into which one looked through a small aperture to see pictures that moved, as a film strip wound on spools passed before a strong light in the opening. This machine was already a popular feature of the penny arcades and was to remain so for years. Edison's latest novelty, the Vitascope, was but a combination of these familiar features, an enlarged Kinetoscope, projecting magnified pictures upon a screen.

Yet, this difference of degree did seem to create a difference of kind, for these large images gave a starling illusion of living, moving figures and the audience showed its approval by tremendous applause. "The effect," said the *Mirror*, "was the same as if the girls were there on the stage; all of their smiles and kicks and bows were seen." "Wonderfully true to life," said the *Herald*.

The short dance ended and was followed by a picture of waves breaking on a shore. As the breakers came tumbling o the sand in showers of spray, "just like the real thing," people sitting in the front rows began to fear a wetting and looked around anxiously for retreat to higher ground. Next came a burlesque boxing bout between two comedians, a short scene from Hoyt's *A Milk White Flag*, in which over twenty persons appeared, an argument between John Bull and Uncle Sam, and finally a skirt dancer performing a serpentine dance.

The audience showed its decided approval of this clever and entertaining novelty, the latest of the many novelties the music hall war was providing. There was general agreement that in bringing it out first Bial had scored a modest victory that should prove quite profitable, at least until the novelty wore off.

That the audience had been present for one of the most consequential events in entertainment in the United States—that in witnessing this first public showing of motion pictures in America, they had in fact participated in a pivotal moment in the social history of the country—of this were wholly unaware. It was a moment that would have come inevitably, if not with an American invention then with the importation of its European counterparts. But the music hall war between Hammerstein and Bial and the rival managers' desperate search for novelties of every kind had unquestionably hastened its advent.

Among theatrical folk. opinion was divided as to the future of the new medium. Most of them predicted a short life span for it. After all, it was only a trick device, entertaining, even fascinating, in its novel illusion, and as with all such clever gadgets, familiarity would soon dull the effect and it would go the way of most novelties.

Others foresaw a permanent place for it on vaudeville programs, even as the illusions of the stage magician were a standard feature of variety bills. And, in fact, for the next ten years motion pictures were to be regarded as part of vaudeville, a type of mechanical illusion act. Charles Frohman, the king of all dramatic managers and producers, predicted that the new invention would permanently replace scenery and lighting effects in producing the illusions of the legitimate stage, a prediction that could not have been more wide of the mark.

That anyone in his right mind would want to go to a theater to sit through an entire performance of flickering shadows on a screen, when he could see real live performers on a stage was too preposterous to consider. That a new medium that could cheaply reproduce, distribute and present news pictures, documentary subjects, entire plays and musical shows with intertitle dialogue or accompanying music, eventually with synchronized sound—that in this invention lay the seeds of a new art form and the basis of a great industry—all this was beyond anyone's imagination.

Bial himself regarded his new living picture machine as only a minor variation on the living picture theme. The solid basis of the living picture he saw in the appeal of the live model, especially when female and undraped. What was needed to restore living pictures to their earlier popularity was a concentration upon these fundamentals.

This was clear from his cabled announcement from Europe of a great new "find." Her name was Mlle. Suzanne Duvenois, a beauty with a stunning figure of formidable womanly development which she knew how to reveal in electrifying solo poses. She would appear next month to show New York the living picture in its noblest and greatest form. And while Bial was announcing this "sensation" he had running in his own theater the greatest and most revolutionary development in living pictures yet made. Stolid, unimaginative Bial—could he ever dream that when all the glories of his music hall had long been faded and forgotten, the name Koster and Bial would still be remembered in the social history of America solely because it was in his theater that the first motion pictures were shown.

Yet Bial could scarcely be blamed if, like all his fellow managers, he had failed to grasp the importance of the new machine. It was a failure of imagination shared by its own inventor. Edison himself was strongly opposed to those of his associates who had plans for developing it. He felt that his basic contribution in this field had been the Kinetoscope, already highly profitable. To further exploit another variant of the same principle was, he was convinced, a foolish way to kill the goose that was just beginning to produce such golden eggs.

Among legitimate theater managers there was rising apprehension over the phenomenal growth of vaudeville. Proctor and Keith's continuous houses were developing a respectable family audience. The music halls were attracting an audience that was both respectable and sophisticated, and as a result of the Hammerstein—Bial rivalry this public was looking to the great music halls rather than to the legitimate theater for the most arresting new stage personalities and the most exciting theatrical novelties.

With well-known performers beginning to leave the legitimate for the high salaries of vaudeville, there was growing alarm that this upstart, vaudeville, might soon engulf the theatrical world.

Such fears were not wholly unjustified, for although vaudeville was developing a new public it was to make serious inroads upon the legitimate theater. Yet, had the managers realized it, the music hall war had just given birth to a new upstart before whom both legitimate and vaudeville managers might well tremble. Within three decades, this sputtering, flickering, moving picture device would grow up into a monstrous giant, to overwhelm vaudeville and drive the legitimate theater into a corner of one city, the Rialto of New York, there to lead a life of precarious glamor as a sick industry—the fabulous invalid of Broadway.

14

Broadway Hits and Misses

In the final week of April, the rising young comedian, Sam Bernard, became another American performer to scale the Olympian heights of vaudeville by a successful appearance at Hammerstein's. The blasé patrons found his jokes, songs and impersonations fresh and amusing—an emphatic hit—and to make a hit at Olympia was to have reached the top.

This was also the week in which another ambitious young American made a second attempt to scale the ladder of success, gaining a foothold only to lose it again Yet eventually, Eva Tanguay was to reach far greater heights than Sam Bernard. Frustrated in her first attempt to make an impression upon New York at Proctor's, she succeeded in obtaining what looked like the big opportunity every young aspirant hopes for. She was engaged to play the lead role in *Hoodoo*, a new musical burlesque opening this week at the Imperial Music Hall. Alas for youthful hope and ambition—all was in vain.

The small music halls were having a difficult time competing with the great music halls on one side and the large continuous houses on the other. Already Tony Pastor's famous establishment had sunk to the level of a second-class house, itself forced to run on the continuous plan. The Imperial, always a second-class music hall, was now third-class, unable to afford any "big name" performers and receiving scarcely any critical attention. Its manager, George J. Kraus, had lost over $70,000 in running it and the new burlesque was a last desperate attempt.

Only the *Herald* bothered to review the new Imperial show and did not fail to notice a talented performer. "Miss Eva Tanguay," it reported, "threw considerable life and anatomy into the part and sang and danced very well." But *Hoodoo* had been appropriately named. Kraus had come to the end of his rope. Even as the production was launched, he admitted that he was bankrupt. There would not be enough money to pay the cast.

At such moments did "Broadway" reveal, again and again, that under the fierce rivalries, the dog-eat-dog competition, under all the professional jealousies and petty spites, there was a heart that could be moved by misfortune. Kraus's friends and managerial associates hastily organized a benefit performance for him. The call went out to the profession to supply talent and, as always, the profession responded. Not only young aspirants eager for every chance to get before footlights, but seasoned performers of established reputation offered to donate their services. Warmhearted charity was not, perhaps, unmixed with self-interest, for amid the uncertainties of the theatrical life, not even the most popular performers could be certain they might not one day be standing in need of a benefit.

Capping all the offers of aid came a gesture of princely generosity from a great manager to a weaker and fallen rival. Oscar Hammerstein cancelled his next Sunday concert and donated the use of his sumptuous Olympia Music Hall for the Kraus benefit that night.

The affair was an emphatic success. The big house was packed for a performance that lasted till midnight. Among the well-known performers were Marie Dressler, Sam Bernard, music hall favorite Clara Wieland, the popular comedian Dan Daly, noted actor John E. Kellard, and the distinguished operatic baritone Signor Giovanni Tagliapietra.

The leading lady and entire cast of Kraus's "Hoodoo" did some numbers from the burlesque. And so, Eva Tanguay, whose career was to be intimately connected with Hammerstein's stage, did actually appear at Hammerstein's theater even in her early abortive attempt to conquer New York. Perhaps Hammerstein noticed her and remembered, for he had a way of filing away in some corner of his mind impressions of promising talent. One performer he surely did notice on this occasion—a child performer who sang and told stores, a little girl named Irene Franklin—for she made the hit of the evening, stealing the show from under the noses of all those well-known artists. He must have made careful note of her, for two years later he was to launch her long and successful career securely by inviting her to play at Olympia.

At 11 p.m., Kraus was called out to make a neat little speech in which he thanked everyone in general and Oscar Hammerstein in particular for his kindness and generosity. That brought concerted and persistent calls for Hammerstein, but the lord of Olympia was not now in his box and a diligent search through the building could not locate him. Hammerstein had quietly slipped out. Ruthless he might be in business competition but his numerous private benefactions he always preferred to make as unobtrusive as possible. This was Kraus's night, not his, and apparently Hammerstein desired neither public expressions of gratitude nor undue publicity in patronizing a defeated rival.

Any benefit whose receipts reached four figures, as this one did, was counted a great success, and such successful benefits generally yielded the recipient anywhere from $1,200 to $2,000. Kraus was able to keep *Hoodoo* running another two weeks so that the cast could receive some pay, after which the Imperial Music Hall closed and disappeared from the New York scene for good. And Eva Tanguay, frustrated, defeated and disgusted, also disappeared from New York. But not for good, for she was not made of the stuff to accept defeat and one day she would be back.

Marguerite (including the Countess and Fatima) was still the big attraction at Olympia, continuing to arouse enthusiastic response. Yet the week of May 4 was announced as the last of its run. Fregoli was coming as the big sensation for the following week and Hammerstein did not want two great star attractions competing on the same program. He would send his ballet-opera to the Harlem Opera House for a week and then put it on the shelf for revival next season.

The first half of the May 4 bill continued to feature such acts as the Tiller Troupe and the electrifying "myriad dancer," Papinta. The one new attraction was the Olympia debut of the two partners Hammerstein was convinced were more than knockabout comics but genuinely inspired comedians. He had given Weber and Fields the place of honor on the bill, the spot before the intermission, the climax of the vaudeville part of the program.

The comedians presented two of the numbers their years of vaudeville experience had brought to a high polish of perfection: their excruciating German dialect specialty "English as She Is Spicked-d-d-dit," and their hilariously slapstick "Pool Table Sketch." The most blasé and exacting vaudeville audience in America howled with laughter and approved with enthusiastic applause.

As an encore, Weber and Fields did their "fiddle number." In this routine one of the partners boasts of his cultural and musical accomplishments, including mastery of the violin. The other derides his pretensions, and, stung to prove himself, the musical one asks the orchestra conductor to lend him his violin. With considerable reluctance, the conductor finally hands over his instrument and the comedian promptly tucks it under his chin and raises the bow in the approved manner. Before he can draw a note, another taunt from his partner causes him to untuck it to reply in kind. He prepares to play again, only to be distracted once more. As the repartee quickens the fiddle travels to and from his chin in rapidly increasing tempo with never a note yet heard. The jibes grow more insulting. Infuriated at last, the would-be musician suddenly exhibits unexpected mastery over his instrument. Grasping the fiddle as a club he brings it down with clean accuracy over the head of his tormentor. There is a wild scuffle, a tangle of thrashing limbs, in the course of which the violin gets stepped on by both combatants. At the end the still unproven virtuoso carefully hands back to the conductor a pitiful bundle of splintered wood and tangled catgut. And how did the Broadway sophisticates of Olympia respond? If left them limp with laughter.

With the seal of approval of this Olympia audience, Weber and Fields were the talk of the town. Their hectic mixture of broad slapstick and sheer fantasy, of low comedy and quick wit, was a fresh and novel combination bordering on genius. Broadway would not see the like again until the advent of the Marx Brothers.

Weber and Fields had become Broadway celebrities. Unlike many who were less grateful, they never had any hesitancy in admitting their debt to the man who had given them their great chance. Felix Isman, their authorized biographer, summed up their long struggle:

> From the Bowery at Chatham Square to Broadway at Times Square is an hour's walk. Weber and Fields had been a quarter of a lifetime on the journey.... At Pastor's and Miner's Eighth Avenue they were on the 10-yard line… at Hammerstein's new Olympia they went over the goal for a touchdown.... It was Oscar Hammerstein who gave Weber and Fields their first chance on Broadway, together with scores of others who made their mark.

And, fittingly enough, their biography is dedicated to Oscar Hammerstein.

With Olympia continuously in the news, its manager was having a particularly busy week. This was the final week of the Fregoli build-up, and to organize the work of his publicity staff to its highest efficiency Hammerstein had recently engaged a new press representative, Edward Burke Scott, the distinguished journalist and former dramatic editor of the New York Press.

Along with the Fregoli material, small driblets of news were released about the work going on up on Olympia's roof, where an army of laborers and artisans were erecting the promised roof garden theater, just enough items to whet public curiosity about what was being planned to be Olympia's crowning glory, but not enough to interfere with public concentration on Fregoli.

Only one event of the week was able to take the spotlight of public interest from Olympia and this was an extraordinary event indeed. A year before, as a benefit for the veteran actor, Charles Couldock, a performance had been given of Sheridan's *The Rivals*, for which an amazing cast of long famous and newly famed actors and actresses had been assembled. Each performer was a star who headed a company of his or her own and the cast was led by the grand old man of the American stage, Joseph Jefferson—truly an all-star cast. Under Jefferson's leadership, substantially the same phenomenal cast had been reassembled and organized for a tour of limited appearances in a selected number of cities.

On rare occasions an entire galaxy could be seen together in a special charitable event such as a benefit, but never had such an all-star company been presented to the American public as a theatrical enterprise. Now, on the Thursday afternoon of this week, Sheridan's classic comedy with this fabulous constellation played a single matinee performance at the American Theatre. The house was thronged with lovers of the theater eager to participate in an event they could treasure in memory and some day recount to their incredulous children, a distinguished audience that included the great Sir Henry Irving himself.

Jefferson played Bob Acres, his most brilliant role, second only in popularity to his beloved portrayal of Rip Van Winkle. Heading the distaff side of the cast was the grand old lady of the American stage, Mrs. John Drew, as Mrs. Malaprop, a role in which she had been famous for years.

Three distinguished stars played the parts of Sir Anthony Absolute, Falkland and Fag—William H. Crane, Joseph Holland and E. M. Holland—and Robert Taber was Captain Absolute. The Sir Lucius O'Trigger was the immensely popular Nat C. Goodwin, whose fame rested equally upon his talent as a comedian and his talent for selecting and marrying a succession of beauteous leading ladies, a list that was to include the exquisite Maxine Elliott. David was played by the most popular of all the masculine comic opera favorites, Francis Wilson. Completing the feminine side were Fanny Rice as Lucy and, Lydia Languish, Julia Marlowe Taber.

Thursday's event made theatrical history out on Friday attention was back to Olympia and upon an event concerning its ruler, an event in the life of the man destined to make more theatrical history than any single man in the American theater.

Outwardly there was nothing in Hammerstein's day at Olympia to indicate anything out of the ordinary. As usual, he spent part of his time up on the roof directing the operations of a swarm of masons, carpenters, bricklayers and glass workers, and in his office, the minutes he could spare from administrative duties saw him at his piano, unconcernedly composing music. But all day long floral pieces addressed to Oscar Hammerstein were arriving at the theater and others were being delivered to the Harlem Opera House and Columbus Theatre. For that Friday, May 8, 1896, was Hammerstein's fiftieth birthday.

Only in the evening was the event duly recognized and celebrated. The mansion at 44 West 120th Street was ablaze with festive light streaming from every window and from the foyer and front door, open like a theater lobby. Carriages were rolling up in a continual procession discharging men and women in gay mood as though coming for a gala performance. And inside, the house was packed with several hundred friends attending a reception at which they shook Hammerstein's had, toasted his health in beakers of wine and heard him respond to their good wishes with what the newspapers called "a short but characteristic speech of thanks."

A fiftieth birthday is a landmark in a man's life, an occasion for reviewing his career, for asking himself if he has been a success or failure and for planning his future. On such an occasion, planning for the future is likely to mean making plans for retirement. Indeed, the very measure of a man's success lies in the possibility at this time to envisage his retirement in comfort or affluence in the foreseeable future.

It is doubtful if Hammerstein gave much thought to his career up to now, for he was not given to dwelling overmuch upon the past. There were too many careers to bother thinking about and he knew he had been successful in all of them: merchant and manufacturer; editor and publisher; inventor; real estate developer; builder, operator and finally manager of theaters.

It was this last career as theatrical showman, his long adumbrated chosen vocation, that must have occupied his thoughts. For this was the present and the future upon which he preferred to dwell. America had been a land of golden opportunity indeed, a country to which one could come as a penniless youth, alone and friendless, and with brains and energy end as a millionaire. Here in this city he loved, his enterprise and initiative had borne fruit in every field he had tilled, ample fruit in personal glory and financial reward.

It was in this present career, his true and final vocation, that he could show his love and gratitude by providing New York with splendid theaters and stage presentations for its people to enjoy—presentations ranging from the most popular forms of entertainment to the highest reaches of musico-theatrical art. It fired his imagination to think of himself as discharging his debt to the city that had rewarded him by assuming the role of showman extraordinary to the people of New York.

He could note with satisfaction that it was barely seven years since he had embraced showmanship as his full-time career and in that short period how many installments on his debt of gratitude he had already repaid. He set little store upon his real estate development of Harlem but he took pride in having given the new northern section of the city two splendid and flourishing theaters, in the Columbus, a house for popular dramatics, and in the Harlem Opera House, the finest first class combination theater in the entire city.

It was barely four years ago that he had stormed down upon Broadway and what an impact he had made in that short time. First, he had provided Broadway with what had been at the time the most beautiful theater in the city and which, through partnership with Koster and Bial, he had made the greatest music hall in America. And now, with the creation of his gorgeous Olympia, this constellation of theatrical showplaces, one of which was already the greatest music hall in the world, he was beginning to pay his final installment on his debt to New York.

Here, upon Olympia all his thoughts were concentrated in making plans for its immediate and long-range future. In none of those plans did his own retirement play a part. He would have laughed at the very mention of retirement. For Hammerstein, just embarked upon his self-appointed mission as showman to New York, at fifty, life was just beginning.

The immediate goal was to bring Olympia to a successful conclusion of its inaugural season. Thus far it had achieved three major triumphs and provided the city with three new sensations. The first had been the unveiling of the great triple-auditorium structure itself, the second the revelation of Guilbert. The third, after that short box-office slump, had been his own *Marguerite*. Now, in seventy-two hours he would present Fregoli who, if all went according to expectations, would provide a fourth great sensation. And in another few weeks he would surprise New York with the fifth sensation he was holding in reserve—the opening of the great roof garden theater, Olympia's fourth auditorium and its crowning glory.

To pilot Olympia successfully through its maiden voyage, this was only the beginning. The next step was to insure the financial stability of the enterprise by freeing it of the heavy load of interest and principal imposed by its mortgage debt. Hammerstein liked to set target dates for his aims and apparently gave himself three years. By the end of that period the profits of three seasons plus the proceeds from the sale of his Harlem theaters and other property would suffice to pay off the entire mortgage or reduce it to minimal proportions.

Yet all this would still be only a beginning and by way of preliminary preparation. To have the greatest theatrical structure in the world free and clear would be merely a clearing of the ground for the start of the real enterprise.

The three-year target date was significant. Only a few weeks ago the Albany Legislature had passed the long-agitated Consolidation Act to unite the City of Brooklyn and the "annexed districts" to the City of New York. In three years, Greater New York would come into being, a vast metropolis of nearly four million, the second greatest city in the world and surely destined to be the first.

Already there was talk of an underground railroad to unite Manhattan and the Bronx and a rapid transit system to unify Brooklyn with Manhattan. Hammerstein had no doubt that Longacre Square would become the focal point of the future city. And coincident with the occasion he would be ready to transform his Olympia into a cultural monument truly worthy of the greater city at whose center it would stand.

The long cherished plan would then be realized when he would convert Olympia into that temple of all the theatrical and performing sets of which he had dreamed, the more popular acts sustaining the nobler and more serious forms of musical and dramatic art. Crowning the whole would be the one art form that in itself combined dramatic art and its sister forms—the dance and the arts of color and form expressed in costume, scenery and lighting—with musical art in all its forms—vocal and instrumental, solo, choral and orchestral—in the splendid synthesis of grand opera. Only then would his debt of gratitude be fully and finally repaid. Then he could regard himself as a benefactor of the city and New York itself henceforth his debtor.

Hammerstein at fifty was full of the confidence of youth. There would be much hard work to be done but the road now seemed clear and the goal in sight. He had as yet no inkling of the disappointments, the frustrations, the heartbreaks that lay ahead. He could not foresee that the three years he envisaged would stretch out into ten years of unremitting toil. He had no premonition that before he could attain the summit of his aspiration, he would first have to traverse the uttermost depths of the valley of despair.

15

The Great Fregoli

The weekend that opened the fiftieth year of Hammerstein's life was a period of high tension, for Monday, May 11 was the date set for Fregoli's debut in America. The Fregoli engagement had been a gamble from the beginning; a far greater risk than the importation of Guilbert. The young Italian "multi-voiced phenomenon" was an unknown quantity with no European reputation and without established success in any place that really counted. But with glowing reports of the man's phenomenal powers and with the tremendous publicity being given him, the odds were in favor of Hammerstein. Yet, as the day of his appearance approached the odds had shortened greatly.

When Hammerstein had first announced the engagement of Fregoli, Bial had been furious with his agents abroad. They had their standing orders from him. If this Fregoli was such a phenomenon—and if Hammerstein was puffing him, he must be—then why had they not snapped him up first. And when Hammerstein was negotiating for him why had they been asleep. They should have had wind of it and topped Hammerstein's offers, doubled and tripled them if need be.

That was spilt milk. Now they must fall back upon the second line of defense. Bial's agents had standing orders for this eventuality also. If Hammerstein did secure an artist with a new and original specialty, they were to find a performer who could duplicate the specialty or learn to imitate it. Soon three continents were being scoured in the search for someone who could provide a reasonable facsimile of Fregoli.

And here Bial had a real stroke of luck. In far off Rio de Janeiro another young Italian had been turned up. His name was Ugo Biondi and he was giving performances that were said to be carbon copies of Fregoli's act. He was even giving some of the identical plays and comediettas in Fregoli's repertoire. Cables were sped back and forth, Biondi's Rio engagement was cancelled by payment of a large indemnity, his advance bookings bought up, shipping schedules consulted. The entire act, bag, baggage and Biondi, was hurriedly packed aboard a ship for New York. It would arrive in time for Biondi to appear at Koster and Bial's May 11, the same night on which Fregoli would open at Olympia.

Bial was throwing down the gauntlet to Hammerstein. If he could not stop him from presenting a new sensation in Fregoli, he could blunt the effect of the novelty by presenting simultaneously an imitation Fregoli to duplicate the sensation. Unlike Hammerstein, who was spacing out his big novelties, Bial was massing all the big guns of his counterattack into one might barrage. Biondi would be added to the costly bill that already included such novel and successful attractions as Loie Fuller's dances (performed by sister Ida) plus Albert Chevalier, plus the Vitascope.

This had been a disconcerting development for Hammerstein, who fully realized its dangers. He had labored mightily to build up public expectation of a sensation novelty.

Bial's maneuver might well halve the effect of his new attraction, and half a novelty was net to no novelty. The Olympia publicity staff had been spurred to intensify its efforts, but everyone was worried. One person alone seemed totally unconcerned—Fregoli himself. Informed of this development by cable, he had replied that he knew all about Biondi, who had been his own pupil. He had himself taught him everything the man knew. Nor was he in the least worried about the competition—he welcomed it. The public would have no difficulty recognizing which as the pupil and which the master.

But Hammerstein was haunted by an even more fearsome specter. Fregoli's Madrid engagement had left a tight timetable, with only one ship available. Biondi was already in New York. Fregoli's steamer was not due till Monday morning. He would arrive the very morning of his debut with only time enough to unpack and get his sets on the stage. He would have to go on without even a rehearsal. And there were all the uncertainties of an overseas voyage. What if the ship were delayed? The consequences were too awful to contemplate. Bial would get his man before the public first. If Biondi made a hit, he might score such a sweeping success that critics and public might then receive Fregoli as an imitation Biondi. That ship had to dock on time. Its captain, at least, would do his utmost for it was rumored he had been promised a sizeable bonus to arrive on schedule.[1]

To counter the array of star acts on Bial's program Hammerstein had prepared an unusually strong bill in support of Fregoli's debut. Even if the Italian should fail to create a sensation, he hoped the rest of the program would contain enough hits to save the day. Only outstanding features of the previous week were retained, among them Papinta, the Tiller Troupe and Weber and Fields. The new acts included a number of novelties and performers making American debuts. Some had been contracted for long in advance, others added only recently. Among the novelties were European high wire performer Ben Abdullah, who did a startling dare-devil act, and a new feature of Hammerstein's own devising called "Marblesques."

During the week just ended something called the Eidoloscope made its appearance in a small hall or converted store on Twenty Sixth Street. It was another moving picture machine, like the Vitascope, the pictures shown over and over from 11:00 a.m. to 11:30 p.m., at an admission of 25 cents. The chief feature was the showing of a complete Mexican bull fight lasting 20 minutes. The enterprise, produced on a shoe-string basis, was unable to afford a theater nor any real advertising. The city ignored its existence and it hardly drew more than a handful of customers off the street. Yet it was certainly the first continuous showing of motion pictures in New York, though not in a theater. Within three days the venture closed its doors and despite the lack of patronage it had not been unprofitable. The entire show-machine, film and operator—had been engaged by Oscar Hammerstein as an addition to the huge vaudeville bill opening on Monday. Hammerstein would be presenting the second showing of motion pictures in an American theater only two and a half weeks after the historic first showing and it would be the first theater presentation of a documentary film on Broadway.

Sunday evening, with Fregoli still on the high seas, Bial attempted to steal a march upon Hammerstein. Copying his rival's method in the promotion of Guilbert, he had invited the press to a special prevue performance by Biondi. But here Hammerstein's great publicity campaign paid dividends. The press did not respond; few important newsmen came and hardly any publicity resulted for Koster and Bial's. After all, if Biondi was an imitation, they could wait 24 hours to see the original and then judge how good the imitation. It would have been better for Bial to brazenly claim Biondi as the original and Fregoli his imitator, but Hammerstein's huge promotion had kept the name Fregoli, the "Multi-Voiced Phenomenon," before the public for weeks and to overtake such a lead was futile.

Monday morning, an anxious Hammerstein was waiting at the dock when, to his unspeakable relief, Fregoli's ship berthed precisely on schedule. The manager welcomed his young star with unconcealed joy. Hammerstein had taken every precaution to ensure there would be no hitches in the clearance of entry and customs regulations. All the papers were ready, and he had come provided with written assurance, guarantees, bonds and ready cash. The young Italian's own entry was smoothly expedited; the next step was to clear his baggage. No single performer had ever arrived in America with such an array of costumes, props and scenery. There were 84 trunks and a score of huge packing cases—several tons of equipment in all.

As the ship's holds steadily disgorged baggage and cargo, the piles of material on the dock grew larger and larger, but still no signs of Fregoli's baggage. A hurried check revealed that by some vexatious contretemps, Fregoli's stuff had been stowed aft in the furthest hold. It could not be reached until everything else had been removed. As the afternoon wore on Hammerstein exhorted foremen and offered bonuses until the stevedores were straining at the double-quick. At last, Fregoli's equipment was reached and taken out ready for inspection and clearance.

Hammerstein raced triumphantly to round up the customs officials. He found them preparing to close up for the day. The frantic manager pleaded, stormed, cajoled, threatened, offered bribes. Fregoli, he told them, had to appear that evening and he could no more go on without his equipment than a magician without his apparatus. But this time the irresistible force of Hammerstein had come up against the immovable object of bureaucratic regulations and official routine. Closing time was closing time—the baggage would have to wait till next morning, was the unconcerned reply. With the inexorable finality of doomsday the officials locked their desks and departed.

Hammerstein was stunned. His worst fears had come to pass. Bial would get his man before the public first after all. All the tremendous publicity promotion frustrated, victory turned to defeat at the very last moment. Now, unless Fregoli should prove immeasurably superior to Bondi, all he could hope for in this battle with Bial was a draw.

The blow once fallen, there was nothing to do but make the best of it. Fregoli himself was a picture of insouciance, although his personal manager, who accompanied him, seemed more concerned. Either this young Italian had good reason for his sublime confidence, or he was a naïve fellow incapable of understanding what was at stake. Hammerstein took his nonchalant star to Olympia where the two presided at a well-attended reception for the press. Fregoli repeated to the newsmen what he had already told Hammerstein—how Biondi was his old friend and pupil, that he welcomed the competition and would let the public be the judge. In fact, having a free evening, he would take the opportunity to go over to Koster and Bial's and attend his friend's opening night.

With theater time approaching, Fregoli departed on foot with a retinue of his own staff, including the little hunchback whom he called his mascot and who always wore Fregoli's name prominently displayed on his hat and jacket. The group was surrounded by a larger entourage of reporters. Like a triumphal procession they set out down Broadway for the rival music hall on Thirty-Fourth Street. Whatever Hammerstein may have felt about such fraternizing with the enemy, he saw that, publicity-wise, this was a masterly stroke. And he must have wondered again, with the thought that either this young fellow was even more alive than he had thought or else he had a very shrewd grasp of public relations.

It was a well-publicized meeting when Fregoli arrived at Koster and Bial's. Biondi came out and there in the lobby, before all the reporters, the two young men embraced each other, kissing each other's cheeks with ardor amid exclamations of delight in voluble Italian. Fregoli wishes his old friend a successful debut and with his retinue passed into the theater. It was Biondi's debut and Biondi's night but already, both in physical presence and in publicity, Fregoli was taking a conspicuous part in it.

Hammerstein, meantime, was having placards put up in his lobby explaining that Fregoli, due to delays in clearing his baggage, would not appear until tomorrow and money would be refunded to all who so desired. Some took advantage of the offer, but the overwhelming majority of a vast audience decided see the monster 13-act bill, which contained so many new features. Hammerstein went to his box to see if despite the missing star attraction, the quality of the program he had provided would arouse enough enthusiasm to counteract the disappointment.

The outstanding holdovers on the bill all made their accustomed hits. There was warm applause for the Tillers, great enthusiasm over Papinta's dances, and hysterical laughter at the antics of Weber and Fields.

Among the new features the most beautiful was unquestionably Hammerstein's own invention and presentation, the Marblesques. This was a new variation on the living picture theme-living statues. Within an illuminated niche a series of famous works of sculpture were revealed, posed by live models, mostly female, whose splendid physiques, mostly undraped, bore eloquent testimony to Hammerstein's artistic standards for the human form. The most interesting feature was that instead of the models posing upon pedestals, the statues themselves were partly plaster sculpture, the whole so subtly joined that it was well-nigh impossible to tell where the plaster ended and the live model began.

The audience found the Marblesques only mildly interesting. As a new twist of the living picture idea, it was a novelty not sufficiently striking. Hammerstein himself had just shown them a more original departure in the animated pictures of his *Marguerite*, pictures that danced and sang.

Much greater enthusiasm was evoked by the animated pictures on the program in the form of the Eidoloscope. Moving pictures on a screen were not, as such, a fresh novelty, this machine being similar to the Vitascope still being shown at the rival music hall. The difference lay in duration and subject matter. The Vitascope views lasted only some two minutes each; the Eidoloscope had a longer span. There were views of Niagara Falls, of the New York Easter Parade before the Vanderbilt mansion, and a Mexican army drill. After these short subjects came the feature with a genuine continuity—the complete Mexican bull fight—which the audience found fascinating and, thanks to the bright Mexican sunlight, remarkably clear. They were the first theater audience to become aware of the possibilities of this new device in presenting interesting newsreel and documentary subjects.

Hammerstein had designed his program to lead up to a climax in his 13th and final act—the debut of the dare-devil wire performer, Ben Abdullah, and his sensational "slide for life." He knew from the rehearsal that it would give the audience an electrifying thrill. Over the audience, a wire with a net under it stretched at a 45-degree angle from the stage to a small platform high up at the third balcony. When the curtain rose for Number 13, this wire was extended into the stage to a platform set up with an arrangement of cushions and springs over a net.

In grace, finish and finesse, Abdullah was no Virginia Aragon on the wire, but he performed a number of daring feats. Finally he began his climactic stunt, walking like a human fly up the sharply sloped wire high over the heads of the audience up the lofty platform. The orchestra began a crescendo drum role and Abdullah began the "slide for life" that would bring him back to the stage up against the springed bumper cushions that would bounce him out into the net.

While the house held its breath, down he came, gathering momentum like an express train. About twenty feet from the stage, his body lurched, he was catapulted forward like a cannonball, struck the soft bumper obliquely and was shot out clear of the net to fall to the stage boards with a sickening thump.

There was a collective gasp of horror from two thousand blanched faces. Women screamed and the curtain was rung down swiftly upon the crumpled figure that lay motionless on the stage. Quickly the stage manager was before the curtain announcing that Abdullah was not seriously hurt and would be all right the orchestra stuck up a jolly tune and the audience began slowly to file out. Even as the announcement was being made, a doctor backstage was pronouncing the performer in a critical condition.

A shaken audience emerged into the square, speaking in hushed tones, the superstitious dwelling upon the ominous number 13. They had been disappointed at missing a promised sensation but they had had their sensational thrill in another form. They would not soon forget what had been a slide for death. And as the last of the audience left they heard the clattering hoofbeats and clanging bell of the ambulance bearing away the unconscious performer from the scene of his American debut.

It was also a shaken Hammerstein who made his way upstairs to his office. What a day! And for the climax, what a night: mischance and mishap piled one upon the other. Sitting down wearily at his desk, the manager wrote out and signed two documents. One was a check for the amount of Abdullah's salary for a full week, addressed to his wife, who, for all Hammerstein knew, might already be his widow. The other was a policy directive to his staff ordering the immediate cancellation of all dare-devil aerial and high wire acts booked for Olympia. He recalled the earlier accident on the night of Guilbert's debut. These acts were sensational attractions, but the theater was a place for entertainment, not an arena for a Roman holiday.

Next morning, Hammerstein was anxiously scanning the newspapers. He was less interested in the reviews of his own show than in what the critics would have to say about the new star on Thirty-Fourth Street, and he was prepared for the worst.

There was no question about it, Biondi had made a big hit. Young, handsome, graceful, his debut was called "unmistakably a success" in one paper, "a hit" in another, "a great success" in a third. "His chief charm," wrote the *World*, "is his ability to change his clothes with lightening rapidity … no more chameleon-like transformation artist ever appeared in this city. But Biondi goes further than other artists of his class… does not confine his efforts to changing garments… performs a dramatic tragi-comedy with four characters, male and female, and assumes them all… and still further throws in some clever singing and ventriloquism." The *Herald* critic stated flatly, "none yet seen in this country has accomplished the astounding feats performed by Signor Biondi," and the *Mirror* noted that "the audience stared open-mouthed at the stage, as he vanished through one door and reappeared through another as an entirely different person."

But there were reservations, too, and the reviewers did not go overboard with enthusiasm. Biondi did not live up to all his billing as a great protean artist and multi-voiced phenomenon. As actor, pantomimist and ventriloquist he was competent, if not outstanding, yet only mediocre as singer and music. The *World* pointed out that he was not multi-voiced by any means. He sang all male singing roles in the same voice—a pleasant, light baritone—and all the female roles in a falsetto that was distinctly unpleasant. The *Mirror* commented: "As a singer he is not a howling success, but as a lightning change artist he is a wonder."

If critical enthusiasm was restrained, this note of reserve must again be credited to Hammerstein's publicity campaign. The critics evidently preferred to wait until they saw the man Biondi was imitating. If Fregoli did not live up to his advance billing either and was merely the same kind of superb technician, then there would be nothing to choose between them. And there was always the possibility which Hammerstein did not care to think about, that Fregoli's performance might be the less skillful. If that were the case, all would be lost and there would be occasion to invoke that special contract clause at the end of the week.

Hammerstein's own newspaper advertising that morning read simply: "Tonight, Positively—Fregoli, the Multi-Voiced Phenomenon—Without Fail." But the harried manager was not quite out of the woods yet. Back to the dock for another session with the customs, there was now no difficulty in smooth processing. This time the trouble was a shortage of handlers and porters on the pier. By the time all of Fregoli's vast equipment had been loaded on trucks, transported and unloaded at Olympia, properly assembled and assorted, stored below stage and arranged backstage by Fregoli's own staff of ten assistants, it was evident that there would be no time for a rehearsal. Nonchalantly, the young Italian said he had no need of one, and Hammerstein, no doubt, was glad to settle for a performance at long last.

Again, that night, the music hall was packed from pit to dome as the lord of Olympia seated himself in his box to await the public's verdict on Fregoli and assess the outcome of his own great gamble—win, lose or draw.

There was a perceptible stir throughout the house when the star's number went up. Those present who had already seen Biondi could notice from the printed program that one of Fregoli's items was his own serio-comic sketch with music called "The Chameleon," the same number the rival performer had presented at Koster and Bial's the night before. And interest was further aroused by a program note Hammerstein had inserted in the playbill which read:

> N.B.—Signor Fregoli desires to announce that every act, play and opera in his repertoire is copyrighted and fully protected against infringement, but that out of pure kindness he has given permission to a performer named Biondi to use a few of his creations only, Biondi having formerly been in Fregoli's employ as an assistant.

Fregoli was cordially greeted when he came out for the first number of his one-man show, a trick vocal number called "An Impossible Duet." Dressed as a nun he sang in a high feminine soprano of surprising richness and purity. Suddenly, turning on his heel, he disclosed the face and garb of a typical operatic baritone, boots and all, singing in deep masculine tones with the conventional gestures of the old-fashioned Italian opera singer. Back and forth he alternated swiftly as the music required switching smoothly from soprano to baritone and back to the conclusion of the duet. It was a clever trick, expertly done with amazing vocal skill and style and the applause was generous.

Hammerstein could heave a sigh of relief. There were special hazards in appearing before a music hall audience where people smoked and drank, could go in and out and, especially in the boxes, eat and converse in informal ease. A performer must win the attention of the house at the start or it could not be won at all. Thereafter it could be lost at any time and once lost it could never be regained. Fregoli's debut, at least, was over the hump.

The star next appeared in a silk hat and smart silk suit to sing a group of popular Italian songs with rapid patter monologues between the verses. He sang them admirably, but the songs were in an unfamiliar style and the foreign language unintelligible. Attention began to flag. The audience was growing restive; there were ominous rustlings and stirrings. The whole debut was hanging in the balance and another five minutes of this would be fatal. The songs—they must have seemed interminable to Hammerstein—came to an end with only perfunctory applause.

Now the curtains parted to reveal the set for a short satirical sketch—a Milanese singing teacher's lesson. Fregoli appeared as the vocal maestro, a fussy, bent, little old man making preparations to receive a pupil. There was spontaneous applause at the perfection of the character as the old man disappeared to sit down behind the piano, only the top of his head showing above the instrument.

Then, through the door came the pupil, a young woman, smartly dressed, a gushing, golden-haired creature full of vitality and awareness of her charms with all the airs of a fore-ordained prima donna. There is conversation, some chords and arpeggios on the piano to which the pupil sings her scales and exercises, interspersed with the maestro's corrections and admonitions, not without some excuses and annoyed rejoinders from the pupil. Finally there is a song, sung by the would-be prima donna with exaggerated archness and much rolling of the eyes.

The audience was now sitting up in disbelief. They could have sworn there were two people on the stage. The man was not only a master of make-up and impersonation, he was also a consummate ventriloquist. Not until the fair pupil's exit, when the dummy head of the maestro was suddenly hoisted high on a stick, did incredulity give way to a storm of applause.

Fregoli's next number was "The Chameleon," a little musical tragicomedy, like all his repertoire, of his own creation. The stage set was a drawing room. A portly elderly gentleman appears, carrying a heavy valise and showing other signs of leaving for a journey. He looks at his watch and calls a hasty but tender last goodbye to his wife, who, from the next room, replies with loving endearments.

No sooner has the husband left by one door than the wife enters by another. She is young, attractive, and sings a gay song of romantic expectancy. A crumpled note is tossed in through the window, she shows a light at the casement, then hurries off to her room to prepare herself for her lover. Almost immediately, a handsome young student jumps in from the window and waits in excited anticipation.

At no time had the stage been empty for more than a few seconds. Fregoli had seemed to walk out one person and come right in again a totally different character. The audience had read the publicity accounts of his ten dressing assistants backstage, lined up between each exit and entrance to help him off and on with clothing and make-up, all timed with split-second precision as he sailed past. But it had to be seen to be believed. It was not merely his technical mastery of time and motion study to produce such quick changes, it was the artistic wizardry of his character transformations. A boy was now standing there where they had just seen a real live woman.

Hearing a noise at the door the youth quickly conceals himself under a table just as the husband returns. He has evidently missed his train, looks for his wife and sees the student's cap. Suspicion turns to rage and a farce-comedy chase begins, the portly husband rushing in at one door, the distraught wife out at another, the youth dodging in and out from under the table.

But suddenly the farce turns serious. The husband is brandishing a pistol, the faces of the woman and student expressing genuine fright. The scene is building up to a catastrophe. Finally, wife and lover follow each other in at the same door. The husband rushes after them; he has them cornered. A shot is heard, a thud, a scream of terror, another shot, a piteous cry, then silence.

Logically, the curtain should fall at this point, but now Fregoli added the little extra touch that bears the authentic stamp of genius. At the very end, a new character appears. A sleepy lodger from upstairs comes down, night-shirted, candle in hand, and complains bitterly of the injustice of it all, that he, a sober, hard-working, respectable citizen should be robbed of his well-earned rest because other people cannot order their domestic affairs with propriety and decorum.

"If Fregoli's success had been in question before this marvelous exhibition of his skill," wrote the *Mirror*'s reviewer, "the applause that thundered through the house at the curtain fall dispelled any such doubt. Nothing so astonishingly clever has been seen here." Those lightning changes were incredible enough, the vocal wizardry itself a phenomenon (four singing voices, male and female), and withal the man was a phenomenal ventriloquist, a superb character actor and master of pantomime.

Fregoli was recalled again and again. The audience would not let him go. Finally he responded with an encore, another one-act sketch. There is to be a theatrical competition, prizes will be offered and preliminary try-outs are being held before judges. The procession begins: composers, impresarios, an old woman bringing her young hopeful, ballad singers, café chantant singers, magicians, soubrettes, each one doing something characteristic. The frisky soubrette, trying her charms on the judges, sent the house into gales of laughter as she sexily wriggled a bare shoulder free of her shoulder strap. And still the wonder grew. When he had done, Fregoli had played a total of fifteen parts, every one a distinct, individualized character.

The huge building fairly shook with the ovation that ensued. A critic described the performer's cumulative effect: after the Chameleon the audience was "ready to salute him as one of the most excellent additions to its amusements New York has had in a decade… when he divided himself into fifteen parts, each one a clever bit of acting and presented the whole as an intelligible sketch, though in a foreign tongue, he was treated as a genius." A one-man show? This man was a one-man theater!

The ovation was still at its height when suddenly Fregoli stepped over the footlights, clambered down into the orchestra pit and bobbed up on the conductor's podium. A small box was placed before him. Back to the audience, he bent down, reaching into it. His hands touched his face swiftly. Then he straightened up, turned around and the astonished house saw the face of Italian composer Gioachimo Rossini. Turning on his heel he raised a baton and led the orchestra into the opening of a familiar Rossini overture. After a dozen bars Fregoli lowered his baton and dived down into his box again, and now he was Richard Wagner conducting a burst of Wagnerian music. Doing his almost instantaneous make-up changes right before the eyes of the audience, he was successively Verdi, Mascagni and a number of other famous contemporary conductors and composers. The more sophisticated among the audience realized he was not merely impersonating the faces but also the mannerisms and conducting peculiarities of each man. They howled with delight.

The Olympia show had come to a dead stop and no one cared. Anything else would now be anti-climax. The whole house was shouting itself hoarse with bravos in one long and sustained roar of approval.

It was hardly necessary for Hammerstein to read next morning's papers. He knew what they would say but it must have made pleasant reading. "Leopoldo Fregoli," the *Herald*'s review opened, "made his bow last night at Olympia, and before he had finished his performance he had his audience in his pocket," and concluded with "Fregoli had become what New York has been looking for, a favorite for her to load with appreciation."

The *World* began with the headline, "Fregoli Scores a Triumph," and ended with the assertion, "Fregoli becomes the sensation of the day." In *The Sunday World*'s follow-up John Dennis, Jr., was to write, "I have seen and admired the wonderful Fregoli at Hammerstein's Olympia. A man who can act a whole opera or play with just himself in the cast is surely a marvel. Fregoli makes the quickest changes I have ever seen, but the point in the performance is not that he changes his dress, but that he changes himself, his gestures, his bearing and his voice."

The *Mirror* critic summed it up: "A more versatile human being than Leopold Fregoli has never been seen on the New York stage…. Fregoli is already the talk of the town… his success was overwhelming. His gifts are of the most diverse nature. He sings in four voices… he can personate people of both sexes almost equally well; he is a ventriloquist, a pantomimist, a musician and a comedian with a genuine sense of humor. Never in the history of the theatre has there been such a many-sided phenomenon. Fregoli is Proteus incarnate."

A startlingly versatile performer, Leopoldo Fregoli (1867–1936) was a one-man theater, convincingly portraying multiple characters through incredibly fast quick-changes of costume and make-up, and speaking and singing in a range of distinct voices. Photograph ca. 1900 (public domain).

In the sensational impact of Fregoli, Biondi was almost snowed under. Yet the pupil was a superb technician who would have been a wonder as a one-man theater in his own right but for the overshadowing presence of the master, a sovereign artist. One commentator, viewing with mock alarm, wrote that with both master and pupil turned loose in the country the entire theatrical profession was facing the threat of mass unemployment. People who had seen Biondi now hastened to see Fregoli and those who saw Fregoli came to see the wonder again and again. There were long lines before the Olympia box-office, the S.R.O. sign was up and tickets were selling for weeks ahead.

The war between the two great music halls had already fired the public imagination, but the battle of the "two Fregolis" had brought it to a dramatic peak. The entire sequence of events—Hammerstein's beating of the drums for the coming of Fregoli, Bial's rushing in of a second Fregoli to stem the advance on the same night, the mischance that left the field open for Bial's successful attack with the imitation Fregoli, and Hammerstein's crushing counterattack the next night with the triumph of the real Fregoli—all this was more than providing magnificent entertainment, it was furnishing the veritable stuff of drama.

Through the crowded week of Hammerstein's birthday and the affairs Fregoli, Hammerstein's trials, troubles and triumphs were all matters of public record and he understood the publicity value of making them public. Yet, during this same period, the one event that was the most sensationally dramatic of all never got into the news, for this was a private matter and Hammerstein saw to it that it remained private.

Despite the manifold cares of Olympia, Hammerstein still exercised personal supervision over his Harlem theaters. Each morning, before going downtown, he would first visit his office in the Harlem Opera House, look over his mail there, receive reports from treasurer Blumenthal and general business manager Rosenberg and give them his instructions. On these spring mornings, he usually drove his two young daughters to school in the family surrey (no doubt with a fringe on the top, the vehicle his infant grandson, Oscar II, would one day celebrate in the words to a Rodgers song). He would stop off at his uptown office, then deliver Rose and Stella to school and set out for Longacre Square.

Rosenberg, manager of both the Harlem and the Columbus, was usually spoken of as Hammerstein's brother-in-law. Actually, the relationship was not quite so close. Mrs. Rosenberg was Hammerstein's half-sister Anna, apparently his father's daughter by his second wife. After the death of Hammerstein's own wife Rose, she had come to America to take care of his brood of four boys and soon married Rosenberg, a harness maker of Selma, Alabama. It was the Rosenbergs who had found for Hammerstein Malvina Jacobi, of Selma, to be his second wife and mother to his children.

When Rosenberg came to New York, Hammerstein had given him the job of general manager of his new Harlem theaters, paying him the generous salary of $200 a week. It was possible to live very well on less than half that sum and the Rosenbergs were able to acquire considerable capital which they increased further by judicious investments and speculations. When such dealings required a large outlay, Mrs. Rosenberg frequently borrowed funds from her wealthy half-brother. Hammerstein, for all that he was a millionaire in property holdings, was often himself short of ready cash for his ventures and, in turn, frequently borrowed from the Rosenbergs to tide himself over. It was an amiably casual arrangement—all in the family.

Of late relations had been a little less amiable than before. There had been some untoward incidents, as when Rosenberg had brought a young man from Alabama to assist Blumenthal in the box-office and shortages had appeared in the accounts. Although Blumenthal was technically responsible, Hammerstein had discharged the newcomer and held Rosenberg accountable for the shortage. It had involved some unpleasantness but no serious rupture.

During the period prior to the advent of Fregoli, Hammerstein was particularly pressed for cash. The mysterious doings up on the roof of Olympia, about which he was not yet ready to make disclosure, involved hundreds of workmen busily preparing his next and final surprise of the season. Despite the success of *Marguerite*, he was hard put for funds to meet the enormous outlay for men and material.

To meet a week-end payroll, he utilized Rosenberg again, borrowing $5,000 from him against his own check and then instructing Rosenberg to hold the check a week so he could pay off some further urgent bills. Hammerstein's enemies on Thirty-Fourth Street had been spreading malicious rumors about his financial difficulties. Whether Rosenberg had become alarmed by these rumors, or whether it was resentment over the shortage incident, for some reason he disregarded his instructions and cashed the check ahead of time. Early Monday morning, Hammerstein was dumbfounded to receive a call from his bank notifying him that his account was overdrawn. The rumors were bad enough without this happening to embarrass his credit standing. Hammerstein was in a towering rage.

That morning when the surrey with the two girls drove up to the Harlem Opera House, Hammerstein jumped down from the driver's seat and made for Rosenberg's office with blood in his eyes. Through the open door Blumenthal heard a first class row: "Rosenberg, you dirty…. How could you do a thing like this to me after all I've done for you!"

The business manager protested that it was all a misunderstanding. The more he tried to explain the angrier Hammerstein became. Next he was chasing Rosenberg around the room trying to lay hands on him and as the other dodged frantically he was picking up and throwing everything movable that came to hand—books, paperweights, inkwells, chairs. Objects came flying out the door past Blumenthal's astonished vision.

At last Hammerstein himself appeared at the door, shouting back: "Now clear out of my sight and don't' ever come near me again. I'm through with you for good!" Calling to his treasurer, "Blumenthal! You are now the manager of this theatre," he strode out of the lobby to the surrey at the curb.

Rosenberg made the mistake of running after him, clutching at Hammerstein just as he reached the side of the vehicle, pleading, "Oscar! Oscar! Listen to me. Let me explain." Hammerstein fairly bellowed at him: "I told you to keep away from me!" Then, seizing the whip from the surrey, he turned and brought it slashing down across Rosenberg's shoulders. Again and again, in his fury, he slashed away at head, neck and shoulders, Rosenberg all the while crying out, "Oscar! Oscar!"

Hammerstein was in one of his terrible rages but as always, fully cognizant of its effects. He saw that the horse, frightened by the cracking of the whip and the loud cries, was rearing nervously. Any moment the animal might bolt, carrying off Hammerstein's terror-stricken daughters. He saw also that passers-by were stopping agape at the bizarre sight. What if the reporters got wind of it? "Oscar Hammerstein Horsewhips Own Brother-In-Law on Street," was one headline he did not care to see. He halted the rain of blows in the very nick of time, sprang into the driver's seat, got the horse under control and drove off to deliver the girls and keep an important date with customs officials on a pier downtown. The ex-manager of the Harlem Opera House and Columbus Theatre, cut, bleeding, staggered back into the lobby, vowing vengeance upon his erstwhile employer.

It was the lurid beginning of one of those long "in the family" hatreds that leave deeper scars than those of a whip. Hammerstein, whose most violent altercations often ended in firm friendships, never forgave Rosenberg for what he felt was an outrageous betrayal by a kinsman. Mrs. Rosenberg was especially bitter over her husband's loss of his lucrative position and became an implacable enemy. And at the time when Hammerstein's troubles were to multiply, it was his own half-sister who would do her utmost to bring about his ruin.

All the public ever knew about his private melodrama was a news item, the next day, announcing that Rosenberg was no longer connected with the Hammerstein theatrical enterprises. They did not know how crowded with drama was that Monday in May, that saw Hammerstein's imbroglio with the customs officials at the dock and a jam-packed theater disappointed at a star's failure to make his debut. They did not know the same day that had ended with a performer's fall from a high wire had opened with the melodrama of Oscar Hammerstein horsewhipping his brother-in-law.

The triumph of Fregoli at Olympia had repercussions, both short term and long. Out of it came a lawsuit and an institution. The suit was only a temporary flurry, but the new institution was to be, for some years, one of the glories of the city and to achieve national fame.

The Koster and Bial organization was still smarting under the crushing defeat at the hands of Hammerstein and Fregoli. When the footnote in the Olympia program referring to Biondi was shown him, Biondi was incensed. He came tearing over to Fregoli, who good naturedly gave him a statement correcting an error in the printed note. Biondi had never actually been employed by him. Biondi then gave out a statement asserting that his family was wealthy and had helped to launch Fregoli's career. Apparently Biondi, bitten by an urge for the stage, later had Fregoli's assistance in preparing his own career. In addition, Biondi also announced the filing of a damage suit for $50,000 against Hammerstein.

An inquiring reporter found Hammerstein jovial and unperturbed. He affected never to have heard of Biondi. The literal-minded newsman identified him as a rival performer in the theater on Thirty-Fourth Street. Hammerstein's eyebrows went up in mock surprise: "Did I understand you to say that there is a theatre running on Thirty-Fourth Street?" He indicated he was much too busy handling the crowds coming to Olympia to be bothered by such trifles as $50,000 lawsuits. But the next day he did delete the offending words from the program note.

Fregoli and his personal manager issued a statement expressing annoyance with Biondi as an imitator seeking publicity by staring controversies with the man he was imitating. Relations between master and pupil were no longer quite so cordial. Of course, the controversy was good publicity—for all concerned. But the lawsuit was quite genuine. Koster and Bial had placed their legal staff at Biondi's disposal to help Bial get back at Hammerstein, at least in some measure.

The chagrin at Koster and Bial's over Fregoli's victory was matched only the intensity of satisfaction at Olympia. On the night of Fregoli's triumphant debut everyone connected with Olympia was joyful, from the Olympia ruler himself down to the ushers—i.e., everyone except two men, one tall and thin, the other short and fat. Weber and Fields were full of resentment and on the verge of despair. They had been one of the big hits of the show. With the coming of Fregoli they expected to be relegated to secondary importance, and, like good troupers, they did not resent it. But they had not expected to find themselves in such a sorry plight.

In a bill of variety acts the presence of a sensational star creates a problem—how to prevent the rest of the program from becoming a total loss. The impact of such a performer almost capsizes the show and only another very strong attraction can bring the program back on an even keel. Hammerstein had deliberately selected Weber and Fields, as his strongest act with the widest popular appeal, for the difficult spot following Fregoli.

It was a cruel spot for the two partners. When they came on the entire house was still buzzing with the wonder of Fregoli. Some, who had come only for the new star, were walking out; the rest, their minds still on the virtuoso performance they had just witnessed, were paying but half-hearted attention. The comedians' best gags fell flat, their most hilarious slapstick aroused only pallid laughter and received tepid applause. Their maximum efforts were rewarded by minimum response. True, by the conclusion of their act they had finally regained the attention of the house. They had saved the rest of the program. But at what a humiliating cost to their professional pride.

Weber and Fields protested vigorously to Hammerstein, pleading to be moved to an earlier spot. Hammerstein was genial but firm. "Anyhow," he joshed them, "you boys are so good they will wait for you all night if they have to." They knew in their hearts that, from the managerial viewpoint, he was right and that in selecting them for the toughest spot he was paying them the sincerest of compliments.

But this was cold comfort. Dejectedly, the two comedians went out into the square, sat on the curb and held their heads in their hands in deepest gloom. After a while, as though thinking aloud, Fields said, "you know, my brother Nat looks a lot like me, and my brother-in-law Bob is the image of you. Maybe they could help us." Together the partners hatched their plan, a plan as dangerous as it was daring.

For the rest of the week they rehearsed in secret while Fregoli continued his smashing success, varying his program with new sketches. Monday evening they were ready to spring their surprise. They had said nothing to Hammerstein but they had arranged for the use of Fregoli's scenery with the stage manager. That functionary naturally assumed Hammerstein's knowledge and permission and they were careful not to disabuse him of the assumption.

Fregoli, beginning his second week that night, outdid himself. He had changed his opening duet into a male trio by means of a dummy cleverly fastened to his back, turning his back to the audience when he sang tenor, his face when he sang baritone, and his side for the bass. And he had introduced a new musical comedy in which one of the roles he played was a ballet dancer, revealing that he was also a graceful and accomplished dancer.

The house was still hoarse from cheering the Italian wonder when Weber and Fields came on. They did their routine number to the now usual half-hearted attention. Then Fields came out before the curtain to make an announcement. He conceded that the Italian star was a wizard and he intended no disparagement. He had come to praise Fregoli, not to bury him. But what these foreigners could do Americans could also do, as well or better They, Weber and Fields, were also experts at lightning changes and they would now proceed to give the audience a demonstration.

The curtain went up and there was the same set Fregoli had just used in one of his sketches. Weber and Fields, in their usual get-up as the two comic Germans, Mike and Meyer, came on, burlesquing the sketch, guttural Teutonic accents replacing the star's liquid Italian. They made their exit and almost immediately returned from the other side of the stage made up as a short, fat woman and a tall, comic gendarme, obvious travesties of two of Fregoli's characters. The house broke into applause. They had made the change every bit as rapidly as the wizard himself.

A few moments of clowning and the two parted in opposite directions, the gendarme leaving by the far right, the fat woman by the left, and instantaneously both reentered as Mike and Meyer from the center door. This time there was no applause. The audience just blinked. Even in Fregoli's lightning changes there was actually an interval of a few seconds. Weber and Fields had seemed to enter at the very moment of their exit! They were out-Fregoling Fregoli!

Out went Mike and Meyer again on the right, only to reappear as gendarme and fat woman on the left. Now the whole house was sitting bolt upright. They could have sworn that two pairs of disappearing heels were still visible when two pairs of toes were coming into view thirty feet across the stage.

The pace quickened, Mike and the woman onstage, the woman vanishing out one side of the stage and Meyer coming in at the other, then Mike out one door, the gendarme in at another. A man's backside would be receding even as the front of him was appearing. Fregoli's feats had been incredible; these were impossible. Amusement changed to amazement as the audience seethed with suppressed excitement. They knew these buffoons were playing tricks on them, but were they doing it with mirrors?

The burlesque whirled into a dizzying climax—Meyer and gendarme transformed into Mike and fat woman, into Mike and Meyer and back into woman and gendarme. When the curtain fell there was a moment of bewildered mystification and then salvos of applause. Weber and Fields, in their Mike and Meyer make-up, came out for a curtain call. More applause, a second bow before the curtain and then a third. The applause continued till, at the fourth call, they came out again, this time arm in arm with the fat woman and the gendarme (Fields' brother and brother-in-law).

The audience took one look at the two "ringers" and let out a howl of delight. Then came a roar of approval and a sustained ovation. Twice that night the show had been stopped dead in its tracks, once by Fregoli, again by Weber and Fields. When they left the theater the two comedians were so happy they even forgot to be apprehensive about Hammerstein.

Back in the theater, the following evening, there was an ominous silence from Hammerstein. The partners, worried but undaunted, did their burlesque and stopped the show again. At their first bow they saw Hammerstein. He was in his box, standing up, and he was joining in the applause. By the time the audience finally let them go, they met Hammerstein striding toward them in the wings. He was shaking a stern finger but his eyes were a twinkle. "I ought to fire both of you for a stunt like this," he told them, "but it was the cleverest thing I ever saw."

But they were not out of danger yet. Another figure had followed Hammerstein and now darted out from behind him. It was Fregoli, gesticulating wildly and pouring out a torrent of unintelligible Italian. And he was making straight for little Joe Weber. Before the rotund comedian could take a step, the Italian was upon him with a bound and both his arms were pinned to his sides. There was a resounding smack, then another. Weber's face was a livid red. Fregoli had soundly kissed him on both cheeks. At last, summoning up his best broken English, the Italian star expressed his rapturous delight. There were some technical tricks, he said, that could make the burlesque even more effective, tricks he would gladly teach them.

There was another rehearsal next morning, not secret this time, with the master, who had taken a special fancy to little Weber, himself coaching and assisting in his own burlesquing That night the spoof was funnier than ever Hammerstein extended the comedy tea's engagement from four weeks to six. His judgment had been correct all along; these men were no mere slapstick buffoons; they were comic geniuses. Gay New York now had two Olympia sensations to talk about. It could see a wondrous performer followed directly by an equally wonderful burlesque of his performance. It was not yet aware that what it now had seen at Hammerstein's was the birth of a new institution, for the next eight years the most unique and distinctive institutions in all the amusements of the city.

Weber and Fields were like Hammerstein in one respect: when they hit upon a successful novelty, they began immediately to think of ways to develop it. They had made a discovery about themselves—their own great talent for travesty. And they had discovered that New York was ready to welcome genuine burlesque with open arms. True burlesque-travesty was almost non-existent. The current musical burlesques were either musical comedy extravaganzas with some parody songs or else nothing but vulgar leg shows, interlarded with coarse and indecent gags. They had, unprecedently, burlesqued a hit performance on the same program. Why not extend this to a wider field?

Every New York season had its outstanding hit performers and shows. What if there were a theater with a permanent company to which the theatergoer, after seeing the season's hits, could go to find them hilariously burlesqued? It would be something novel and they were obviously the men to provide it. They had saved enough capital to lease a theater and organize such a stock company and they would be the stars of their own theater.

Lew and Joe went straight to the man who had done so much for them already. To Hammerstein they freely confided all their plans. And they had a concrete proposition. The Olympia Theatre next door was now untenanted. Would he lease it to them? They were prepared to obligate themselves to a long-term lease at any price within reason.

Hammerstein had other plans for his own theater, and though he liked their idea he liked them too well to advise them to try it. Paternally, he told them:

> Take the advice of an expert at losing money. You're actors, not business men. You're getting $500 a week and you have two other shows of your own. Don't gamble a sure thing like that away for a Broadway wildcat. Betting on the horses is a parlor game alongside guessing which way the cat will jump on Broadway. Your idea's never been tried. You believe New York would like it. Maybe it would, maybe it wouldn't.

It was prudent advice but they were like him in another way, too. Once they had their hearts set upon a bold attempt they didn't take advice. Hammerstein probably suspected as much and probably liked them the better for it. Certainly he did not suspect that one day he would not only lease but build a theater for one of them, and it would because the famous partnership had finally split up.

The partners lost no time in setting their ambitious plan in motion and there were moments when they must have wished they had heeded Hammerstein's advice. Kraus's old Imperial Musical Hall was standing empty, with a lease he was eager to be rid of. They took it off his hands, undertaking the obligation even before their Olympia engagement was up. They had their theater now and after the expenditure needed to renovate the house for their purposes they would have just enough money left to engage a company, mount their first production and begin their risky speculation. Then they discovered there was a mortgage on the house and unless they could meet it their lease was worthless.

Frantically, the partners scurried to borrow money from relatives, friends, anyone. Somehow they managed to raise the amount but they had now mortgaged themselves to the hilt. If the venture is the coming fall was not an immediate success they would be utterly ruined. They would have to begin the long climb to security all over again. Hammerstein had warned them it would be a gamble and they had been willing to risk it. They had never thought it would hang upon a single throw of the dice.

The war of the music halls continued without let-up. On one side were Hammerstein's forces, including Weber and Fields and the Eidoloscope, led by Fregoli. On the other side, Bial's array, including Biondi and the Vitascope, headed by Chevalier, with both rival houses drawing immense crowds. At Olympia, the season's big sensations had been well spaced; the final one, the opening of the Roof Garden Theatre, was coming within a month. On Thirty-Fourth Street, Bial's heavy artillery had all been concentrated behind Chevalier, whose engagement was nearing its close, but now he would bring up his two remaining big guns from Europe.

The first of these was Bial's "discovery," the French beauty, Mlle. Duvernois, whose four-week engagement was to restore the living picture of its former glory. He was confident that the opulence of her figure and the daring of its revelation would create a sensation. She made her American debut at Koster and Bial's the same night on which Weber and Fields introduced their Fregoli burlesque at Olympia. Without question she was a beautiful woman with symmetrical charms of formidable womanly development which she displayed to the fullest in undraped solo poses such as "Phryne," "The Slave," "The Triumph of Venus."

"If I had never seen a living picture, I should have been startled by her nudity," wrote the *Herald* reviewer, adding that as a matter of fact, "I didn't feel any more like applauding then my neighbors" All the critics agreed it was a startling display of the female form. Yet the *World* noted the audience's "appalling lack of enthusiasm" and the *Mirror* observed "the entire act passed on comparative silence," concluding "This means that the living picture craze is dead and buried as far as New York is concerned." It was a remarkable demonstration of how quickly the theater public could become jaded. New York had seen Kilanyi's and Hammerstein's pictures and now even a beautiful woman in the most daring of nude poses evoked only boredom. After three nights the voluptuous Frenchwoman was withdrawn from the bill, the worst "flop" in the history of Koster and Bial's.

That left one last European celebrity for the season, the English singing comedienne, Jenny Valmore, for whom Bial also expected a sensational success. Her American debut, the week after the fiasco of the French "sensation," drew critical comments to the effect that her songs were commonplace or vulgar, and from the *World* the summary edict: "Judging from her performance there is no reason why Miss Valmore should have come to this country and a great many why she shouldn't." At least she lasted out her engagement, but as another big gun in Bial's war with Hammerstein, she was another dismal dud. If it was any comfort to Koster and Bial's, the night of her unspectacular debut saw a debut at another theater that was an even worse failure.

Tony Pastor's once famous theater, too poor to complete with the great music halls, too small to compete with the large continuous vaudeville houses, was steadily losing ground. Driven to desperate expedients, Pastor was also presenting a "sensation." Her name was Lady Sholto Douglas, a former waitress in a Bakersfield, California, concert hall before she married the youngest son of the Marquess of Queensberry. She was billed to do a song and dance act and she had every advantage of publicity for achieving a sensational success, all the glamor of a poor girl marrying into the nobility, all the notoriety of the eccentric Marquis who gave his name to the rules of the prize ring, and the notoriety of other members of the family—the poet Lord Alfred Douglas, partner in the scandal that had just ruined and sent to prison his friend, Oscar Wilde.

Despite these advantages and great expectations, Lady Douglas, "a stalwart young woman with an uncertain voice," was a flat failure. She sang such numbers as "Won't You Play House with Me?" and one reviewer, who found her singing "colorless and not enhanced by her disposition to raise her skirts and display her noble nether limbs," observed gently that there were no violent demands for encores. Her dancing was fully on a par with her singing. The audience had been drawn largely by curiosity as to just what it was the English aristocrat had seen in this girl. Whatever it was, though she lifted her skirts and kicked up her heels, they failed to discover it.

During these weeks, European theatrical news and stage personalities figured prominently in the headlines. In Paris, Cleo de Merode, whose beauty had made her the idol of the public and the favorite of a king, was again in the newsprints as the most talked about woman in Paris. She had given Paris a brand new scandal, centering around a piece of sculpture, Falguiere's *La Danse*, a statue exhibited at the Champs Elysees Salon.

The beautiful dancer had admitted posing for the work before it was placed on exhibition and had turned out to be a nude figure of a dancing woman, very lovely if somewhat on the slender side by current ideals of the female form. It was the sensation of the Salon and, whatever the indignation of the respectable, added immeasurably to the gayety of Paris. De Merode herself vehemently denied having posed nude—the sculptor had tricked her—and alternatively wept, threatened to bring lawsuits and to retire to a convent, while Paris made her the butt of jokes, quips and jibes. One prominent commentator announced he was quite willing to believe the young lady had not actually posed for the statute. He had no doubt the sculptor had done it from memory.

Typically malicious was the comment of another Parisian celebrity, Yvette Guilbert. Asked her opinion of the notorious Merode statue, she told an American reporter: "The face is vairy good—but the body—Mon Dieu! If she is like to that—eet is a vairy poor—how you say—advairtisement."

Another lady of the European stage was in the news at this time—a woman poles apart from the Parisian dancer. Long one of the great ladies of the concert stage, all Clara Schumann had done to make headlines was quietly to die at the age of seventy-six. A distinguished pianist in her own right, the widow of the great romantic composer had devoted herself to popularizing the works of her husband, some of whose loveliest compositions she had herself inspired.

Of all the theatrical news from Europe, the most theatrical was a scene in which the central actor was not of the professional stage. Amid barbaric pomp and splendor in the Kremlin, Nicholas II was crowned Czar of all the Russias. Yet even this opening scene of the drama was to be outdone by the lurid melodrama of this same actor's final scene, to be played, more than two decades later, before the guns of a revolutionary firing squad.

And another actor upon the stage of history was making his first appearance in the news, when a youthful British lieutenant of Hussars broke into print at the age of twenty-one with his first literary effort, a sea story published in *The Century Magazine*. The event was of interest to the New York press only because young Winston's American mother, Lady Randolph Churchill, was the daughter of a famous New Yorker, the late financier Leonard Jerome. Some thought it anomalous that a young army officer's first literary effort should be a naval story, but a later generation would be quite familiar with the interest of a British prime minister who liked to sign himself "former naval person."

What intrigued New York most about the European theatrical world at the moment was to know which of its celebrities would be brought over next by the rival music halls. If hopes for enlightenment were raised by the almost simultaneous arrival from Europe of Albert Bial and Willie Hammerstein, they were quickly dashed.

Bial was highly secretive about the foreign performers he had secured for next season and would announce nothing beyond the American reappearance of Cissy Fitzgerald, the English song and dance "girl with the wink."

Willie never spoke for publication at any time. He had come to report on the work of the London Hammerstein office and to assist his father with Harlem bookings and the new roof garden before returning to Europe. Oscar was not talking about his future attractions either. So tense, now, was the rivalry for European performers that both managers were playing their cards very close to the chest.

With the approach of summer, theatrical anticipation centered increasingly about the great music halls as the legitimate theater season began to peter out. Only two legitimate events made a stir. At the Casino, Gustave Kerker and Hugh Morton turned out the annual summer musical revue typical of that house—a tuneful succession of songs, jokes, ballets and burlesques called "In Gay New York." A brilliant cast included such feminine charmers as Virginia Earle, Sylvia Thorne and Madge Lessing (once the reigning beautify of the Old

Koster and Bial Cork Room), and, on the ale side, the popular singer, Julius Steger and a whole group of clever comedians, including Walter Jones, Richard Carle and Lee Harrison. In all this array of talent the greatest hit was scored by the young Hebrew comic, David Warfield, in a dazzling display of versatility. Besides his Hebrew specialty, he did a hilarious travesty of Mrs. Leslie Carter's big scene in *The Heart of Maryland* (one of the season's great successes) and topped it with a burlesque of Sir Henry Irving in *Macbeth* that was not only a bit of clever parody but an example of perfect mimicry. He literally stole the show.

The other event occurred the same night as the new Casino opening. This was another all-star benefit performance of *The Rivals*, but this time a kind of burlesque version of the now famous cast headed by Jefferson and Mrs. Drew. All the parts were taken by popular musical comedy and farce-comedy comedians, including Willie Collier and Dan Daly as Bob Acres and Captain Absolute and, in the roles of Lydia Languish and Mrs. Malaprop, Ada Lewis and Marie Dressler. The performance was so successful it had to be repeated several times.

This was the tail end of what had been, financially, an unexpectedly poor season. The two great music halls had both done well, as had the large Proctor and Keith houses devoted to continuous vaudeville. The small music halls were in serious straits, one of them, Kraus's Imperial, having already gone under. In the legitimate sphere, a few Broadway shows had been profitable successes, many had been disastrous failures and most managers and producers had suffered severe financial losses. Outside of New York, many road tours had done poorly and it was freely predicted that before the season was out some theatrical firms with lesser resources would be forced to the wall.

Yet when the news came in the latter part of May of the first significant failure, the entire theatrical world was stunned. It was not one of the weaker vessels, it was the richest, most firmly established and greatest theatrical enterprise in the land. The theaters it controlled in New York included the foremost house for drama—Abbey's Theatre—and the established shrine of grand opera—the august Metropolitan Opera House. The attractions it managed ranged over drama and comic opera, the concert stage and grand opera. The stars it presented this season alone included Sarah Bernhardt, Irving and Terry, Lillian Russell, the de Reszkes, Melba and Calve, and it had at various times managed the American tours of Patti, Mrs. Langry, Modjeska, Coquelin, Beerbohm Tree, Sarasate, d'Albert and the boy wonder Josef Hofmann.[2] The great firm of Abbey, Schoeffel and Grau was bankrupt. And Henry E. Abbey, the famous manager who had introduced so many great foreign artists to America, had been lying ill at the Gilsey House for weeks, a worn-out and broken man.

There was considerably mystery as to why this should have been such a disastrous season. All the leading managers were interviewed—Miner, Palmer, Harris, Lederer, Klaw, Erlanger, Hayman, French, Pito, Hammerstein—and their explanations published. Some blamed it upon a general business depression, some on the bicycle craze, others on an oversupply of theaters. Hammerstein alone had no explanation, although he effectively disposed of the reasons given by the others.

"It is not due to bad trade," he pointed out, "for I have seen the theatres doing immense business in times of panic... effort has been made to blame the bicycle.... Bicyclists are not theatregoers as a rule. Besides they don't ride in the dark.... Nor do I think the increase in the number of theatres has done any harm, for my experience is that for every new theatre created an old one will come down. I cannot offer an explanation. I only know that throughout the country the effect has been the same.... It is inexplicable."

Most inexplicable of all was the reason for the failure of the greatest managerial firm in the country. Outside the profession, many, recalling Abbey's earlier ruin after managing the Metropolitan's first season in 1883, concluded that his operations in the rarified heights of grand opera had again brought disaster. Theatrical insiders knew this was very far from the case.

Since the return to the management of the Metropolitan in 1891, grand opera—thanks to Grau, who took charge of this department of the firm—had been consistently profitable. In the current opera season, Abbey's firm had made a profit at the Metropolitan of nearly $100,000. In addition, Bernhardt's tour had netted over $50,000 and Irving and Terry not much less. The losses had been in other ventures, especially those in the "popular" field of comic opera and with its most popular star. Abbey, Schreffel and Grau had lost almost $200,000 on Lillian Russell.

The fair Lillian was still America's sweetheart, her pink and gold loveliness still the ideal of feminine beauty, her silvery voice as pure as ever and her vocal skill at its height (she could have had a career in grand opera had she sought it). But her salary, too, was at its height, and after enticing her away from her former managers, Abbey's firm was forced to pay them a large indemnity. The productions given here were lavishly mounted, as fitting vehicles for the presentation of so great a favorite. Yet, though the public was always eager to talk about her and read about her, it was apparently no longer eager to go to see her, at least not in sufficient numbers to prevent this golden-haired lorelei from causing the greatest theatrical shipwreck of the day.

It was in the very week of the failure of Abbey, Schoeffel and Grau that Hammerstein was presenting their great and fatal star at the Harlem Opera House in *The Little Duke*. Fully aware of Lillian Russell's diminished drawing power, Blumenthal was under instructions to play up her publicity value to the utmost.

There was her famous gold-plated bicycle, a gift from her devoted admirer and presumed lover, the flamboyant "Diamond Jim" Brady,[3] one of the best known of New York's more fantastic personalities. Blumenthal rang all the changes on that; the shining wheel was ridden through the streets by its owner, was exhibited in a window, was stolen, recovered—all to no avail. The opening of the star's engagement drew only fair-sized houses.

Blumenthal decided upon something more drastic. He put out the story that the golden "bike" had been in a serious collision and the golden beauty knocked down with painful injuries. At the theater, the curtain was delayed and then an announcement made that despite a badly sprained ankle and bruised leg the star would go on with the show and her engagement as scheduled. Twice during the performance, the audience gasped as the lovely Lillian slipped and fell, only to continue bravely and uncomplainingly. (Blumenthal had greased two spots on the stage to make it easier.)

That did it. Anxiety about the beauty's injuries and admiration for her pluck brought capacity houses for the rest of the engagement. And at each performance, the fair Lillian cooperated by slipping or stumbling at least once. Blumenthal was inordinately proud of his publicity stunt. Though Hammerstein must have smiled at its crudity, it had worked, and he did not withhold his commendation.

With the departure of Chevalier and the abject failure of Duvernois and Valmore, Bial had shot his bolt for the season. He had no further surprises and no other sensations from Europe to offer, and capacity houses at Koster and Bial's were no longer in evidence. The Olympia Music Hall, however, was still packing them in with Fregoli, and Hammerstein was announcing the imminent unveiling of his final surprise for the season—the opening of the roof garden theater.

At the same time Hammerstein was also announcing some surprises for next season at the Olympia Theatre. Since *Excelsior, Jr.*, the opening hit show, it had proved difficult to find suitable attractions for this house. Hammerstein had decided to solve the problem by producing his own shows. For this purpose he was forming a permanent stock company to be known as the Olympia Comic Opera Company, and every few days announcing the engagement of prominent performers. The caliber of the company was sufficient to arouse anticipation. To head the organization he had secured on of the leading comic opera prima donnas of the day, the soprano, Camille de'Arville. Other leading artists included the contralto, Lucille Saunders, the popular tenor, Julius Steger and the comic favorite, James T. Powers. One day of each week Hammerstein was auditioning applicants for the chorus and minor roles. The first show this company would present in the fall would be "Santa Maria," a romantic comic opera written and composed by Hammerstein himself. He was now working on the book, lyrics and music in his spare time, although where he managed to find spare time was a secret he did not divulge.

The one announcement that should have evoked the greatest surprise came from both Olympia and Koster and Bial's, yet elicited hardly a raised eyebrow, only mirthful chuckles. This was the news that the two rival theaters were applying for hotel licenses and would be converted into hotels!

Up on the fifth floor of Olympia, behind the top gallery, Hammerstein was fitting up fourteen rooms as bedrooms for the Olympia Hotel, and Bial was preparing a dozen rooms for sleeping accommodations at Koster and Bial's Hotel. The public took the announcement as another neat little jest. It was all part of the great Raines Law joke.

The Raines Law,[4]4 recently passed in Albany, was one of a long series of futile and misguided attempts to curb the evils of drink through regulating the saloons. It brought into existence two new institutions that subtracted little from the consumption of liquor but added much to the gayety of the metropolis: the Raines Law sandwich and the Raines Law hotel.

One provision of the law prohibited the sale of liquor without food. At places normally serving food (including the music halls), this merely meant that patrons were compelled to order food with their drinks. In the saloons it brought forth the incredible Raines Law sandwich—two pieces of moldy bread enclosing a scrap of desiccated ham or cheese that was passed out with each full glass of beer or whiskey and passed back with each empty glass, black and grimy from handling as it passed from customer to customer.

Another provision of the law enforced the closing of all bars at midnight and all-day on Sundays. Hotels were exempt, privileged to supply their lodgers with sold or liquid refreshment at any hour or day. Hence the Raines Law hotel. Saloons by the hundred put a cot or two into their back rooms, obtained licenses and operated as hotels. The music halls played out the comedy on a larger scale, providing actual, if never used, bedrooms.

The lowly saloons and the gay music halls were not alone in this subterfuge. Even the proud and dignified Metropolitan Opera House applied for a hotel license. The great opera house was also rented out for social events, including gala balls that were all-night affairs in which the bar was a central attraction. The management had no intention of curtailing its revenues from this source and took steps more akin to the methods used by the saloons than to the alternative practiced by the music halls.

One day the great opera singers, Melba, Eames, Calve, the de Reszkes, and the others, discovered that into each of their dressing rooms a cot and washstand had been moved. The stars' dressing rooms were now, technically, bedrooms for hire. And in an inconspicuous place in the lobby a small sign announced the existence of the Metropolitan Opera Hotel. On only one known occasion did an innocent stranger naively seek a night's lodging, only to have his request met with gales of laughter from the convulsed attendants.

Hammerstein's Olympia "Hotel" had acquired at least one apparently permanent lodger. Fregoli was staying on through his third, fourth and fifth weeks with standees six deep every evening. Each week he was introducing fresh tricks, new plays, comediettas and operettas in which he assumed from four to fifteen roles, concluding each performance by clambering down into the pit to conduct the orchestra in the guise of Wagner, Verdi, Mascagui and other famous musicians. Although the audience fully appreciated the accuracy of his make-up in these concluding impersonations, few were sufficiently familiar with the originals to appreciate the subtle points of his mimicry. By the opening of his fifth week in America Fregoli was remedying this situation by adding figures known by sight to a New York audience.

He swung the orchestra into the familiar opening bars of a rousing march and there was John Phillip Sousa himself on the podium, the face, the manner, the movements, to the life. A shift to a symphonic selection and it was Anton Seidl conducting in the characteristic Seidel manner. Now it was the fiery, Leonine Paderewski, and finally, as the orchestra launched into one of the numbers from "Marguerite," there was Oscar Hammerstein conducting his own music, Hammerstein down to the last idiosyncratic detail—the way he held his head, moved his body, smiled, bowed, the expression on his face, even, one could have sworn, the Hammersteinian twinkle in his eyes. The house literally went wild with shouts of acclaim. Fregoli always stopped the show, but this time it seemed it would never resume again.

It was one day during this week that everything went wrong at Olympia. Behind the scenes and in the front offices everyone on the administrative staff appeared to be working at cross purposes and there was a grand mix-up. It took an irate Hammerstein hours to straighten out the tangle and he minced no words in reprimanding the heads of his departments for their bungling. Yet they stoutly insisted they had only carried out his own personal instructions and it was not their fault if the orders were contradictory.

Hammerstein's anger mounted to fury. Then, as the light dawned, he suddenly began to laugh. Fregoli had been up to his tricks again. He had been impersonating Hammerstein all over the building that day, issuing conflicting instructions until all was confusion. But knowing the cause was no solution. Now no one could be sure of Hammerstein's personal orders. Everyone was on guard against a hoax. The entire Olympia staff was paralyzed until Hammerstein called his lieutenants to his office and gave them a secret code word for the duration of Fregoli's engagement. If the code word was used, they could be sure it was the master of Olympia himself; if not, they would know they were in the presence of the master of all impersonators.

Epilogue

This book ends on a high note with success but the story continued for many years after with upsets, foreclosures, triumphs and manipulations. The birth of Broadway and the reference to Hammerstein as the Father of Times Square shall stand forever in history.

The Olympia building still stands as well. It has gone through many changes and its purpose has been broken up for multiple uses over the last 100 years.

Let us always be reminded of the genius and creative efforts using basic human ingenuity to capture our attention. Looking at the wonders of today's technology, visual effects and musical expression, we can see the striking resemblance to the theatrical innovations of the late 1800s.

Chapter Notes

Adolph S. Tomars began researching the manuscript on which this book is based in the 1950s. He died in 1985, leaving the work uncompleted. The text was painstakingly reconstructed from the original, badly yellowed and faded pages, with many hours of editing.

Tomars' unfinished typescript contained no notes or bibliography. All of his research materials—six boxes of them—are housed in the New York Public Library Manuscripts and Archives Division, call number JPB 03-8, "Adolph S. Tomars Oscar Hammerstein I research papers, 1878–1980." The contents of the collection are cataloged on the NYPL website here: http://archives.nypl.org/mus/20318#overview.

The following annotations have been added by the editor.

Chapter 1

1. American writer and critic Gilbert Seldes (1893–1970) was editor of the modernist political and literary magazine *The Dial*, published in various forms and during various periods from 1840 through 1929.

2. According the periodicals directories at Duke University's Perkins Library, the *United States Tobacco Journal* became the *United States Tobacco and Candy Journal* in 1983, then the *U.S. Distribution Journal* in 1987 or 1988. Publication ceased in 1999.

3. In the landmark 1901 case *Cherry v. Des Moines Leader*, the Supreme Court of Iowa found: "A public performance may be discussed with the fullest freedom, and may be subject to hostile criticism and hostile animadversions, provided the writer does not do it as a means of promulgating slanderous and malicious accusations." The decision is still cited as precedent in court cases today, confirming the right of fair commentary and criticism in the press.

4. American writer and artistic photographer Carl Van Vechten (1880–1964), a Harlem Rennaissance patron and Gertrude Stein's literary executor.

5. Huneker (1857–1921) was a well known theater, art and literary critic.

6. A prima donna in both senses of the term, Scottish soprano Mary Garden (1874–1967) was famous for her flamboyant persona and public feuds with colleagues.

7. A prankster figure of German folklore, Till Eulenspiegel first appeared in print in a 1515 chapbook. Then a well-known music critic, Pitts Sanborn (1879–1941) wrote for the *New York Globe*, *New York Mail* and the *New York World-Telegram*.

Chapter 2

1. Hammerstein built his first Manhattan Opera House in 1893; it soon failed, later to be revived as Koster and Bial. His second Manhattan Opera House—today the location of Manhattan Center at 311 West 34th Street—was opened in December 1906.

2. George Ehret (1835–1927), an immigrant brewer from Germany, established his famous New York brewery in Hell Gate in 1866.

3. The great Shakespearean actor Edwin Thomas Booth (1833–1893), older brother of actor and Abraham Lincoln's assassin, John Wilkes Booth.

4. Giacomo Meyerbeer (1791–1864), among the most successful composers of grand opera in the nineteenth century.

Chapter 3

1. Irish nationalist Joseph Ignatius Constantine Clarke (1846–1927) was an American journalist, poet, playwright and author, and at various times an editor for the *New York Morning Journal*, the *Criteron* and the Sunday *New York Herald*.

2. Manager Ariel Barney handled theater and musical performers, and appeared as a performer in at least one stage production, *The Twin Sister* (1902). John Russell (c. 1856–1925) performed in Broadway musicals, including *Sweet Marie* (1901) and *The Hired Girl's Millions* (1907).

3. Famed Polish pianist and composer Ignacy Jan Paderewski (1860–1941).

Chapter 4

1. The Panic of 1883, a severe, four-year long depression affecting every sector of the economy—except, it seems, the New York theater industry.

2. It is unclear which of Hammerstein's daughters, Stella or Rose, is here referred to.

Chapter 5

1. French music hall singer Eugénie Fougère (1870–?) made her fame as a *chanteuse épileptique* (epileptic singer), parlance of the day for a performer whose main attraction was sexually provocative singing, movements and facial expressions.

Chapter 6

1. Tammany Hall, seat of the perennially corrupt Democratic Party machine that exerted huge influence over New York City politics, business and labor for generations.

2. Clarence Lexow (1852–1910) served in the New York Senate 1884–1898 and as chair of the internal affairs committee sponsored a bill calling for state investigation of the New York City Police.

3. Abbott, real name Matilda Tatro, was one of a number of young women, typically of slight build, performing the "magnet act" on the late 19th century vaudeville circuit.

4. August Belmont, Sr., (1813–1890), born August Schönberg, was a German-American financier, foreign diplomat and Democratic National Committee chair in the 1860s.

5. "King of Comedy" Mack Sennett (1880–1960) was a Canadian-American film director, producer, and studio head, famous as the originator of slapstick pie-throwing.

Chapter 7

1. The New York Society for the Prevention of Cruelty to Children, better known as the Gerry Society, after founder Elbridge T. Gerry (1837–1927), pushed for legislation prohibiting children under 16 from dancing, juggling, performing acrobatics, etc. on stage in theaters or amusement parks.

Chapter 9

1. French actor Benoît-Constant Coquelin (1841–1909), known as "Coquelin the Elder," whose *New York Times* obituary called him "one of the greatest theatrical figures of the age."

Chapter 12

1. English romantic painter Joseph Mallord William Turner (1775–1851), famous for his colorful, expressionistic watercolor landscapes.

2. Stanford White (1853–1906) was shot to death on the roof of Madison Square Garden by Harry Kendall Thaw, the mentally unstable heir to a railroad fortune who became obsessed over White's romantic past with actress Evelyn Nesbit, Thaw's wife.

Chapter 15

1. The reward presumably offered by Hammerstein.

2. Polish-American composer Josef Casimir Hofmann (1876–1957) began his career as a five-year old piano prodigy touring Europe and America.

3. The son of West Side saloon owner, James Buchanan Brady (1856–1917) worked his way up from bellhop to financier and philanthropist, as well as celebrated personality among New York society high and low.

4. Authored by reformist New York lawyer and politician John Raines (1840–1909), the law had the unforeseen consequence of encouraging prostitution in hotels.

Index

Aarons, Alfred E. 166, 172
Abbey, Henry 49, 51, 105, 121–23, 132, 144, 150, 198–99
Abbott, Annie 80–81, 204
Abdullah, Ben 182, 184–85
Adams, Maud 103, 107
Adgie (The Lion Tamer) 11
Albani, Emma 123
Allen, Viola 102, 162
Aragon, Virginia 11, 147, 152, 164, 184
Arliss, George 9
Aronson, Rudolph 44, 91, 95, 101
Avril, Jane 126

Bacaresco family 65
Baidis Sisters 116
Barney, Ariel 39, 203
Barnum 16, 81, 143, 150
Barrett, Lawrence 102
Barrymore, Ethel 61, 103, 107, 162
Barrymore, Lionel 9, 55
Barrymore, Maurice 9, 25, 93
Bayes, Nora 11
Beekman, James Hyde 132
Beere, Bernard 25, 34
Belgrave, Lord 43–44
Bell, Hillary 87, 140
Bellew, Kyrle 161
Bellicose, Oscar 88
Bellwood, Bessie 53, 54-57
Belmont, August 82, 204
Bernard, Sam 11, 104, 175–76
Bernhardt, Sarah 93, 97, 140, 144, 161, 165, 172, 198
Bertoldi, Mlle. 57
Bigelow, Charles A. 117
Biondi, Ugo 181–86, 189, 192, 195
Blum, Leon 97
Blumenthal, George 85–86, 190–91, 199
Bly, Nellie 80
Bonci 17
Booth, Edwin 9, 81, 203
Booth, John Wilkes 203
Borge, Victor 147
Boucicault, Aubrey 164

Bradna, Ella 11
Brady, Diamond Jim 199
Brahms, Johannes 91
Brandeis, Marie 152
Bressler-Gianoli, Clotilde 13
Brodie, Steve 91, 99
Brown, Buster 11
Brummel, Beau 128
Bull, John 173
Burke Scott, Edward 177
Byrne, Charles Alfred 37, 38, 41, 49

Caicedo, Juan 57, 59
Calve, Emma 13, 49-50, 54–55, 123–24, 131, 135, 141, 145–46, 150, 198, 200
Camille 63, 93, 109, 128, 161
Campanini, Cleofonte 13, 14-15
Campbell, Patrick 9
Cantor, Eddie 11
Cantori, Maestro 123
Capitaine, Alcide 56-57
Carle, Richard 117, 198
Carter, Leslie 9, 198
Caruso, Enrico 3, 17, 98
Casino 37–38, 49, 56, 62, 94, 197
Cavalieri, Lina 12, 13
Cavalleria Rusticana 49, 53, 62
Charpentier, Louise 13
Chase, William 138
Cherry Sisters 11
Chevalier, Albert 97, 143, 149, 151, 163–66, 181, 195, 199
Chopin 147
Churchill, Winston 197
Cinquevalli, Paul 11, 95, 143, 160, 163–64
Clarke, Joseph Ignatius Constantine 203
Clarke and Lederer 38–39, 43
Clemencean, George 97
Cleveland, Pres. Grover 92, 132
Cline, Carver 36, 45, 47, 72, 79-80, 163
Cline, Maggie 11, 56, 97
Coghlan, Charles 53, 63, 161

Cohan, George M. 8, 57
Cohan, Josephine 11
Cohan, Josie 57
Collier, Willie 198
Colman, Ronald 107
Comstock, Anthony 102
Conried, Heinrich 61- 62
Conti, Nina 167
Corbett, James J. 63
Cork Room 29–32, 37
Couldock, Charles 177
Court of Special Sessions 91–92
Coxey, Jacob S. 59
Crane, William H. 178
Croker, Richard Wellstead "Boss," 93
Crossman, Henrietta 9, 161
Cunard, Lady 18

Dalmores, Charles 13
Daly, Dan 198
"La Dame Blanche" 160
Damrosch, Leopold 122
Damrosch, Walter 14, 162
Daniels, Frank 9
Dauset Moreno, Carmen 30-32, 36, 67, 149
De'Arville, Camille 200
De Koven, Reginald 161
Della Rocca, Giacinta 118, 127, 130
De Merode, Cleo 110, 149, 196
Dennis, John 189
Depew, Chauncey M. 142
de Reszke, Edouard 49, 54, 57, 95, 123–24, 141, 145, 198, 200
de Reszke, Jean 49, 54, 57, 95, 123–24, 141, 145, 198, 200
De Wolfe, Elsie 103, 107, 162
Diaz, Pablo 168
Di Dio, Mlle. Marietta 9, 65–69, 71–74, 76–78, 80, 88, 90, 93, 135
Didur, Adamo 13
Dixey, Henry E. 11, 101
Docksteder's Minstrels 63
Donnay, Maurice 126
Douglas, Lady 196
Douglas, Lord Alfred 196

Index

Dresser, Louise 11
Dressler, Marie 11, 164, 176, 198
Drew, John 9, 55, 63, 81, 103, 107, 178
Drew-Barrymore, Mrs. 61
Dreyfus Case 97
Dufranne, Hector 13
Dumas, Alexandre 93, 109, 128
Dunbar, Lady 43-44, 47
Dunn, Arthur 117
Duse, Eleanora 9, 93, 135, 140, 144, 161, 165
Duvernois, Suzanne 173, 195, 199
Dvořák 53

Eames, Emma 49, 55, 123, 98, 200
Earle, Virginia 197
Edison, Thomas 8, 56, 171-72, 174
Edison's Kinetoscope 172
Edwards, Gus 11
Ehret, George 28, 203
Eidoloscope 182, 184, 195
Electric Lady Bicyclist 59
Elliott, Maxine 161, 178
Eltinge, Julian 11
Époque, Belle 50
Erlanger, (Manager) 198
Evening Mail 16, 18
Evening Sun 135

Fatima 168, 176
Faust 49, 122-23, 152-54
Faversham, William 101-2, 162
Finck, Henry T. 124
Fiske, Harrison Grey 120, 138
Fiske, Minnie Madden 162
Fitch, Clyde 128
Fitzgerald, Cissy 197
Fougere, Eugenie 29, 66, 204
Francioli 152, 155
Franklin, Irene 176
Fregoli, Leopoldo 166, 167, 171-72, 176-77, 181-201
Frohman, Charles 63, 173
Frohman, Daniel 107
Fromme, Isaac 73, 79, 81, 83-84, 87-92
Fuller, Loie 10, 149, 151, 160-61, 163-165 169, 181
Furst, William Wallace 49

Gadski, Johanna 162
Garden, Mary 203
Garden Theatre 47, 49, 57-59, 101
Garrison, William Lloyd 86
Gentle, Alice 13-14
Gentleman Jack 63
George, Grace 9
Gerry Law 102
Gerson, Edmund 95
Gildersleeve, Judge 86, 89, 92

Gilmore's Band 172
Gilroy, ex-Mayor Thomas 132
Gilsey House 35, 37, 39-41, 43, 45, 47, 61, 68, 73, 152, 198
Goodwin, Nat. C. 178
Grady, Judge 92
Grant, General 60
Grau, Maurice 49, 55, 105, 121-23, 132, 145, 150, 198-99\
Gregory, Josie 29
Guilbert, Yvette 51, 54, 67, 80, 95, 97, 100, 104, 111, 120-121, 123-125, 126-129, 130-135, 136, 138, 139, 141-146, 149, 151, 165-166, 169, 185

Hamilton, May 57, 117
Hammerstein, Arthur 7, 109, 132
Hammerstein, Elaine 7
Hammerstein, Harry 158
Hammerstein, Oscar II 7, 86
Hammerstein, Willie 7, 18, 55, 84-86, 166, 197
Hammerstein Living Pictures 59, 64, 67, 80
Hare, John 138
Harlem Opera House 25-26, 47, 55, 63, 97, 102, 124, 128, 176, 178-79, 190-91
Harned, Virginia 102
Harrison, Lee 198
Harrison, Louis 38-39, 49
Harrold, Orville 13
Hart, William S. 107
Havemeyer, Charles F. 132
Havemeyer, Theodore 132
Hearst, William Randolph 136
Held, Anna 9
Henderson, William J. 123
Hengler Sisters 117
Henry, Prince 162
Herbert, Victor 9, 146
Hertz (magician & illusionist) 147
Hill, Senator David B. 92
Hirsch, Jack 39-42
Hoffman, Gertrude 10
Hofmann, Josef 198
Holland, E.E. 117, 178
Holland, Joseph 178
Holmes, Oliver Wendell 86
Hooty-Tootie Girl 104
Hope, Anthony 107
Hopper, De Wolfe 9, 63, 103, 107, 172
Hopper, Edna Wallace 9, 163
Horzowski, Mieczyslaw 14
House, Fred 159
Howe, Julia Ward 86
Howells, William Dean 162
Hoyt, Charles 43, 54, 87-88, 173
Hummel, Abe 18, 81-83, 86, 88, 92, 102, 162-163

Huneker, James 5, 16, 18, 20, 37, 203
Hussars 154-56, 197

Inaudi, Giacomo 56
Ingenues, Les 126, 133-34
Ingersoll, Robert 18
Irving, Sir Henry 47, 81, 110, 128, 178, 198
Isman, Felix 177

Jacobi, Malvena 190
Janis, Elsie 11
Jaures, Jean 97
Jefferson Market Court 72, 87-89
Jefferson, Joseph 9, 102, 177
Jerome, Leonard 197
Jerome, William Travers 19, 82
Johnson Troupe 118
Jones, Walter 117, 198
Jouy, Jules 133
Juan, Don 129

Kellard, John E. 176
Kerker, Gustav 37-41, 43, 45, 54, 142, 197
Kern, Jerome 7
Kessler, George 63, 68-77, 79, 140
Kielmansegg, Countess 167
Kilanyi, Edouard Von 57-61, 116-17, 127-28, 171, 196
Kinetograph 56
Kinetoscope 171, 174
Kohinoor 42-45, 47, 50, 59, 63, 75, 153
Kraus, George 138, 175-76, 195
Krehbiel, Henry Edward 123
Kudlich, Magistrate 159

Lackaye, Wilton 102
Lane, Sargeant 72, 87
Langtry, Lillie 82, 101
Languish, Lydia 178, 198
Larie, Adrienne 59
Lasalle, Jean 49, 129
Leckaye, Wilton 90
Lederer, (Manager) 39, 41, 43, 198
Lehmann, Lilli 13, 122, 123
Leigh Sisters 172
Leoncavallo 53
Lescot, Edmee 36
Lessing, Madge 29, 197
Lewis, Ada 198
Lexow, Senator Clarence 79
Lexow Committee 78, 82-83, 84, 204
Lind, Jenny 138, 143, 150
Lipman, Clara 168
Little Egypt 82, 168
Lloyd, Alice 11

Lockhart's Comedy Elephants 107
Loftus, Cissy 11, 97–98, 101
Longacre Square 94, 96, 101–2, 104, 106, 108, 113, 116, 119–20, 180, 190
Lyne, Felice 13

Manhattan Opera House 3, 13, 16, 22, 26–27, 31, 34, 98, 124, 140, 203
Mann, Louis 168
Mansfield, Richard 9, 79, 102, 128, 140
Mantell, Robert B. 9
Mapleson, James Henry 26
Marguerite (the musical) 9, 142–43, 151–57, 160, 163–64, 166–69, 171, 176, 179, 184, 190
Marks, Ted 106, 131–33, 145
Martinettis 67, 160, 163, 164
Marx Brothers 177
Materna, Amalie 122
Maurel, Victor 95, 98
May, Edna 9
Mazarin, Mariette 13
McCarthy, Justin Huntley 97
McCormack, John 13
McCormick, Cyrus H. 121
McCreery, James 105
McElfatricks, J.B. 98
Melba, Nellie 13, 22, 26, 49, 53, 95, 123, 141, 145–46, 150, 198, 200
Mellers, Raquel 139
Meltzer, Charles Henry 135, 161
Mendl, Lady 103
Miller, Henry 9, 101–2, 138, 162
Milton, Ellie 47
Modjeska, Helena 9, 82, 93, 107, 162, 198
Moore, Laura 157
Moore, Victor 11
Morton, Hugh 197
Mott, Magistrate. 138, 153
Mullins Bill 102

Neagle, Henry 37
Nesbit, Evelyn 204
Nethersole, Olga 9, 90–91, 93, 97, 128, 138
Neuendorff, Adolph 26, 61, 62
Neumann, (ballerina) 57
New York Globe 15, 203
New York Herald 16, 18, 33, 53, 58–59, 73, 75, 118, 120, 146, 164–65, 172, 175, 203
New York Mail 203
New York Mirror 128
New York Morning Journal 203
New York Press 33, 83, 177, 197
New York Sun 9, 67, 135
New York Times 8, 204

New York World 33, 67, 80, 83, 90, 114, 135, 138, 154
Nicholas II 197
Niemann, Albert 122
Nilsson Aerial Ballet 66
Nimmo, Alice 84
Nordica, Lillian 13, 95, 123, 145

Oelrichs, Herman 132
Olcott, Chauncey 9, 63
Olschansky 164
Olympia 9, 99–103, 105–6, 108–11, 113–16, 119–21, 124–25, 127–32, 138–42, 146–47, 151–53, 155–58, 160–61, 164, 166–72, 175–81, 185–86, 188–92, 195, 199, 200–201
Olympian Splendor 107–19
Otero, Belle 149

Paderewski, Ignacy Jan 40, 117, 136, 203
Paderewski, Leonine 201
Palmer 39, 42, 162, 198
Papinta 169, 176, 182, 184
Parkhurst, Rev. Dr. Charles H. 78, 82, 93
Pastor, Tony 56, 63, 81, 97, 104-105, 110, 175, 177, 196
Patti, Adelina 13, 100, 123, 145
Petrosini, Officer 70–72
Philadelphia Orchestra 14, 111, 152
Piff, Duke 43
Potter, Cora 161
Powers, James T. 200
Priganza, Trixie 11
Proctor 105, 169, 170, 174–75

Qualitz, Clara 32, 34, 50, 57
Querker, August 43–45

Raines Law 200
Randolph Churchill, Lady 197
The Rawsons 57
Reeve, Ada 36
Rehan, Ada 9, 128
Réjane, Gabrielle 101
Renaud, Maurice 22
Reuss, Prince 65
Rice 49, 102, 109, 117–18, 167, 168
Rice, Fanny 178
Rice's burlesque extravaganza 57
ichardson, Leander 37, 39
Ring, Blanche 11
Ritchie, Adele 101
Robson, May 162
Rockefeller-McCormick, Edith 121
Rooney, Pat 11
Roosevelt, Theodore 7, 93, 162
Rose, Alice 152, 154, 157
Rosenberg, Henry 55, 100, 190-191
Rossini, Giochimo 188

Routt, Cora 104
Rovere, Richard 82
Rudolf, Prince 107
Russell, John 39, 40
Russell, Lillian 9, 18, 28, 36, 49, 51, 56, 63, 82, 161, 164, 198–99

Sabel, Josephine 57
Salvini, Alexander 25, 63
Sandersonm, Julia 11
Sandow, Eugen 51–53, 55–57, 60–61, 63, 67, 74, 80
Saunders, Lucille 200
Scalchi, Sofia 95
Scheel, Fritz 14, 111, 115, 127, 130, 136, 142, 152, 155
Schmittberger, Captain 84
Schoeffel 198–99
Schumann, Clara 197
Schumann-Heink, Ernestine 13
Segommer 108–9, 116
Seidl, Anton 14, 53, 122-123, 201
Seldes, Gilbert 7, 16
Sembrich 49
Sennett, Mack 87, 204
Shaw, (George) Bernard 79, 95, 102, 110, 123
Sheridan 63, 128, 140, 177
Sholto Douglas, Lady 196
Siegfried, fearsome Wagnerian 124
Siegmund 86–87
Skinner, Otis 9
Sloane's burlesque 115, 117
Solomon, Fred 28, 32
Sothern, E.E. 9, 63, 102, 107
Sousa, John Philip 9, 11, 28, 172, 201
Spencer-Churchill, Consuelo 110
Stanton 122
Steger, Julius 198, 200
Stein, Gertrude 203
Steinhardt 82–83, 90
Stella 190, 203
Stevenson, Adlai 58, 92
Stevenson, Mamie 58, 117
Stone, Fred 11
Strauss, Johann 91
Strong, William Lafayette 92
Sullivan, John L. 56
Svengali 102
Sylva, Marguerite 13

Taber, Julia Marlowe 9, 162, 178
Taber, Robert 162, 178
Tagliapietra, Signor Giovanni 176
Tammany Hall 79, 93, 204
Tanguay, Eva 9, 11, 170, 175–76
Tannen, Julius 11
Tannhauser 122, 124
Tatro, Matilda 204
Teazle, Lady 128

Tempest, Marie 47, 63
Templeton, Alec 147
Templeton, Fay 9, 82, 109, 117, 139-140, 151, 164
Terry, Ellen 47, 110, 128, 136
Tetrazzini, Luisa 13, 22
Thaw, Harry Kendall 204
Thomas, Theodore 14
Thorn, Stephen 93
Thorne, Sylvia 197
Thornton, Bonnie 56–57
Thornton, Jim 56
Tiller Troupe (sisters) 10, 169, 176, 182, 184
Times Square 3, 8–9, 15, 22, 116, 119, 177
Tortajada, Senorita 33
Toscanini 13
Toulouse-Lautrec 126
Tschernoff (and trained dogs) 67
Tubaus, Maria 139

United States Tobacco Journal 8, 203

Unthan, Carl 56
Urdohl 147

Valentin (Jacques Renaudin) 125
Valmore, Jenny 196
Vanderbilt 110, 121, 184
Van Vechten, Carl 15, 16, 18, 20, 136, 203
Vaughn, Therese 117
Verne, Jules 80
Vernon, Harriett 36, 37, 45, 63, 66, 74, 104, 163-164, 172
Vesta, Tilley 97, 104, 110
Vesta, Victoria 11, 110
Victoria, Queen 110
Vitagraph, Edison 11
Vitascope 171–72, 181–82, 184, 195
Von Januschowsky, Georgine 26, 105
Von Tilzer, Harry 9
Voorhis, Judge 73, 81, 88

Wagner, Richard 20, 122-123, 188, 201

Wainwright, Marie 63
Warfield, David 9, 104, 198
Weber and Fields 11, 169–70, 176–77, 182, 184, 192–95
Wentworth, Fanny 147, 152
Wernig, C.A. 42
White, Stanford 162, 204
Whitty, Dame May 110
Wieland, Clara 176
Wilde, Oscar 53, 102, 196
Williams, Bert 11
Williams, Jesse 39
Wilson, Francis 9, 103, 140, 157, 178

Zeisloft 114
Zélie 98
Zenda 107
Zentaello, Giovanni 13
Ziegfeld, Florenz 51, 169
Zola, Emile 97, 107, 109, 126

www.ingramcontent.com/pod-product-compliance
Lightning Source LLC
Chambersburg PA
CBHW080805300426
44114CB00020B/2835